Cruising Historic San Francisco Bay with FDR's Presidential Yacht *Potomac*

Franklin Delano Roosevelt on the *Potomac*, Port Everglades, April 8, 1936

Cruising Historic San Francisco Bay with FDR's Presidential Yacht *Potomac*

David Lee Woods

Foreword by
Michael Roosevelt

Summerset
Books

**Cruising Historic San Francisco Bay
with FDR's Presidential Yacht *Potomac***

David Lee Woods

Foreword by Michael Roosevelt

First Edition revised, Second Printing
Copyright © 2003 by David Lee Woods

Published by
Summerset Books
PO Box 2252
Walnut Creek CA 94595

ISBN 0-9715509-0-5 18.95 (paper)
Library of Congress Control Number: 2001119967

The author has tried to ensure that all the information in the book is accurate and the copyrighted photographs and text have been used with permission. However, if I have inadvertently used materials without credit, have used non-released copyrighted materials, or if there are errors or omissions I would appreciate your writing me at Summerset Books.

Printed and bound in the United States of America by DeHart's Printing Services Corporation, Santa Clara, California. (3/25/03) The United States Government Style Manual, the Chicago Manual of Style, and the American Psychological Association (APA) style guide were used as references in the design of the book. The type is set in Antique Olive and New Century Schoolbook.

Front cover photograph: In 1995, John Ravnik took the cover photograph of the *Potomac* on her post-restoration maiden voyage on the San Francisco Bay.
Back cover photograph: On October 14, 2001, Mia Chambers took the photograph of the author.

Contents

Foreword by Michael Roosevelt

In the year 2000, two generations after the death of my grandfather Franklin Delano Roosevelt, a poll of Americans across the nations voted him the most important American of the twentieth century. No one else was even close: not Albert Einstein, not Babe Ruth, not Dwight Eisenhower.

Here at the Port of Oakland's Jack London Square, the community-based, not-for-profit corporation informally known as the Potomac Association is entrusted with one of the most significant artifacts of the life and momentous presidency of Franklin Delano Roosevelt. The *Potomac* is now stationed at her berth alongside the FDR Pier, ready to serve the next junior high school class visit, or the next two-hour history cruise of San Francisco Bay, or the next port of call.

Because the *Potomac* was my grandfather's "Floating White House" and he enjoyed it so much, I have a great affinity for this vessel. I am sure that he would be proud to know the level of affection that is felt by all those who are involved in the preservation and current public connection made by this National Historic Landmark. In this book, which was originally written as a history cruise guide for the *Potomac* docents, David Lee Woods captures the importance of the vessel to FDR and the nation, and its character as well. This book includes a comprehensive pictorial history of the Bay Area as seen on the *Potomac* cruise. It also has photographs of other vessels you might see on the bay, including historic vessels and WPA and CCC projects from the 1930's and 1940's.

The *Potomac* is a superb educational vessel. It helps bring to life those crisis-ridden years of the Great Depression and World War II when it was a part of great events in our nation's history. FDR spent much of his leisure time aboard the *Potomac*, reflecting about decisions that would change the world. Read this book. Then come and visit the *Potomac* as it continues to honor FDR and to serve our nation, inspiring generations to love America the beautiful.

Michael A. Roosevelt, Chairman
Board of Governors
Association for the Preservation of
the Presidential Yacht *Potomac*

Author's Preface

The presidential yacht *Potomac* is berthed at Jack London Square in Oakland, California, and provides two-hour history cruises on the San Francisco Bay. As a docent narrator, I started this book as my narration notes for these history cruises. Over several years, I have added materials based on my research, questions asked and information supplied by passengers and other docents. My primary concern was to make this a brief, interesting and historically accurate coverage of the history of the Bay Area as seen from the decks of the *Potomac*. Because the *Potomac* was Franklin Delano Roosevelt's presidential yacht, there are many references to FDR. The narration is of a general nature, with additional information included in the endnotes and reference section.

This book has three sections. The first section, **History Cruise on San Francisco Bay**, includes photographs of some of the areas covered by the narration. With a copy of the book in hand, the format of the narration section will help interpreters who are assisting people with limited ability in English. It will also help those with a hearing impairment who would like to read the narration. The second section, **What You Might See Afloat on San Francisco Bay**, includes photographs and descriptions of many of the typical types of vessels on the bay. The third section, **For More Information**, includes additional information on FDR and other presidents, all of the presidential yachts, Bay Area points of interest, historical landmarks, a time line, websites, bibliography, and index. The historical sites are sequenced by location as seen from a boat and are not in chronological order.

San Francisco Bay Area Map

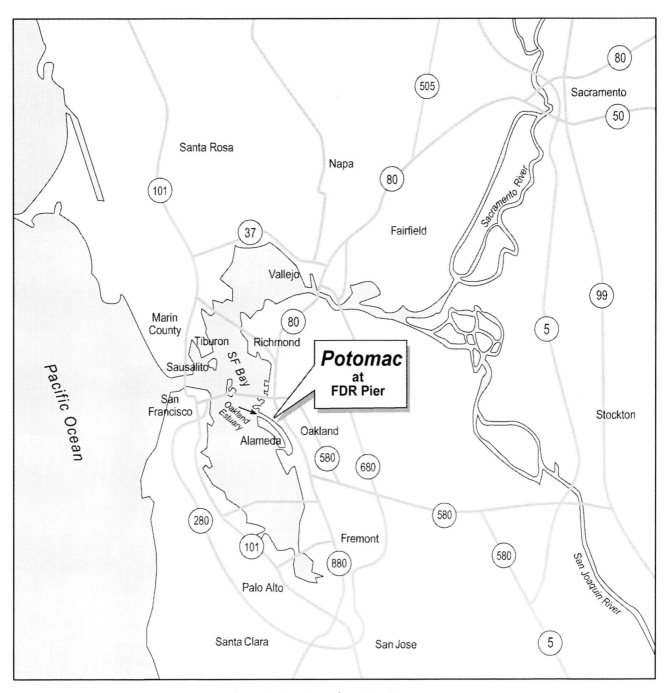

Figure 1 - **San Francisco Bay Area map**

Points of Interest on SF Bay Map

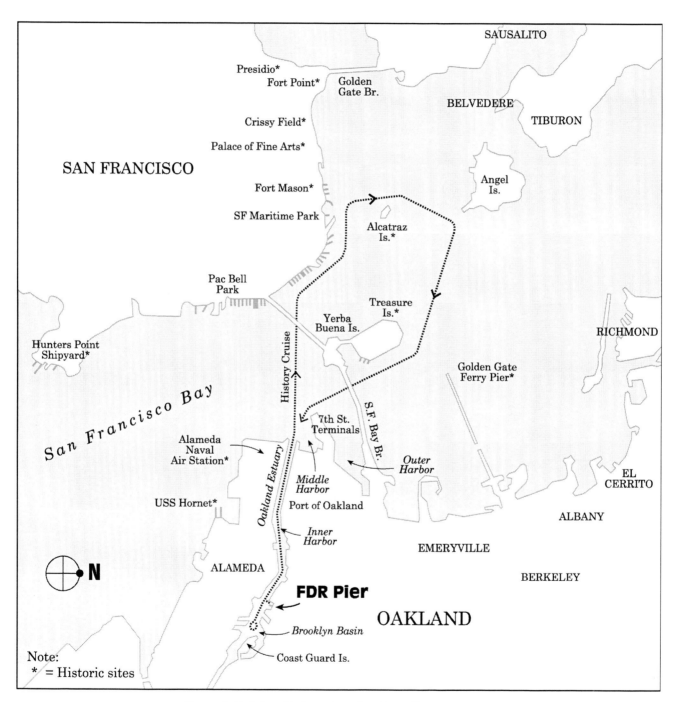

Figure 2 - **Points of Interest on San Francisco Bay Map**

History Cruise on San Francisco Bay

1 - FDR's "Floating White House"

A Short History of the *Potomac*

The USS *Potomac* was originally built in 1934 as the Coast Guard cutter *Electra*. The 165-foot vessel, weighing 376 gross tons, with a cruising speed of 10 to13 knots, was converted to the presidential yacht USS *Potomac* for Franklin D. Roosevelt, who had her recommissioned as a U.S. Navy vessel in 1936. As former assistant secretary of the navy, FDR had a deep love for the sea and navy tradition. He hated to fly and chose either trains or ships as a preferred means of transportation throughout his presidency.

FDR suffered from sinusitis most of his adult life. Particularly during the sultry summer days in Washington D.C., he preferred to cruise on the USS *Potomac* rather than stay in the White House. The USS *Potomac* gave the nation's thirty-second president much needed relaxation from the cares of governing the United States through the Great Depression and World War II. He loved informal strategy sessions with close advisors and congressional leaders in the privacy and seclusion of the USS *Potomac*. Recreation aboard the vessel included fishing, poker games, and family gatherings, plus endless hours with his beloved stamp collection.

A paraplegic since he was stricken with polio in 1921 at the age of thirty-nine, FDR's greatest fear was being caught in a fire, unable to escape because he could not walk. He therefore preferred the all-steel *Potomac* over the ornate all-wooden *Sequoia*, the 100-ton presidential yacht used by his predecessor Herbert Hoover. For Roosevelt's convenience, a hand-operated elevator was installed inside a false stack that was added during the conversion. The president, who had developed an extremely strong upper body, was able to use the pulleys to move up and down between the saloon and upper boat deck. There are few records of President Roosevelt's wife Eleanor sharing her husband's "Floating White House." In 1941, she celebrated her fifty-seventh birthday with family members aboard the USS *Potomac*. She also came aboard during the June 1939, visit by King George VI and Queen Elizabeth, cruising with the royal couple past Williamsburg, Virginia, and George Washington's home at Mount Vernon. This was an historic first visit to the United States by reigning British royalty. Other royalty who came aboard the presidential yacht were Crown Princess Martha of Norway, Queen Wilhelmina of the Netherlands and Crown Prince Gustav of Sweden.

At least one of FDR's national radio broadcasts or "fireside chats," as these broadcasts came to be called, originated from the USS *Potomac* on March 29, 1941.

In August 1941, four months before Japan's attack on Pearl Harbor, FDR boarded the USS *Potomac* ostensibly for a fishing trip and a visit to Martha's Vineyard. The president was secretly transferred that evening to the heavy cruiser USS *Augusta*, which took him to the historic first meeting with British Prime Minister Winston Churchill off the coast of

Newfoundland. During this top-secret rendezvous, the two world leaders forged the principles of the Atlantic Charter, forming the allied partnership during World War II, and what Roosevelt called the "United Nations" to plan the post-war peace.

After America's entry into the war, the president's recreational use of the USS *Potomac* decreased; both his schedule and security precautions dictated the decline.

After the president's death in April 1945, the USS *Potomac* endured a long and ignominious history. At one point she fell into private hands and later in 1980 was seized in San Francisco Bay as a front for a drug smuggling operation. In 1981, while impounded at Treasure Island during a heavy storm, the proud vessel's hull was pierced and she sank.

She was refloated by the navy two weeks later and sold by the U.S. Customs Service to the only bidder, the Port of Oakland, for just $15,000. The Port of Oakland then spearheaded a cooperative effort with organized labor, maritime corporations and dedicated volunteers to complete a $5 million restoration.

With restoration completed, the *Potomac* was opened to the public on April 12, 1995, the fiftieth anniversary of FDR's death.

The Association for the Preservation of the Presidential Yacht *Potomac* now operates this National Historic Landmark as an active memorial to Franklin Delano Roosevelt and the momentous times through which he led our nation.

For more information about the vessel, see Historic Vessels on page 148, touring the *Potomac* on page 178, presidential yachts on page 193, and refer to Capt. Walter W. Jaffee's book *The Presidential Yacht Potomac*.

▪ Dockside Tours

The *Potomac* is open for guided dockside tours January through mid-December on Sundays, 12:00 noon to 4:00 P.M., and Wednesdays and Fridays from 10:00 A.M. to 2:00 P.M., with the last ticket sold 45 minutes before closing. Tours are approximately 45 minutes long. A reservation is required for group tours of ten or more.

▪ History Cruises

Two-hour narrated history cruises along the San Francisco waterfront, around Treasure Island and Alcatraz are offered from April through early November. These trips are on the first and third Thursdays, and the second and fourth Saturdays, of the month. Departure times are 10:00 A.M. and 1:30 P.M. with boarding 15 minutes before departure. Prior to boarding a 15-minute video is shown in the Visitors Center.

In addition, several special holiday cruises are offered.

▪ Special School Tours and History Cruises

In addition to special dockside tours for students, a limited number of one-hour history cruises are available to schools at no charge. Both dockside tours and cruises must be arranged in advance.

- *Potomac* **Financial Support**

The *Potomac* is an important cultural and educational resource for the Bay Area's many communities, and with public support will continue to be available for a diverse and ever expanding audience. The *Potomac*'s small size, unique history and design combine to create a rare museum setting. It offers small-scale yet intimate and scholarly lectures; in-depth educational curricula designed to forge long-term relationships with visitors of all ages; and community outreach that targets local communities.

Funding provided by dedicated patrons has been critical to its success. By making the vessel accessible and relevant to ever-increasing and diverse constituencies, the *Potomac* is making a valuable contribution to its immediate community and beyond.

You may help support these efforts by becoming a member of **Friends of the *Potomac***.

Cruise Route Map Index

The two-hour history cruise leaves Jack London Square, goes into Brooklyn Basin, then out the estuary across the bay to the San Francisco waterfront. It goes along the waterfront past the San Francisco Maritime Park, circles Alcatraz Island, and then returns by Treasure Island. It continues up the estuary and back to the FDR ier.

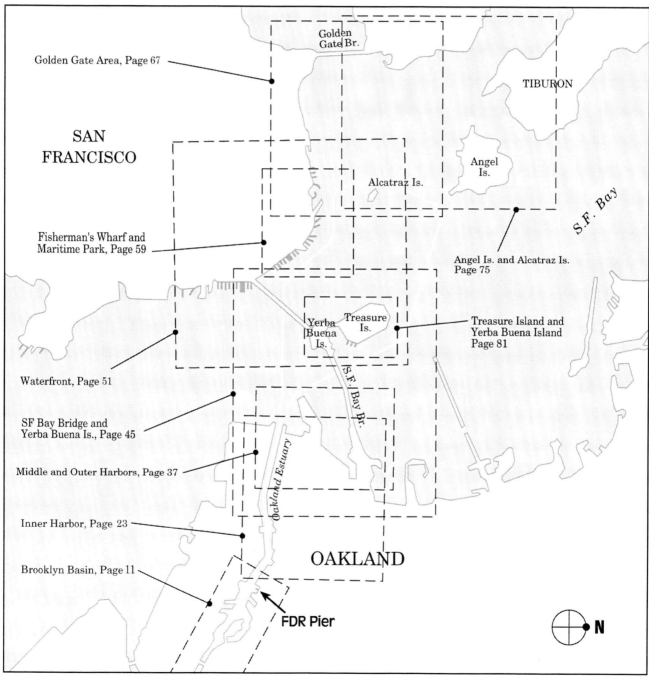

Figure 3 - **Cruise Route Map Index**

Welcome Aboard

Welcome aboard the Franklin Delano Roosevelt presidential yacht *Potomac* for a cruise on historic San Francisco Bay. Join FDR vicariously in one of his most enjoyable pastimes, a cruise on his beloved *Potomac*. Though FDR never sailed on the *Potomac* in San Francisco Bay, he did visit the Bay Area on a number of occasions. Many of the things that we see on our cruise were here when he visited.

Our cruise will take us into Brooklyn Basin, then out the estuary across the bay to San Francisco. There we will sail by the city-front, past the San Francisco National Maritime Historic Park, and around Alcatraz.

Figure 4 - **Passengers boarding the Potomac**

Next, we go past Treasure Island, the home of the legendary China Clippers, past the largest container cranes in the world, and finally back to the FDR pier at Jack London Square.

As the crew casts off the lines and we pull away from the dock, we start our tour with a look at the historic *RELIEF* lightship which is moored next to the *Potomac*. Though this particular lightship was not built during FDR's lifetime, he would have seen this ship's predecessor anchored in the Atlantic keeping vigil in fair weather or foul. As we pull away from the dock, we have a view of Jack London Square.

Figure 5 - **Kurt Lauridsen as FDR with his dog Fala, and in the background, a 1943 Liberty ship** [1]

Figure 6 - **1951** *RELIEF* **lightship at Jack London Square, moored next to the** *Potomac*

▪ 1951 RELIEF Lightship

The WAL 605 is one of six lightships constructed by the Coast Guard in 1951. From 1898 to 1971 a series of lightships named *SAN FRANCISCO* marked the entrance to the bay.

The WAL 605 first served as the *OVERFALLS*, stationed off Delaware. In 1959, she was renamed the *BLUNTS* and transferred to a station off Cape Mendocino, California. In 1969, she became the *RELIEF*, relieving all West Coast lightships when they left station for overhaul.

The ship was decommissioned by the Coast Guard in 1975 and given to the city of Olympia, Washington in 1976. Olympia was unsuccessful in making the ship a museum and sold the vessel to Mr. Alan Hosking of Woodside, California in 1979. He in turn donated the ship to the United States Lighthouse Society in San Francisco. They have restored the historic lightship as a museum.[2,3]

Figure 7 - **1951** *RELIEF* **lightship as seen from the** *Potomac*

Figure 8 - **Jack London Square and marina as seen from the *Potomac***

Jack London Square

We will start with a little history of Jack London Square. The area was named after Jack London, an Oakland native and well known writer. Though he was born in San Francisco in 1876, he grew up in Oakland.[4] He died at his Beauty Ranch near Glen Ellen, Sonoma County, in 1916 of kidney disease when he was only forty years old.[5]

He left more than fifty-two books, numerous stories and essays, many of which have been translated and continue to be read around the world. He is best known for *Call of the Wild, White Fang,* and *The Sea-Wolf.*

Oakland was the home base for Jack London and his fellow teenage "oyster pirates"; his favorite saloon, Heinhold's First and Last Chance, still stands today at Jack London Square, adjacent to a portion of his 1898 Yukon cabin, which was moved to Oakland in 1969.[6]

When Jack London was here at the waterfront with his small sailboat *Razzle Dazzle* and later on his 30-foot yawl, the *Roamer,*[7, 8] this area was mostly an industrial area with shipyards, factories and warehouses.

The waterfront started in the early 1850's as two wharves jutting out into San Antonio Creek, which we now know as the estuary. It grew as an industrial and shipping area through World War I; then in 1927, the Port of Oakland organization was established to manage growth along the waterfront.

During World War II there was additional significant industrial development in the area to support wartime needs. After World War II many of these businesses closed and there were a number of unused, decrepit industrial buildings in the waterfront area.

The Port of Oakland cleared the area and in 1951, ninety-nine years after the founding of Oakland, named it Jack London Square and dedicated its use to restaurants and entertainment. Within four years the square attracted a million visitors annually. New constructions can be seen on the waterfront and more are planned.

The 1960 marina was rebuilt in 2000, and a new berth for the *Potomac* and other historic vessels is in the construction stage. As we go on our tour we will be seeing many more examples of how the foresight of Oakland's founders paid off. [9, 10]

---

[1] Kurt Lauridsen is a docent on the *Potomac*; the Liberty ship is the *Jeremiah O'Brien*.
[2] For more information on United States Lighthouse Society, see Historic Data Sources on page 259.
[3] Glover (2001).
[4] Kingman (1979) page 15 [Jack London born in San Francisco January 12, 1876], page 28 [He moved to Oakland at nine].
[5] Jack London was born January 12, 1876 and died November 22, 1916.
[6] Historical Landmark No. 824 – San Leandro Oyster Beds, Alameda County names Jack London. See page 227.
[7] Jack London, *His Life and Books*. [01/05/03] from website www.parks.sonoma.net/JLStory.html.
[8] Jack London traveled in the South Pacific on his ketch *Snark* from 1907 to 1909.
[9] Allen (1996) *Jack London Square*.
[10] Minor (2000).

2 - Brooklyn Basin

Brooklyn Basin Map

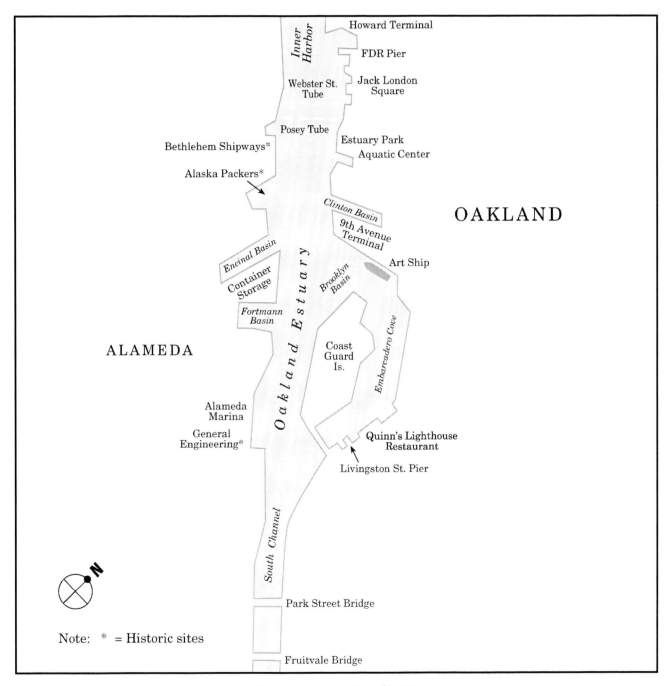

Figure 9 - **Brooklyn Basin Map**

Figure 10 - **Brooklyn Basin from Jack London Square**

Polyglot Population

In prehistoric times, the Bay Area was one of the most densely populated regions in North America.[1]

With the coming of the Spanish in the late eighteenth century, the Bay Area began to embrace a polyglot mix of people as unique as anywhere in the world.[2,3] On our history cruise, we will be seeing some of the things that this growing and diverse blend of people has accomplished.

Even before the gold rush, San Francisco's population in 1848 of 800[4] came from twenty different countries. Then there was the influx of people for the gold rush. By 1849, San Francisco's population was more than 100,000.[5] Its reputation for diversity remained intact, with settlers from everywhere in the Union and several thousand more from South America, Asia, Europe, Mexico and even the British penal colony of Australia.

Many of these settlers came to the East Bay, and by 1852 the towns of Oakland and Brooklyn were established on the banks of San Antonio Creek.[6] That was the same year Wells Fargo opened an office in San Francisco.[7] Within a year Oakland established police and fire departments, opened a school, and linked the two towns by means of a bridge across the creek. On Broadway there were hotels and commercial wharves on the estuary.[8] Oakland, in particular, grew rapidly, embracing most of the East Bay population. The town of Brooklyn was annexed in 1872, although its name survives as Brooklyn Basin.

Because the bay dominated the geography of the region, ferry service quickly became a reality; this was the first manifestation of a commitment to shipbuilding and overseas trade that became the twin hallmarks of East Bay development.

The Rail and Ferry

Back in the 1850's, there were piers in both Oakland at Broadway and in Brooklyn at Thirteenth Avenue. However, at low tide a sandbar blocked the mouth of the creek and larger ships could not come to Oakland or Brooklyn.[9] Ships had to anchor in deeper water and shuttle the cargo by using small boats. Also in 1850, the Episcopal Church of St. James the Apostle was completed, and services are still held in the original building.[10] By 1853, the steam sternwheeler *Kangaroo* made a trip twice a week between San Francisco and Oakland.[11, 12]

The City of Oakland started dredging the estuary in 1859, and this helped the East Bay become an international maritime shipping hub. By 1877, the U.S. Army Corps of Engineers had deepened the estuary to twenty feet at high tide, allowing both Alameda and Oakland to become major ports and shipbuilding areas.[13, 14, 15]

In 1863, a steam railroad took passengers and freight from Broadway along Seventh Street to Oakland Point and from here to the ferry to San Francisco.[16, 17]

By 1864, an additional rail-ferry system took passengers and freight from the East Bay via a ferry pier in Alameda to San Francisco, and in 1869, the transcontinental railroad came to Oakland. By 1875, horse-cars were running from Alameda across the Webster Street Bridge to Piedmont.[18, 19, 20, 21]

By 1880, the rail-ferry system allowed commuters to go from their homes in Alameda's East End to the Ferry Building in San Francisco in forty minutes. One hundred and twenty years of progress has not improved the time for that commute.[22]

During the Great Depression when FDR was in office, a pipe manufacturer in Oakland had excess pieces of large pipe. About two hundred jobless men made their homes in these pieces of pipe, and called it Pipe City, or Miseryville. This is one symbol, and a very local example, of the deep economic and social crises FDR faced as he took office.[23, 24, 25]

The New Deal

FDR visited the Bay Area several times during the Great Depression. The first visit was during his first run for the presidency in 1932; at that time he delivered the major policy speech before the San Francisco Commonwealth Club, laying out the blueprint for what became the New Deal's policies to address the woes of the depression.

The Bay Area was a recipient of these New Deal policies in the 1930's. The "alphabet soup" of New Deal programs, NRA (National Recovery Act), WPA (Works Projects Administration) and the CCC (Civilian Conservation Corps), were all represented in the Bay Area.[26] They built or helped build Treasure Island, San Francisco's Aquatic Park, the Berkeley library and post office, the Alameda County courthouse with its distinctive WPA-commissioned murals, the Berkeley Rose Garden and Oakland's Woodminister open-air theater. These are but a few examples of the rebuilding of the area (and the nation) that the New Deal undertook.

We will see some of the fruits and problems of this century and a half of Bay Area growth and change as we proceed on the history tour.

Lumber Mills and Wharves

KTVU Channel 2, several condominium developments, and the Estuary Park now use part of the waterfront.[27] This area was at one time used by a number of lumber companies receiving logs for the lumber mills and shipping the lumber via both rail and ships.[28]

Figure 11 - **Condominiums, KTVU Channel 2, and the City of Oakland's Estuary Park**

Ninth Avenue Terminal

The Ninth Avenue Terminal, berths 82–84, does not have container cranes, so ships must have onboard cranes to load and unload their cargo. It handles break-bulk cargo, the type that cannot fit into containers, such as steel, lumber, cotton, and large or heavy items.

Figure 12 - **Port of Oakland Ninth Avenue Terminal**

Long-term plans call for the Ninth Avenue Terminal operations to be relocated, part of the terminal removed and this entire area to be upgraded for more commercial and recreational uses. The old part of the terminal may be preserved for historical displays.[29]

Figure 13 - **1939 *ARTSHIP* retired Maritime Academy T/S *Golden Bear***

The ARTSHIP

The *ARTSHIP* on the Oakland side of the estuary is moored on the east side of the Ninth Avenue Terminal.

She is the Maritime Academy's retired training ship *Golden Bear*. An extensive renovation project is underway to convert the ship into theaters, gallery space, classrooms, meeting space, studios, and other facilities necessary to support various types of arts programs. For more information on the *ARTSHIP*, see Historic Vessels on page 149.[30, 31, 32, 33]

The Land of Cotton

Starting in 1893, the area near Embarcadero Cove was the site of the California Cotton Mills company. The mills grew into a very large factory and started the West Coast textile industry. They milled California-grown cotton hauled in from the valley by rail. A new state-of-the-art facility replaced the original mill in 1917. Much of the factory was demolished for construction of the Nimitz Freeway in 1954.[34] However, part of the old brick wall lines the freeway near the Twenty-third Avenue off-ramp.

Coast Guard Station

Alameda was not an island until 1902, when the tidal canal was excavated to help flush out the estuary. The dirt from excavating the canal between San Antonio Creek and San

Figure 14 - **Coast Guard cutter *Boutwell* moored at Coast Guard Island**

Leandro Bay was used to reclaim marshland along the estuary. Between 1915 and 1917 dredging materials were deposited behind levees in the center of Brooklyn Basin to make a seventy-five-acre island.

One of the first uses of the island was shipbuilding. To save steel during both World Wars I and II, concrete ships were built. On a 1920 map, the U.S. Concrete Shipbuilding Plant is shown on Government Island.[35, 36]

In 1934, both the Coast Guard and the Customs Station were opened on the renamed Coast Guard Island.[37] That was the same year the *Electra* was launched and eventually became the *Potomac*.

Alameda Marina

The Alameda Marina now occupies the site of the General Engineering and Dry Dock Company, which was here from 1922 to 1948, and repaired nearly 4,000 ships during World War II.[38]

The Alaska Packers

On the Alameda side of the estuary is a container storage area between the Fortman Marina and the old Encinal Terminals. A year after FDR's birth in 1882, the Alaska Packers started in San Francisco. The organization was formed as a coalition of twenty-six salmon canners.[39] They started with two sailing ships that sailed to Alaska for salmon.[40] They moved to Alameda in 1905 to what is now the Fortman Marina, and the fleet grew to twenty-two vessels by 1910. However, by 1926 the fleet was down to twelve vessels. The *Alaska Star* made the last commercial sailing trip from Alameda in 1930, and the last four sailing vessels were sold in 1935. The Alaska Packers used steamships until World War II, when they moved to Seattle. [41, 42, 43]

Alaska Star has been restored and renamed the *Balclutha*. She is berthed at the National Maritime Historical Park in San Francisco.

The *Star of India* was her sister ship and made her last trip for salmon in 1923. The *Star of India* has also been restored and is now berthed at the San Diego Maritime Park.[44]

Figure 15 - **Alameda Marina—1922–48 General Engineering and Dry Dock Company**

Most of the other sailing ships were not so lucky; many wooden vessels rotted at the end of Coast Guard Island. At low tide, some of their rotted remains can be seen sticking out of the water. These sunken ships are indicated on the nautical chart of Brooklyn Basin.[45]

Figure 16 - **Container storage next to Fortman Marina, Alameda**

In 1959, Matson Lines built the first container loading facility at the Encinal Terminals with a gantry crane built specifically for loading and unloading containers from cargo ships.[46, 47]

The California Packing Company Del Monte warehouse was built in 1927 behind the Encinal Terminals and processed food under the brand name Del Monte.[48] The buildings are on Buena Vista Avenue and are being redeveloped for commercial and mixed-use development.

Shipbuilding

Figure 17 - **Encinal Terminals started in 1925; in 1959 the site of the first gantry container crane**

Throughout FDR's lifetime, shipbuilding had been going on in Alameda, where the first shipyard started in 1890.[49]

From 1900 to 1916, United Engineering Works had a small shipyard where the four long slanted ramps, called shipways, are now. In 1916, Bethlehem Shipbuilding took over the site, building and repairing ships during World War I. Bethlehem did ship repair between 1922 and 1937, but with new contracts they added the shipways and built and repaired ships during World War II.[50]

Figure 18 - **Wooden ship graveyard at Coast Guard Island**

Figure 19 - **1916 to 1948 Bethlehem Shipbuilding shipways in Alameda**

During World War II, Bethlehem built eight troopships and repaired more than 1,000 damaged vessels here.[51] After the war, American President Lines (APL) bought two unfinished troopships and outfitted them for civilian passenger service, naming them the *President Cleveland* and *President Wilson*.[52] These 610-foot luxury liners were designed to carry 550 passengers and a crew of 352. They were launched in 1947 and served until 1973 when APL terminated its passenger line service.[53] These two ships were the last ships built on these shipways.

Both the Bethlehem[54, 55] and Moore[56] shipyards were here on the estuary during World War I and World War II. General Engineering Dry Dock Company,[57] Hurley Marine Works,[58] Hanlon Dry Dock,[59] the Stone Boat Yard,[60] and other small yards on the estuary joined them to build or repair ships. After World War II, the site of United Engineering Company shipyard, next to the present Alameda ferry terminal, was first used by Matson Navigation, and later by Todd Shipyards. It is now owned by Alameda Gateway Limited.[61, 62]

There were twelve major shipyards in the Bay Area during World War II, plus many smaller repair facilities.

Shipyards were built in record time. Marinship went from mudflats in Sausalito to the launching of its first ships in just nine months.[63] Starting in December 1940,[64] Kaiser converted Richmond mudflats into four shipyards and built 727 ships during the war.[65]

In 1938, it took many months to build an average cargo ship; by 1945 it took only a few weeks.

In November 1942, Kaiser Richmond set an all-time record of building and launching the liberty ship *Robert E. Perry* in four days, sixteen hours and twenty-six minutes.[66] The war lasted 1,365 days and the Bay Area shipyards produced 1,400 vessels, averaging a ship a day during the war years.[67] The Bay Area shipyards built 45 percent of the cargo ships and 25 percent of the warships built in America during World War II.[68]

This production outnumbered the 1,220 U.S. flag merchant ships that were lost during the war.[69] In addition, thousands of ships were damaged, and many were repaired in various Bay Area facilities. As a result of these losses, the U.S. Merchant Marine suffered the highest rate of casualties of any services in World War II.[70]

Figure 20 - **Floating homes at 5ᵗʰ Ave. Marina, Oakland**

Shipbuilding and other wartime employment increased the population of the Bay Area by over 25 percent between 1940 and 1945.[71]

Floating Homes

There are a number of floating homes on the bay like those here at the Barnhill Marina and the 5th Ave. Marina. These do not have engines and must be towed to a new location. They are connected to city utilities to preclude pollution of the bay.

Figure 21 - **Floating homes at Barnhill Marina, Alameda**

Bulk Cement Elevators

These cement elevators were built about 1934, then after World War II, the Lone Star Cement Corporation built these bulk cement elevators to handle cement brought in by ship from Davenport, which is just north of Santa Cruz. The frontage road from Davenport to Davenport Landing is named Cement Plant Road. After the cement was loaded into the elevators, it was bagged and then shipped out by rail or truck. The plant closed in the early 1960's.[72]

Figure 22 - **Lone Star Cement bulk cement elevators and bagging plant**

[1] Port of Oakland *Room With a View* Exhibit.

[2] Local References page 201, "The Early Days in San Francisco Area."

[3] Appleton (1855) page 106, *The Annals of San Francisco*.

[4] March 18, 1848, *California Star* reported that non-native population of San Francisco was 575 males, 177 females, and 60 children (total 812). From San Francisco Museum website [01/06/03] www.sfmuseum.org/hist/chron1.html.

[5] December 31, 1849, population of San Francisco was estimated at 100,000 including 35,000 people who came by sea; 3,000 sailors who deserted ships; and 42,000 who came overland. From San Francisco Museum [01/05/03] www.sfmuseum.org/hist/chron1.html.

[6] Bagwell (1982) pages 47–49. [The town of Oakland was incorporated on May 4, 1852 by a special act of the state legislature. The City of Oakland was incorporated March 25, 1864.]

[7] July 13, 1853, Wells Fargo office Montgomery Street in San Francisco. [01/05/03] www.wellsfargohistory.com.

[8] Bagwell (1982) Hotels page 40, Pier page 43. Horace W. Carpentier owned the Oakland Waterfront.

[9] Bagwell (1982) pages 36, 224. [The 13th Ave. wharf was in the town of San Antonio, which became part of Brooklyn in 1852.]

[10] Historical Landmark No. 694 - Church of St. James the Apostle, Oakland. See page 226.

[11] Bagwell (1982) page 38.

[12] Harlan (1976) page 74.

[13] Bagwell (1982) page 192. [In 1877, the U.S. Army Corps of Engineers made major dredging improvements to the channel in the estuary.]

[14] Cooper (1996) *Estuary Transformed*.

[15] Bagwell (1982) page 192.

[16] Bagwell (1982) page 41.

[17] Cooper (1996) *Birth on the Water*.

[18] Minor (1993) page 3.

[19] The Panama trans-isthmus railroad was completed in 1855.

[20] Minor (1993) page 6.

[21] Minor (1996) *Bridges Become Tunnels*.

[22] Minor (1993) page 5.

[23] Oakland Public Library, Oakland Room, Photo Archives and Oakland, CA: Oakland Museum Photo Archives. Display photograph *Potomac* Office.

[24] Cooper (1996) *Homeless Shelter in Pipe City*.

[25] At the foot of 19th Avenue, the American Steel and Concrete Pipe Co. had many unsold pieces of 3-foot diameter pipe. The pipe was sold in 1933.

[26] See "FDR's New Deal Agencies in the Bay Area" on page 169.

[27] Estuary Park was opened in 1972.

[28] Lavoie (1996) *Loading Lumber*.

[29] Jack London Area Development Plan *OAK-4.4: Promote development of commercial-recreational uses in the vicinity of the Crescent Park and Clinton Basin*. From website [01/05/03] www.estuaryplan.com/jack_lon.htm.

[30] Jack London Area Development Plan *OAK-4.4: Promote development of commercial-recreational uses in the vicinity of the Crescent Park and Clinton Basin*. From website [01/05/03] www.estuaryplan.com/jack_lon.htm.

[31] Fassel (1996) *ARTSHIP*.

[32] For more information on the Maritime Academy see page 95.

[33] For more information on the *ARTSHIP* see Historic Vessels on page 149.

[34] Lavoie (1996) *The Land of Cotton*.

[35] Bonnett (1999) page 17.

[36] Minor (1993) pages 30–31 [1920 map].

[37] Cooper (1996) *The Government Builds an Island*.

[38] Minor (1996) *From Shipyard to Yacht Harbor*.

[39] Braznel (1982) page 163.

[40] Minor (1996) *The Alaska Packers*.

[41] Alaska Packers vessel history from The Maritime History Virtual Archives website [01/10/03] http://pc-78-120.udac.se:8001/WWW/Nautica/Nautica.html.

[42] For more information see Historic Vessels - *Balclutha* page 159.

[43] Minor (2000) pages 12, 26.

[44] For more information see Historic Vessels - *Star of India* page 163.

[45] NOAA Nautical Chart 18650 *San Francisco Bay Candlestick Point to Angel Island Jan 31, 01.*

[46] Minor (1996) *Cranes Alight at Encinal Terminals*.

[47] Minor (2000) page 146. (1930's photograph of square-riggers berthed off Coast Guard Island).

[48] Braznel (1982).

[49] Minor (1996) *Victorian Shipyards*. [Charles G. White and Hay & Wright came from San Francisco to Alameda in 1890.]

[50] Bonnett (1999) page 18.

[51] Minor (1996) *Alameda's Bethlehem Shipyard*. [Opened in 1916 on the site of United Engineering Works, opened in 1900.]

[52] Bonnett (1999) pages 152, 153.

[53] Information from website [01/05/03] www.apl.com.

[54] Bonnett (1999) page 12. [Bethlehem Shipyards was in Alameda from about 1916 to 1946.]

[55] Minor (1996) *Alameda's Bethlehem Shipyard*.

[56] Moore (1994). [The Moore Dry Dock Shipyard was in Oakland from 1908–1961.]

[57] Minor (1996) *From Shipyard to Yacht Harbor*.
[The Alameda Marina is on the General Engineering shipyard site (1922–1948) near Coast Guard Island at the estuary end of Chestnut Street, Alameda.]

[58] Bonnett (1999) page 141. [Hurley repaired over 400 ships on their single marine railway haulout.]

[59] Hanlon Dry dock was near the 9th Avenue Terminal in 1920; data from Port of Oakland.

[60] "The Stone Boat Yard: Three Generations of Quality," Wooden Boat 109, November/December 1992, pages 60–68.

[61] Southern Pacific Co. (before 1874 –1942). United Engineering (1942–1945), Matson Navigation (1945–1959),Todd (1959–1983), AGL (1983 to present). Alameda Gateway, LTD (AGL), plaintiff, v. The United States, defendant, and Port of Oakland, No. 97-160L, December 23, 1999. Website [08/12/00] www.contracts.orc.doc.gov/fedcl/opinions/99opin/97-160L.html.

[62] United Engineering Works was at the Bethlehem shipbuilding site east of Webster Street; United Engineering Company was west of Webster Street next to the Alameda ferry terminal. These were different companies.

[63] Wollenberg (1990). [Broke ground March 28, 1942; launched first ship November 23, 1942; built 93 ships, the last launched October 1945.]

[64] Johnson (1993) page 33.

[65] Bonnett (1999) page 32.

[66] Johnson (1993) page 66. [November 12, 1942 in Richmond Yard Two.]

[67] Bonnett (1999) page 6.

[68] Bonnett (1999) page 6.

[69] U.S. Merchant Ships Sunk or Damaged in World War II, information from U.S. Merchant Marine website [01/20/03] www.usmm.org/shipsunkdamaged.html,
Bonnett (1999) page 31 gives a number of 764; these would be ships over 1,000 tons.

[70] U.S. Merchant Marine Casualties during World War II, information from U.S. Merchant Marine website [01/20/03] www.usmm.org/casualty.html.

[71] Johnson (1993) page 33.

[72] Information supplied by phone with Barnhill Marina 12/17/01 (510-521-8387).

3 - Inner Harbor
Inner Harbor Map

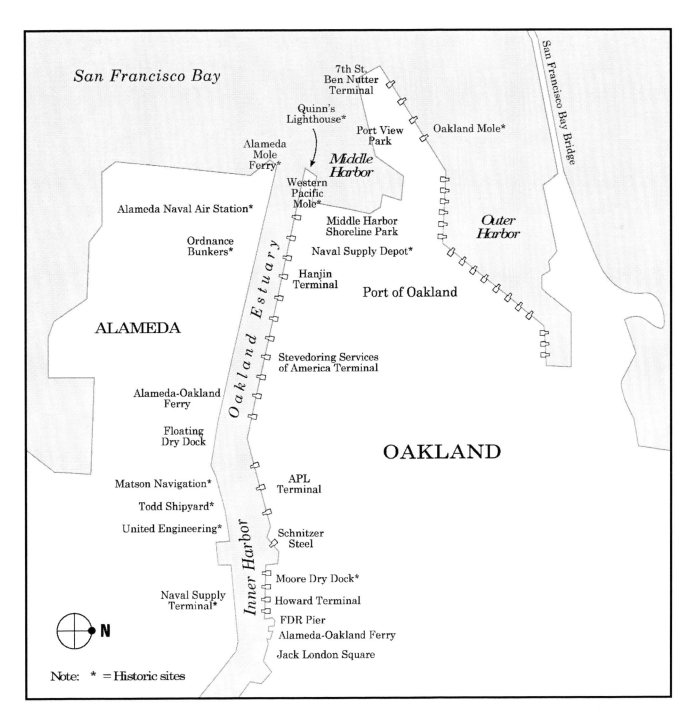

Figure 23 - **Inner Harbor Map**

Port of Oakland

Starting in 1852, the entire Oakland waterfront was privately owned, including piers at Seventh Street and the foot of Broadway. It was not until 1909 that the City of Oakland gained control of the waterfront area.[1] In 1927 the City established the Port of Oakland agency to bring in shipping revenues and control growth on the waterfront. The Port now has three divisions: maritime, aviation, and real estate.[2] Starting at the Livingston Street Pier in Embarcadero Cove and extending to the outer harbor, the Port of Oakland has 19 miles of waterfront and more than 1,000 acres of marine terminal facilities. There are more than 20 berths with 40 container cranes and room for more than 30,000 containers, which come in standard sizes from 20 to 53 feet long.[3] There are four new deep-water terminals on the estuary, with ten new large cranes (the largest in the world) able to service the new post-Panamax container freighters that are too large to go through the Panama Canal.[4, 5, 6] The Port of Oakland is the fourth busiest container port in the United States, and handles 98 percent of all container cargo in the Bay Area.

Charles P. Howard Terminal

The container terminal next to the FDR pier is the Charles P. Howard Terminal. It was originally a privately owned terminal; built in 1900, it enabled Oakland to compete with San Francisco in handling cargo.[7] In 1978 the Port acquired the old terminal and expanded it to include the old Grove Street Terminal. The new Charles P. Howard container terminal was opened in 1982.[8]

A lot happened a century ago when Charles P. Howard built a new terminal: President William McKinley was assassinated, and Theodore Roosevelt became president. The American flag had only forty-five stars. Arizona, Oklahoma, New Mexico, Hawaii, and Alaska had not yet been admitted to the Union.

Also in 1901, Guglielmo Marconi sent the first radio signal across the ocean

Figure 24 - **Charles P. Howard Terminal**

between England and Newfoundland;[9] settlers were given vast Native American lands in the Oklahoma Territory, and the Boxer Rebellion in China ended.[10]

Container Cranes

In New Jersey, SeaLand Services started using "sea chests" or containers in 1956. However, in 1959 at the Encinal Terminal in Alameda, Matson Lines installed the first container crane made specifically for loading and unloading standardized containers from cargo ships.[11, 12, 13]

In 1962, SeaLand started using containers for shipping by truck to the terminal. In 1966, they modified four ships to handle their 5000 new trailer-mounted shipping containers, and switched from shipboard cranes to two new land-based cranes at the Outer Harbor.[14] In 1968, the first trainload of containers arrived at the Seventh Street Terminal.[15]

These large ship-loading container cranes not only look big, they are big.

The cranes at the Charles P. Howard and American President Lines (APL) terminals are more than 190 feet tall and 90 feet wide. The cranes at the new terminals are more than 200 feet tall.[16] All of these cranes can load or unload a

Figure 25 - **Container crane loading ship**

Figure 26 - **Container crane loading ship**

container in less than two minutes.

All of these cranes can lift a 40-ton load up to 100 feet off the dock and can reach more than 130 feet over the water and 50 feet back over the dock.[17]

The United Engineering Company Shipyard was across the estuary, near the old Naval Supply Terminal.[18] These transit sheds at the old terminals and those in San Francisco are typical of the pre-container break-bulk cargo facilities.

These are the types of terminals that were in use during FDR's lifetime.

Figure 27 - **Old Alameda Naval Supply Terminal "Refer Dock"**

Figure 28 - **Pier 31 in San Francisco**

Schnitzer Steel

Those big piles of brown stuff are scrap iron. Your old car may well have passed through Schnitzer Steel, which processes scrap metal for shipment. They are one of the largest ferrous metals recyclers in the United

Figure 29 - **Schnitzer Steel crane and car shredder**

States. The Oakland center is just one of their more than forty collection and processing facilities nationwide. On the West Coast, they export over 50,000 tons of scrap iron a month with their twenty-nine ships.

Cranes with big claws or magnets handle the steel, and the big yellow car shredder takes only fifteen seconds to turn a car into little pieces. Then, either the large crane or the long yellow conveyor belt loads the scrap steel into the ship's hold.

In 1909 the Moore Dry Dock Company started here. During World War II they expanded and included the area now used by the APL terminal.[19]

Moore built ships for both World Wars I and II and continued operation until 1961.[20]

From 1909 to 1954 Moore launched more than two hundred vessels of every size and description. In 1919 they set a shipbuilding record of launching six ships during one high tide.[21] In addition to building ships, they fabricated steel used in buildings and bridges.[22] During World War II more than 125,000 workers were employed here by Moore. Schnitzer opened their facility here in 1961 after the Moore Dry Dock Company closed.[23, 24]

Figure 30 - **Schnitzer Steel's conveyor belt loading a ship**

Figure 31 - **Schnitzer Steel's conveyor belt loading a ship**

Figure 32 - **Schnitzer Steel's dump bucket crane**

Inner Harbor Turning Basin

We are now passing through the Inner Harbor Turning Basin. Container ships turn here before or after visiting their individual berths in the Inner Harbor. This area is being enlarged to handle the new larger ships that will be using these terminals.

On the Alameda side of the estuary the Port will remove part of the old navy terminal, clear away part of the area, and construct shoreline improvements for the City of Alameda.

APL Terminal

American President Lines (APL) has five container cranes, and their pier is more than 2,000 feet long. It was built on the site of the Moore Dry Dock Company.

The company has room to store almost 4,000 containers on trailers, with another 4,000 stacked.[25]

The terminals can handle post-Panamax container ships. These ships can hold 4,300 twenty-foot containers, or enough to fill a train seventeen miles long. The new ships that will use the port will be much larger.

APL and its predecessors have been in the shipping and passenger business since 1849, although APL closed its passenger service more than twenty-five years ago.[26, 27]

Figure 33 - **Ship in Inner Harbor Turning Basin**

Figure 34 - **Removing part of the Old Naval Supply Pier in Alameda for Inner Harbor Turning Basin, May 7, 2002**

Figure 35 - **APL Terminal with two ships**

Another shipping line that we may see today has also been around for a long time. Matson Navigation, an important sponsor of the *Potomac*, was established in 1882, the year that Franklin Delano Roosevelt was born. It provided passenger service from 1908 to 1970.[28, 29]

Alameda Ferry Terminal

Figure 36 - **Matson Navigation employees on the *Potomac***

Next to the former Alameda Naval Supply Terminal is the Alameda Ferry Terminal.

Alameda has had ferry terminals since 1864. During the Civil War, the first railroad ferry terminal was on the south side of Alameda, near where the USS *Hornet* is now docked. The town of Woodstock was there, and a long wharf went out to deep water. The Woodstock wharf was used from 1864 until 1873.[30]

Two events occurred in 1869 that made the Bay Area an important link in worldwide commerce. The Suez Canal opened, giving us direct access to Europe, and completion of the transcontinental railroad gave us access to the U.S. market.[31, 32, 33]

The first transcontinental rail service in the area was to the Woodstock wharf in Alameda, where passengers boarded the ferry to San Francisco. Travel time between coasts was cut from more than 120 days by ship around the Horn of South America to 6 days across the continent by rail. There is an historical landmark in Alameda commemorating this event.[34, 35, 36, 37]

The Woodstock terminal served for a few months until the Central Pacific started using its depot at Broadway and Seventh Street in Oakland and the Oakland Point ferry terminal. Then, starting in 1871, passengers used Oakland's new Seventh Street Long Wharf; passenger service was moved to the new Southern Pacific Mole in 1882, while the Long Wharf was used for freight until 1918.[38, 39, 40]

Figure 37 - **Alameda Ferry Terminal with a ferry and old Southern Pacific maintenance shop**

The big sawtooth building behind the Ferry Terminal was built in 1910 by the Southern Pacific as a maintenance shop for the Red Trains, one of the streetcar lines. It later served as machine shop of United Engineering and Todd Shipyards. Rosenblum Cellars Winery now occupies part of the building.

The Old Alameda Ferry Terminal

In 1878, a year after the Statue of Liberty was dedicated, a new Alameda railroad ferry terminal was opened at the site of the current terminal.[41]

A railroad trestle crossed the Alameda marsh to the landfill made from dredging material. Here, at what was then the mouth of the estuary, the South Pacific Coast Railroad (SPC) built a new ferry terminal and freight wharves.[42]

In 1884, the year Eleanor Roosevelt was born, the rail line was extended two and one-half miles on a long trestle out to a deep-water wharf near a point that is now the end of the estuary.[43, 44]

End of Land in Alameda

On a 1920 map of Alameda, the area beyond the Alameda Ferry Terminal was open bay, and the Alameda side of the estuary was mostly marsh. On the Oakland side of the estuary the end of land was about where the new Cypress Freeway curves near the former army base.[45, 46]

Floating Dry Dock

The Bay Ship and Yacht Company operate floating dry docks that sink partway, allowing a vessel to float in; it is then re-floated, leaving the vessel above water and ready for repairs. This is where the *Potomac* gets her hull inspected and painted.

NOTE: The two Canadian Coast Guard ships that were berthed near here were moved in March 1999 (for more information see Local References on page 215).

Figure 38 - **Alameda Bay Ship and Yacht floating dry dock**

Alameda Naval Air Station

In 1917 the United States entered World War I, and Congress authorized emergency shipbuilding in the Bay Area.[47] That same year the navy expressed interest in building a base in the East Bay. In the 1930's the City of Alameda started filling 2,800 acres of marshy land and mud flats at the west end of Alameda to make a site for a large naval base.[48, 49, 50]

The Alameda Naval Air Station opened in 1940,[51] just in time for World War II. For almost fifty years, it was an aircraft repair station for a berthing base for the navy. The last

Figure 40 - **Ready Reserve fleet in Alameda at Pier 3 near the USS *Hornet***

aircraft was overhauled in 1996, and the aircraft carrier USS *Carl Vinson* was the last carrier berthed in Alameda; it left there in 1997.[52, 53]

Now owned by the City of Alameda, the Alameda Naval Air Station has been renamed Alameda Point with only a few Ready Reserve ships berthed at Pier 3, next to the USS *Hornet*. Looking across the runway you can see their onboard cranes reaching up in the air.

Airports

After World War I, there were several landing fields in the East Bay and a few airports with hangars and support facilities.[54]

Alameda had an airport in 1920 west of Webster Street on the site of College of Alameda and later a second airport on

Figure 39 - **Closed Alameda Naval Air Station, now known as Alameda Point**

a narrow strip of reclaimed land next to the Alameda Mole.[55] In 1927, Oakland opened one of the first commercial airports, and it became the western terminus for transcontinental airmail. In 1927, just a month after Charles Lindbergh had flown across the Atlantic, Albert Hegenberger and Lester Maitland[56] completed the first transpacific flight to Hawaii. In 1928, the first transpacific flight to Australia also originated in Oakland.[57, 58]

Air passenger service also started in 1928, and by 1929, with its 7,000-foot runway and five hangars, Oakland was one of the finest airfields in the world.[59]

Amelia Earhart first flew into Oakland in 1931, completing the first transcontinental flight of an autogiro.[60] She also made the first solo flight from Hawaii to North America in 1935, landing at Oakland.[61]

In 1937, Amelia Earhart flew west from the Oakland Airport on her first attempt to circumnavigate the world. In Honolulu, an accident extensively damaged the plane, and it was shipped back to the factory for repairs. When it was ready, she changed her flight plan and started her second attempt from Miami going east, with plans to end her around-the-world flight in Oakland on July 4, 1937. Unfortunately, the plane disappeared at sea on June 29, 1937.[62]

During World War II, Oakland Airport was known as Oakland Naval Air Station and was used exclusively by the military; all passenger service shifted to San Francisco Airport.

The airport was renamed North Field when the new Oakland Airport opened in 1962. Now the Oakland International Airport serves nearly 10 million passengers a year.[63]

The Western Aerospace Museum is located at North Field.[64]

Trains to Deep Water

In the years before airplanes and trucks, people and cargo traveled by wagon or train to the ships. However, in the 1800's it was more than two miles from Oakland and Alameda to deep water. To reach deep water it was necessary to build railroad trestles out to where larger ships and ferries could dock at deep-water wharves. As the estuary was dredged, rock walls were built on each side of the estuary and the dredged material was put behind these jetties; these fingers of land became known as the Alameda Mole and Western Pacific Oakland Mole. An additional Southern Pacific Oakland Mole went out to deep water from Seventh Street. In this case, the word *mole* is from Latin and means a structure in the water that serves as a breakwater or pier.

Alameda Mole

The Alameda Mole started in 1884 as a trestle that paralleled the estuary out to a deep-water wharf.[65] The Alameda Mole had ferry service for both passengers and freight. After a fire destroyed the old ferry terminal, the Southern Pacific Railroad opened a new terminal in 1905. It served until 1939, when the Bay Bridge access to San Francisco made the ferry service unprofitable.[66, 67]

By 1940, much of the area behind the mole had been filled in to make the Alameda Naval Air Station. The navy demolished the abandoned ferry terminal building in 1941 to clear the flight path for the runway. By 1960 the runway had been extended to the site of the old ferry terminal.

Oakland Moles

At Seventh Street Oakland Point there were both the Long Wharf, opened in 1871, and Oakland Southern Pacific Mole, built in 1882. After the Central Pacific bought all of the small railroads in the area and formed a partnership in the Oakland Waterfront

Company, it had a complete monopoly on both rail shipping and the Oakland waterfront. The Central Pacific reorganized in 1885 as the Southern Pacific.

Figure 41 - **Oakland Western Pacific Mole, September 1999**

In 1859, Oakland citizens raised $14,000 to dredge a makeshift channel through the sandbar. Starting in 1874, the Army Corps of Engineers began dredging the estuary and by 1894 had built stone jetties two miles out to deep water on both sides of the estuary.[68]

Figure 42 - **Estuary dredging new deep-water terminals, March 2000**

In 1903, the Western Pacific Railroad was founded, and the first spike was driven in 1906 at Third and Union streets in Oakland.[69] To break the Southern Pacific monopoly, the Western Pacific soon started laying track on the north estuary jetty using armed guards. Southern Pacific lost the legal battle and both the City of Oakland and the Western Pacific gained control of a large portion of the waterfront, including all of the landfill areas.[70]

Western Pacific freight service started in 1909, and passenger service started in 1910 at the new Oakland Third and Washington Street station with passengers taking the ferry to San Francisco from the Western Pacific Oakland Mole.[71, 72] In 1911 ships started sailing directly from the Western Pacific Mole to Japan.

Western Pacific passenger ferry service from Oakland to San Francisco continued until 1917, when the U.S. government took over the railroads and Western Pacific was required to close its ferry and barge service.

Figure 43 - **New terminal under construction, April 2002**

All Western Pacific passenger trains then went to the Southern Pacific Oakland Mole. After World War I, Western Pacific ferry service resumed and continued until 1939. The most memorable Western Pacific passenger train was the *California Zephyr*, which ran between Oakland and Chicago from 1949 to 1970. In 1982 Western Pacific merged with Union Pacific, thus ending eighty years of Western Pacific railroad service to Oakland.[73, 74]

Figure 44 - **Two new cranes on delivery ship, May 10, 2002**[75]

For those who like railroads, there is the Golden Gate Railroad Museum at Hunters Point Naval Shipyards in San Francisco[76] and the California State Railroad Museum in Sacramento.[77]

New Terminals

On the Oakland side of the estuary new large container terminals are being built between the APL terminal and the end of the estuary. These will handle new large ships with a 46-foot draft.

When these are completed, they will have ten of the largest cranes in the world. In October 2000, the first four cranes were delivered by ship from China.[78] During the summer of 2001, these new terminal cranes started handling containers. The second ship arrived with two smaller cranes and two large cranes in May 2002, and the third shipment of four large cranes arrived in June 2002.

Figure 45 - **New terminal cranes on delivery ship, December 18, 2000**

New cranes were braced on the delivery ship. Note the size of the employee compared to the size of the wheels and braces.

Figure 46 - **New terminal crane bracing on delivery ship**

Figure 47 - **New terminal cranes bracing on delivery ship**

[1] Much of the waterfront had been extended with landfill beyond the 1852 low water line. The court ruled that Southern Pacific Railroad owned only to the 1852 low water line and the City of Oakland owned between the 1852 low water line and the current low water line.

[2] For more information see website [01/06/03] www.portofoakland.com.

[3] Containers are 20, 24, 40, 45, 53 feet long, 8 feet wide and from 8 to 9.6 feet tall. All shipping is measured in TEU's or Twenty Foot Container Equivalent Units.

[4] Panamax freighters are the largest vessels that can go through the Panama Canal, post-Panamax are larger vessels, see "Container Freighters" on page 98.

[5] For more information on container freighters see "Container Freighters" on page 98.

[6] The last shipment of four cranes arrived from China on June 14, 2002.

[7] Bagwell (1982) page 192.

[8] Minor (2000) pages 25, 56. [Dedicated on October 20, 1982 and named in honor the founder of the old terminal.]

[9] Information from website [12/17/01] www.invent.org/book/book-text/71.html.

[10] Daniel (Ed.) (1982) page 30. [President McKinley was shot on Sept. 6, and died on September 14, 1901. The Chinese Boxer Rebellion started in 1898 and ended Sept. 7, 1901. First Oklahoma land rush was in 1889; on Aug. 9, 1901,the Oklahoma Territory gave 6,500 new homesteaders 160 acres each.]

[11] Westerlin (1996) Containers Transform the Waterfront.

[12] Minor (1996) Cranes Alight at Encinal Terminals.
    Minor (2000) page 48.

[13] Schwendinger (1984) page 152.

[14] From Port of Oakland Overview Brochure, Sept. 27, 1962. [Can unload ships in one-sixth the time of conventional ships.]

[15] Port of Oakland, Room With a View Exhibit, panel #8. First trainload of containers arrived Sept. 12, 1968.
    Minor (2000) page 54.

[16] Schwendinger (1984) page 134. [History of APL.]

[17] Port of Oakland Terminal Specifications Brochure.

[18] Southern Pacific Co. (before 1874 –1942), United Engineering (1942–1945), Matson Navigation (1945–1959),Todd (1959–1983), AGL (1983 to present). Alameda Gateway, LTD (AGL), plaintiff, v. The United States, defendant and Port of Oakland, No. 97-160L, December 23, 1999. Website [08/12/00] www.contracts.orc.doc.gov/fedcl/opinions/99opin/97-160L.html.

[19] Moore (1994) page 74. [Purchased a small shipyard belonging to the Boole family.]

[20] Moore (1994) pages 238, 275. [The last powered vessel launched was a ferry hull #308, on January 22, 1954.]

[21] Moore (1994).

[22] Cooper (1996) Moore Dry Dock Co. Becomes Schnitzer Steel. [Park St. Bridge (1934–35), High St. Bridge (1938–39).]

[23] Information from Hoover's the Business Network. Website [01/06/03] www.hoovers.com.
    (Gary Schnitzer confirmed data by phone on 10/10/01.)

[24] Cooper (1996). [Schnitzer Steel uses Moore Dry Dock site.]

[25] Port of Oakland Terminal Specifications Brochure, available from the Port of Oakland.

[26] Niven (1987) page 26. [Pacific Mail Steamship Company started service between San Francisco and Panama in 1849. Passenger service ended in 1973.]

[27] Pacific Mail 1848 to 1899; The Dollar Line 1900 to 1950; American President Lines 1950 to present.

[28] Capt. William Matson sailed his first ship out of San Francisco April 10, 1882. [01/06/03] www.matson.com.

[29] Goodwin (1994) page 76. [January 30, 1882.]

[30] Minor (1993) page 3.

[31] Harrison (1971) page 792.

[32] Ambrose (2000).

[33] The 47 ½ mile Panama Railroad from the Atlantic to the Pacific was completed January 28, 1855. From website [01/06/03] www.trainweb.org/panama/historyc.html.

[34] Cooper (1996) The Transcontinental Railroad Comes to Town.

[35] Historical Landmark No. 440 - Alameda Terminal of the First Transcontinental Railroad, see page 225.

[36] Bagwell (1982) page 52. [First train arrived Alameda Sept. 6, 1896. First train arrived Oakland Nov. 8, 1869.]

[37] The Panama trans-isthmus railroad was completed in 1855.

[38] Bagwell (1982) page 47. [In 1863, steam trains went from Broadway down Seventh Street to new Oakland Point ferry landing.]

[39] Cooper (1996) The Transcontinental Railroad Comes to Town.

[40] Bagwell (1982) page 59. [Central Pacific opened Long Wharf in 1871.]

[41] Minor (1993) page 4.

[42] Minor (1993) Page 4.

[43] Minor (1993) page 4.

[44] Bean (1988). [Born Oct. 11, 1884; Died Nov. 7, 1962.]

[45] Bagwell (1982) map on pages 34, 35.

[46] Oakland City Library, Oakland Room, Map File.

[47] Bean (1988).

[48] Fulbright, Leslie. "Tied to the Bay," *Alameda Times-Star*, Sunday, July 4, 1999, page 8, special section.

[49] Minor (1993) page 30.

[50] Minor (2000) page 2. [1923 map shows area as "Naval Base Site."]

[51] November 1, 1940. [Alameda Naval Air Station opened.]

[52] January 14, 1997. [Aircraft carrier USS *Carl Vinson* left Alameda.]

[53] "A Fond Farewell," *Alameda Times-Star*, Sunday, July 4, 1999, page 12, special section.

[54] Campbell, Ace (2000). [Northern California Chapter of the American Aviation Historical Society, 1-408-251-5936. During the 20th century, there were over 700 landing fields within 75 miles of the Golden Gate.]

[55] Minor (1993) page 31. [1920 map with aviation field and aeroplane hangar.] Minor (2000) page 97. [1928 airport.]

[56] Bagwell (1982) page 198. [On June 28, 1927, U.S. Army Lieutenants Lester J. Maitland and Albert F. Hegenberger made first nonstop flight to Hawaii.]

[57] Cooper (1996) *Oakland Builds an Airport*.

[58] Cooper (1996) *Pioneer Aviators at the Oakland Airport*.

[59] Bagwell (1982) page 200.

[60] Cooper (1996) *Pioneer Aviators at the Oakland Airport*.

[61] Minor (2000) pages 95–96.

[62] Amelia Earhart data from website [01/06/03] http://ellensplace.net/eae_intr.html and from website [01/06/03] www.incwell.com/Biographies/Earhart.html.

[63] Cooper (1996) *Oakland Builds an Airport*.

[64] For more information on the Western Aerospace Museum see Historic Data Sources on page 259.

[65] Minor (1993) page 6.

[66] Minor (1993) page 6.

[67] Ford (1977) pages 191, 213. [At 1: 23 a.m. January 15, 1939, the ferry *Oakland* made the last trip from the Alameda Mole.]

[68] Minor (2000) page 11. [The jetties were called training walls to train the water to clean the estuary.]

[69] First Western Pacific spike driven January 2, 1906, last spike November 1, 1909. Freight service started December 1, 1909 and passenger service started August 22, 1910. [01/06/03] www.wprrhs.org.

[70] The courts ruled the Southern Pacific owned up to the 1852 low tide line and the City of Oakland owned all filled land.

[71] Bagwell (1982) page 59, map on pages 201–202. [Map at Oakland Public Main Library, Oakland Research Room.]

[72] Minor (2000) page 19.

[73] Western Pacific Railroad Historical Society [01/06/03] www.wprrhs.org.

[74] The California Zepher cars *Silver Crescent* and *Silver Stag* are in the Gold Coast Railroad Museum. See page 259.

[75] Photograph by David Dibble, May 10, 2002.

[76] Golden Gate Railroad Museum from website [01/06/03] www.ggrm.org.

[77] California State Railroad Museum from website [01/06/03] www.csrmf.org.

[78] Rubenstein (2000, Oct. 20). [Delivered October 20, 2000. Height of cranes about 220 feet.]

4 - Middle and Outer Harbor
Middle and Outer Harbor Map

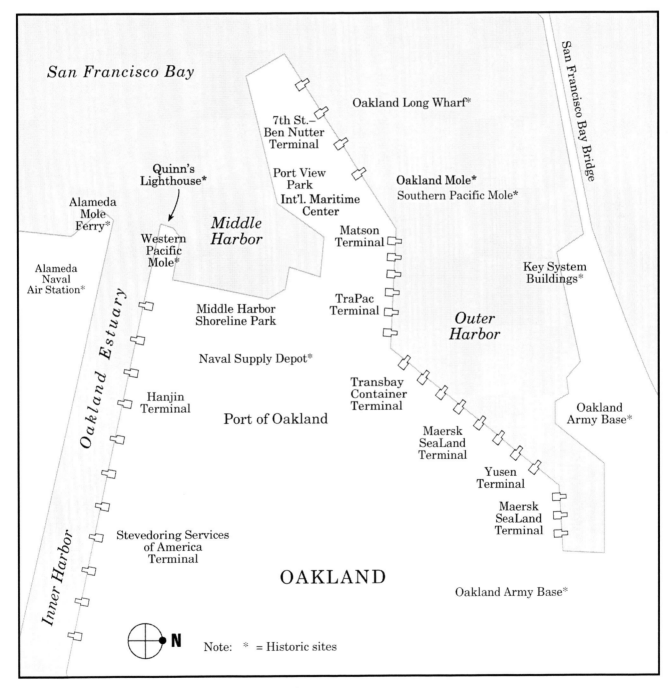

San Francisco Bay

San Francisco Bay Bridge

Oakland Long Wharf*

7th St.–
Ben Nutter
Terminal

Quinn's
Lighthouse*

Port View
Park
Int'l. Maritime
Center

Oakland Mole*
Southern Pacific Mole*

Alameda
Mole
Ferry*

Middle
Harbor

Western
Pacific
Mole*

Matson
Terminal

Alameda
Naval
Air Station*

Key System
Buildings*

Middle Harbor
Shoreline Park

TraPac
Terminal

Outer
Harbor

Naval Supply Depot*

Hanjin
Terminal

Port of Oakland

Transbay
Container
Terminal

Oakland
Army Base*

Maersk
SeaLand
Terminal

Yusen
Terminal

Maersk
SeaLand
Terminal

Stevedoring Services
of America
Terminal

OAKLAND

Oakland Estuary

Inner Harbor

Oakland Army Base*

N

Note: * = Historic sites

Figure 48 - **Middle and Outer Harbor Map**

Old Naval Supply Center

The area just the other side of Oakland Western Pacific Mole was the Naval Supply Center. It was commissioned in 1941 and at the end of World War II there were 14,000 employees.[1]

Figure 49 - **Naval Supply Center, Oakland, September 1999**

The buildings were demolished in 1999, and the area now includes the Middle Harbor Shoreline Park, tidelands restoration project, and new rail and marine terminal facilities.

L. J. Quinn's Lighthouse

In the late nineteenth century, deep water was several miles from shore and the channel to the estuary was marked by the ferry terminals on the Alameda side. On the Oakland side of the estuary stood the Oakland Entrance Lighthouse. It was

Figure 50 - **Estuary channel Green Light #7, 1903–65 site of Quinn's Lighthouse**

about two miles from shore, though there was a jetty going part way out to mark the channel.

In 1902, the United States acquired perpetual control over the Panama Canal Zone; that same year a new lighthouse was built at the end of the estuary. It became known as the L.J. Quinn's Lighthouse, named after one of the lighthouse keepers.

By 1950, the Western Pacific Railroad ferry slip went out a little beyond the lighthouse. It was the only lighthouse in the world directly connected to a transcontinental railroad.

In 1965, the Coast Guard replaced the lighthouse with an automated green light on a white tank-like structure. It marks the entrance to the estuary and the site of the old lighthouse.[3]

The unused lighthouse was sold and then barged to the new Embarcadero Cove development in 1970.

Figure 51 - **L. J. Quinn's Lighthouse, about 1903** [2]

At the Restaurant and Pub, you can enjoy a meal or a drink and see old photographs showing how the lighthouse looked before and during its move.[4]

Middle Harbor Shoreline Park

Since the Naval Supply Center closed in 1998, the Port of Oakland has been redeveloping the Middle Harbor.[6]

The Middle Harbor Shoreline Park includes the former navy wharf, Point Arnold, and a tideland restoration project that will deposit dredged sand in the basin in order to provide shallow water and shoreline habitats for marine plants, animals and birds.[7] The *Room With a View* exhibition center is also located there, in the former Southern Pacific Oakland Pier Train Tower, which was moved from the SP Mole at the end of Seventh Street.

Figure 52 - **L. J. Quinn's Lighthouse and Western Pacific ferry slip, about 1950** [5]

Figure 54 - **L. J. Quinn's Lighthouse Historic Landmark Restaurant and Pub.**

Figure 53 - **Middle Harbor Shoreline Park and the Tidelands Restoration Project for marine life and birds**

Seventh Street Terminal

The Seventh Street Terminal extension was developed between 1965 and 1971, using excavated materials from Bay Area Rapid Transit (BART) construction projects. This included materials from building the tunnels and dredging the BART tube under the bay. Here in 1968, container trade began between the United States and Japan.

Figure 56 - **Middle Harbor *Room With a View* Exhibition Center**

This was the last major bay fill before the formation in 1965 of the Bay Conservation and Development Commission (BCDC).[8]

The Seventh Street Terminal is part of the Outer Harbor, which includes the old army base.

In 1941, the army opened Camp Knight on the Outer Harbor shoreline. The army base served as an induction center during the Vietnam War and is now being converted to civilian use.

Maersk SeaLand Terminal

At the far end of the Outer Harbor are the oldest container cranes at the Maersk SeaLand Terminal.[9] The switch from onboard cranes to land-based cranes was made in 1966.[10]

Two more container cranes have since been added to this terminal.

Figure 55 - **The first cranes at the Port Of Oakland are at the Maersk SeaLand Terminal**

Nutter Marine Container Terminal

The Ben E. Nutter Marine Container Terminal is at the west end of the Seventh Street Terminal. The cranes have a low profile so they did not interfere with the flight path of planes from the Alameda Naval Air Station.[11]

Figure 57 - **Ben E. Nutter Marine Container Terminal**

Matson Terminal

The Matson Terminal is adjacent to the Nutter Terminal and uses two different types of cranes.[12]

TraPac Terminal and Transbay Container Terminal have the next five cranes.[13]

Figure 58 - **Matson Terminal**

Three Types of Cranes

The three types of cranes along the center section of the Outer Harbor belong to Maersk SeaLand[14], Yusen[15], and the second Maersk SeaLand[16] terminal at the end.

Figure 59 - **Three different types of cranes**

Burma Road Terminal

The Burma Road Terminal is on the site of the old army base. It has one crane designed to lift break-bulk cargo that is very heavy or too bulky for container shipping.

Figure 60 - **Burma Road Terminal with break-bulk crane**

The Long Wharf

At Oakland Point, the Central Pacific Railroad extended the Seventh Street pier to become the Long Wharf to deep water in 1871. They used it for both passengers and freight until the Central Pacific passenger mole was completed in 1882.[17, 18] The Long Wharf was subsequently used only for freight until 1918, when it was closed.[19] The wharf was south of the current Bay Bridge and extended into the Outer Harbor.[20] In 1885 the Central Pacific reorganized and became the Southern Pacific Railroad. An 1882 "bird's-eye view" of the city of Oakland also shows the proposed 40th Street Long Wharf, which later became the Key System ferry terminal.[21] At 40th street, in 1903, the Key System added a three-mile trestle, almost to Yerba Buena Island, for its new ferry terminal.[22] The Bay Bridge is just north of the old Key System ferry terminal and some of the old Key System buildings are still in use near the Bay Bridge.[23]

The 1880's brought many changes that would have a long-term effect on the Bay Area. With the enactment of the 1882 Chinese Exclusion Act, the ethnic diversity of the Bay Area labor force started to change.[24] Edison invented the light bulb in 1883, and Eleanor Roosevelt was born in 1884.[25] The labor movement changed forever with the founding in 1886 of the American Federation of Labor.[26] People arriving in New York saw the world with new hope after the Statue of Liberty was dedicated in 1886.[27]

[1] Lavoie (1996) *Oakland Naval Supply Depot*.

[2] Photograph of Quinn Lighthouse courtesy of United States Lighthouse Society. See Historic Data Sources on page 259.

[3] The 1965 date is from data supplied by the United States Lighthouse Society & L.J. Quinn's Lighthouse Restaurant & Pub.

[4] From materials supplied by the L.J. Quinn's Lighthouse Restaurant & Pub.

[5] Photograph of Quinn Lighthouse courtesy of United States Lighthouse Society. See Historic Data Sources on page 259.

[6] The Naval Supply Center was later known as the Fleet & Industrial Supply Center Oakland (FISCO).

[7] NOAA Nautical Chart 18650 *San Francisco Bay Candlestick Point to Angel Island Jan 31, 01*.

[8] Cooper (1996). *Tunnel Becomes Terminal*.

[9] Port of Oakland Map, Maersk SeaLand berths 20–21.

[10] Minor (2002) page 52. [SeaLand switched from shipboard cranes to land-based cranes.]

[11] Port of Oakland Map, Ben E. Nutter Terminal berths 35, 37, & 38.

[12] Port of Oakland Map, Matson Terminal berths 32–34.

[13] Port of Oakland Map, Trapac Terminal berth 30 with three cranes; and Transbay Container Terminal, berths 25 & 26 with two cranes.

[14] Port of Oakland Map, Maersk-SeaLand Terminal berth 24.

[15] Port of Oakland Map, Yusen Terminal berth 23.

[16] Port of Oakland Map, Maersk SeaLand berths 20–21.

[17] Bagwell (1982) page 58. [Central Pacific opened the Oakland Mole for passenger service on January 22, 1882.]

[18] Kemble (1957) page 39.

[19] Bagwell (1982) page 58. [Long Wharf was removed to help Outer Harbor vessel traffic.]

[20] Bagwell (1982) map on pages 34–35. [Map available in Oakland City Main Library, Oakland Room.]

[21] Bagwell (1982) view on page 129.

[22] Bagwell (1982) map on pages 202–203; Long wharf and Oakland SP Mole on page 59; Key System on page 165.

[23] A photograph on page 48 shows the Key System trestle and ferry terminal and the Bay Bridge in 1935.

[24] Chinese Exclusion Repeal Act of 1943, Approved December 17, 1943. From website [01/06/03] www.cetel.org/1943_repeal.html.

[25] Eleanor Anna Roosevelt (October 11, 1884 to November 7, 1962). From website [01/06/03] www.whitehouse.gov/history/firstladies/ar32.html.

[26] American Federation of Labor started in Columbus, Ohio in 1886. From website [01/06/03] www.pittsburghaflcio.org/founding.html.

[27] Statue of Liberty dedicated on October 28, 1886. From website [01/06/03] www.nps.gov/stli.

5 - Bay Bridge and Yerba Buena Island (YBI)

Bay Bridge and YBI Map

Figure 61 - Bay Bridge and Yerba Buena Island (YBI) Map

Bay Bridge History

The Bay Bridge is an FDR legacy and was funded in part as a New Deal WPA project.[1] Construction started in 1933, the same year FDR became president, and ended in 1936, two years ahead of schedule. The project employed more than 6,500 men; unfortunately, 24 lost their lives.

It was then the longest, biggest, and most expensive bridge in the world, and used almost 7 percent of the entire steel output of the United States. The Golden Gate Bridge was built at the same time. Bay Area bridge construction helped depression recovery by putting people to work, both directly on bridges and roadways, and nationwide in the production and shipping of materials for these massive projects.

The Tunnel

In 1936, the tunnel through Yerba Buena Island (YBI) was the largest single bore in the world, 76 feet wide and 58 feet high.

Until 1958, there were six lanes of automobile traffic on the upper deck. On the lower deck, there were three lanes of truck traffic and the Key System's two train tracks. (See page 214 for a photograph of the underside of the bridge.)

In 1958, when the train tracks were removed to make one-way traffic on each deck, the roadway through the tunnel was lowered by two feet to allow room for trucks on the upper deck. This was done without stopping traffic during the day; each night the "bump" moved farther through the tunnel. As you drive over the bridge toward San Francisco the roadway dips just before you get to the tunnel.

Four Types of Bridges

The Bay Bridge actually consists of four different types of bridges, connected by a tunnel through Yerba Buena Island. Starting from Oakland, there are two types of truss bridges joined to a cantilever bridge. On the San Francisco side of the island there are two suspension bridges connected by a large central anchorage.[2]

Figure 62 - **Bay Bridge truss sections with expansion joint between the two types of truss bridges**

Figure 63 - **Bay Bridge cantilever sections and short truss section going to Yerba Buena Island**

Figure 64 - **Bay Bridge East suspension span**

Expansion Section That Fell

Between the two types of truss bridges, a short expansion section allows the bridge to flex during an earthquake. During the 1989 Loma Prieta earthquake, the bridge flexed beyond its engineering limits. The expansion section of the upper deck slipped from its supports and came to rest with one end on the lower deck.

Expansion section

Figure 65 - **Bay Bridge expansion section that fell in 1989 earthquake**

The Bent Bridge

The bridge does not go straight from Oakland to Yerba Buena Island (YBI), but has a bend in the middle. This bend was necessary to go around the Key System ferry terminal.

Suspension Bridge

At almost two miles,[4] the suspension bridge is the longest crossing of navigable water in the world. Two 28-inch[5] diameter suspension cables hold up the bridge, and each cable is made of approximately 18,000[6] pencil-sized wires.

Center Anchorage

The central anchorage is the largest and deepest bridge pier ever constructed. It is more than 500 feet tall, almost 100 feet wide and 200 feet long, and rests on the bottom 250 feet below.[7]

From top to bottom the anchorage is taller than the Great Pyramid.[8]

It was built by sinking steel caissons into a hole dredged in the bottom. Engineers put 15-foot diameter pipes in each of the holes in the caissons. After pumping out the water, they filled the pipes with concrete.[9]

All of the anchorages and piers have been seismically retrofitted, and all of the critical bridge rivets are being replaced with stronger bolts.

Figure 66 - **Bay Bridge and Key System Ferry Terminal, 1935** [3]

Figure 67 - **Bay Bridge central anchorage**

Figure 68 - **Bay Bridge tower seismic retrofitting, September 1999**

History of Yerba Buena Island

Yerba Buena Island (YBI) has been called Wood Island, Sea Bird Island, and Goat Island. During the 1830's and 1840's, there was a herd of goats on the island. On an 1847 map it is named Yerba Buena Island.[10] However, on an 1869 map it is named Goat Island.

During the Civil War, the island was a military base.

During World War II, the navy transformed Treasure Island into a naval base, maintaining it until the base closed in 1999.

Figure 69 - **Coast Guard Vessel Traffic Control Center and antennas**

Coast Guard Vessel Traffic Control

On top of Yerba Buena Island (YBI), you can see a building and several large antennas; this is part of the Coast Guard Vessel Traffic Control Center, with radio, radar, and video coverage of the bay.

All commercial ships must check in before moving between locations.

Figure 70 - **Yerba Buena Island with Coast Guard Buoy Tender Station and Vessel Traffic Control Center**

[1] WPA (Works Projects Administration). See "FDR's New Deal Agencies in Bay Area" on page 169.

[2] Dupré, J. (1997) page 78.

[3] Associated Oil Company photograph from San Francisco Museum website [02/21/02] www.sfmuseum.org.

[4] The suspension part of the bridge is 1.78 miles long.

[5] The cables are 28¼ inches in diameter.

[6] There are 17,464 wires in each cable.

[7] Center pier is 502 feet tall, 197 feet long and 92 feet wide, and is 242 feet in the water. The total volume is 571,387 cubic yards. The upper part of the pier is hollow, with a construction raft floating on the water.

[8] The Khufu Pyramid of Gizeh is 480 tall and 755 feet at the base. The total volume is 15,200,666 cubic yards. From website [01/06/03] www.geocities.com/athens/sparta/2622/html/gizeh.htm.

[9] Moore (1994) page 207.

[10] Bagwell (1982) 1820 map pages 12–13, 1869 map pages 34–35.

6 - SF Waterfront
San Francisco Waterfront Map

Figure 71 - **San Francisco Waterfront Map**

A Little San Francisco History

San Francisco has a colorful history, where unexpected events became commonplace. Though we think of the Hudson's Bay Company as being in Canada, in 1841 it established a California headquarters in San Francisco. An historical landmark marks the site.[1]

In 1847, Yerba Buena had seventy-nine buildings[2] and a population of 800[3] when it was renamed San Francisco, and Jasper O'Farrell, an engineer, drafted the first city plan. A street is named in his honor. The next year San Francisco opened the first public school in California.[4] Then, with the gold rush in 1849, the population of San Francisco went from 800 to 30,000, and the next year an additional 65,000 people arrived.[5] During part of this time, the population doubled every ten days.

The gold rush thus not only promoted a rapid movement to statehood, but also a notoriously wild city that came to be called the new "Barbary Shore." An historical landmark shows the site of Fort Gunny-Bags, which was the headquarters for the Vigilance Committee.[6]

In 1852, the What Cheer House opened as a hotel for men only, and no liquor was allowed on the premises; it housed California's first free library and the first museum.[7]

In 1876, Alexander Bell invented the telephone, the same year that the cable cars were started in San Francisco.[8]

Giants New Pacific Bell Ballpark

The home of the Giants is the new 41,000-seat SBC (Pacific Bell) ballpark. Construction started in 1998, and the first baseball game was played there in April 2000. The *Potomac* visits here occasionally.

Figure 72 - **China Basin and the Giants SBC (Pacific Bell) ballpark**

China and Central Basin

Commercial shipbuilding in the Bay Area began in gold rush days. In 1850, the Pacific Mail Steamship Company, the predecessor of American President Lines (APL), opened a shipyard in Benicia.[9] In 1854, the U.S. Navy opened a shipyard in Vallejo on Mare Island and in the next 142 years the Mare Island Shipyard built more than 500 ships for the navy.[10, 11]

The Hunters Point Shipyards have also been involved in shipbuilding since the 1850's. The Stone Boat Yard started in 1853 at Hunters Point, eventually moved to Alameda, and is now the oldest ongoing boat-building business on the Pacific Coast.[12, 13]

Union Iron Works built its first 750-ton vessel in China Basin in 1885, where the ballpark is now located, a year before the Statue of Liberty was dedicated.[14] For comparison, the *Potomac* is a 337-ton vessel.

In 1892, the year Grover Cleveland was elected president, Union Iron Works built the navy cruiser *Olympia*, Admiral Dewey's flagship in the 1898 battle of Manila Bay.[15]

Over a sixty-year period, hundreds of navy and merchant ships were built in shipyards from China Basin to Central Basin.

In 1923, the year before FDR formed a law practice and managed Al Smith's presidential campaign, the Stone Boat Yard built a 138-foot schooner, the last large commercial wooden sailing ship built in the United States. During World War II Stone built wooden minesweepers and tugboats in Alameda.

New San Francisco Shoreline Planned

Looking south, the big Mission Rock Terminal is Pier 50. Pier 52 is just south of Pier 50 and is being developed into a new public boat-launch ramp, café, fishing and bait shop, and parking lot for trailers.[16]

Just south of the Bay Bridge, Piers 30–32 will become a $270 million cruise ship terminal and retail complex, with a 400-room hotel, jazz club and movie theaters.[17]

Just north of the Bay Bridge will be a new Rincon Park and two new restaurants.[18]

Old Shoreline

As we cruise by the piers on the San Francisco shoreline, it is hard to realize how much of this area was open water before 1850. As San Francisco grew, the City filled in marshlands and built new land on the remains of ships that had been abandoned by their crews during the gold rush.[19]

In 1846, two years after FDR's mother, Sara Delano, was born, Captain J.B. Montgomery landed the sloop-of-war *Portsmouth*[20] at Montgomery and Clay and raised the Stars and Stripes on the plaza.[21] The site is called Portsmouth Square; now because of landfill it is eight blocks from the water.

In 1848, the year gold was discovered at Sutter's Mill, a pier existed where Market and Bush Streets meet. This is now six long blocks from the water. There is an historical landmark at the location.[22] By the 1850's, the bay had been filled out to Front Street.

Ferry Building

The Ferry Building was dedicated in 1898, five years after the electric streetcars replaced horse-cars in Alameda and Oakland.[23, 24]

Because it was a steel-framed structure, it survived the 1906 earthquake with only moderate damage. It was modeled after the Gheraldi tower in Italy.

In 1957, a double-decker freeway was built along the Embarcadero from Folsom Street to Broadway, blocking views of the Ferry Building. The 1989 Loma Prieta

Figure 73 - **San Francisco Ferry Building, dedicated in 1898**.

earthquake damaged the freeway, and it was torn down. Begun in 2001, a $66 million renovation of the Ferry Building includes shops, restaurants, offices, and new ferry landings.[25]

Coit Tower

Coit Tower is a 180-foot-tall reinforced concrete column built in 1933 on Telegraph Hill. It is open to the public, and the observation gallery on top gives a good view of the Bay Area. On the ground floor walls nineteen murals are products of FDR's Public Works Art Project.[26]

There was controversy over the social criticism represented by the murals, and they were not always popular.

Figure 74 - **Telegraph Hill with Coit Tower, built in 1935**

The tower was named after Lillie Hitchcock Coit who in 1929 left $125,000 to San Francisco to "add beauty to the city I have always loved." Lillie is best known for her lifelong passion for fire fighting. After becoming a mascot to the Knickerbocker Hose Company #5 in 1863 at age 20, she rarely missed a blaze. She smoked cigars and dressed in men's clothes in order to gamble in the North Beach saloons, publicly ice-skated in short skirts and was even discovered by her husband on a men's camping trip. [27]

Telegraph Hill

In 1849, Telegraph Hill was one of a number of connected flag semaphores which let merchants know when a ship was nearing the bay.[28] Telegraph Hill was used for only five years, but it kept its name when, in 1854, an electrical telegraph system replaced the flag semaphores.[29, 30]

However, the Bay Area was still a frontier; in 1850 a grizzly bear was caught near Mission Dolores,[31] and in 1853 a man was mauled by a grizzly bear in the City of Oakland.[32]

SP Golden Gate Ferry *Santa Rosa*

The Southern Pacific Golden Gate Ferry *Santa Rosa* is permanently berthed at Pier 3 and is used for commercial office space.[33]

Figure 75 - **Southern Pacific Railroad Golden Gate Ferry** *Santa Rosa*

Ship Pilot Service

All commercial ships on the bay must have a pilot on board, and the San Francisco Bar Pilot Service uses Pier 9 as its headquarters and base for its orange-hulled vessels. The San Francisco Bar Pilot Service started in 1836 and in 1850 was commissioned by the California state government. They started with two pilot boats, the *Rialto* and the *Relief*.[34]

Figure 76 - **Pilot boats at Pier 9**

Ro-Ro Ship

The USS *Cape Henry* is a Ro-Ro, or Roll-on-Roll-off, ship which can dock at most piers and drive trucks or army tanks off the ship like a ferry, or it can also be unloaded with forklifts or with the crane on the foredeck.

The red, white and blue stripes around the upper structure indicate that is it a navy ship, maintained by civilians as a part of the Ready Reserve fleet.

As we go by you can look up the ramp into the ship. One ramp goes to the upper deck and two ramps go below.

Figure 77 - **USS *Cape Henry* foredeck crane**

Figure 78 - **USS *Cape Henry* with red, white and blue stripes of Ready Reserve fleet**

1 Historical Landmark No. 819 - Hudson Bay Company, San Francisco. See page 242.

2 April 1, 1847, count of structures in Yerba Buena showed 79 buildings that included 22 shanties, 31 frame houses and 26 adobe dwellings. From San Francisco Museum [01/06/03] www.sfmuseum.org/hist/chron1.html.

3 March 18, 1848, *California Star* reported that non-native population of San Francisco was 575 males, 177 females, and 60 children (total 812). From San Francisco Museum website [01/06/03] www.sfmuseum.org/hist/chron1.html.

4 Historical Landmark No. 587 - First Public School in California, San Francisco. See page 238.

5 December 31, 1849, population of San Francisco was estimated at 100,000 including 35,000 people who came by sea; 3,000 sailors who deserted ships; and 42,000 who came overland. From San Francisco Museum [01/05/03] www.sfmuseum.org/hist/chron1.html.

6 Historical Landmark No. 90 - Fort Gunny-Bags, San Francisco. See page 236.

7 Historical Landmark No. 650 - Site of the What Cheer House, San Francisco. See page 239.

8 See 1876 Time Line Reference on page 248.

9 Kemble (1957) page 60.

10 Vallejo Naval & Historical Museum website [01/06/03] www.vallejomuseum.org.

11 Kemble (1957) page 39.

12 "The Stone Boat Yard: Three Generations of Quality," *Wood Boats*, November/December 1992, pages 60–68.

13 "Stone Boat Yard Begins a New Chapter," *Alameda Journal*, February 15, 2000, page A6, Business Section.

14 Bonnett (1999) page 10.

15 Bonnett (1999) page 11.

16 "Envisioning a New Look for the Waterfront," *San Francisco Chronicle*, February 16, 2000, front page.

17 "Envisioning a New Look for the Waterfront," *San Francisco Chronicle*, February 16, 2000, front page.

18 "Envisioning a New Look for the Waterfront," *San Francisco Chronicle*, February 16, 2000, front page.

19 Kembel (1957) page 11 [map of old and new water front].

20 Dictionary of American Naval Fighting Ships, Vol. V pages 360–361. From website [01/06/03] www.hazegray.org [Sloop-of-war *Portsmouth* was built in 1843 and served until 1915. She was 153 feet long with a beam of 38 feet. A Sloop-of-war is a small sailing warship with guns on only one deck.]

21 See Historical Landmark No. 81 - Landing Place of Captain J. B. Montgomery, San Francisco, on page 233.

22 See Historical Landmark No. 83 - Shoreline Markers, San Francisco, on page 234.

23 Olmsted (1998) page 20 [dedicated July 13, 1898].

24 Minor (1993) page 6. [1893 electric streetcars, or trolleys, began running between Park Street and Oakland.]

25 "Envisioning a New Look for the Waterfront," *San Francisco Chronicle*, February 16, 2000, front page.

26 See "FDR New Deal Agencies" on page 169.

27 Lillie Hitchcock Coit lived from 1843 to 1929.

28 Semaphore is an apparatus for visual signaling (as by the position of one or more movable arms), or a system of visual signaling by two flags held, one in each hand.

29 Kemble (1957) page 12. [An electric telegraph system replaced the flags on September 22, 1853.]

30 May 27, 1854, Marine telegraph from Fort Point to San Francisco completed. From San Francisco Museum [01/06/03] www.sfmuseum.org/hist/chron3.html.

31 June 22, 1850, 500-pound grizzly bear was caught today near the Mission Dolores. [01/06/03] www.sfmuseuorg/hist/chron2.html.

32 Bagwell (1982) page 36.

33 For more information on the *Santa Rosa* see page 161.

34 Information from *San Francisco History* website [01/06/03] http://zpub.com/sf50/sf/hd850b.htm#post-office.

7 - Fisherman's Wharf and Maritime Park

Fisherman's Wharf and Maritime Park Map

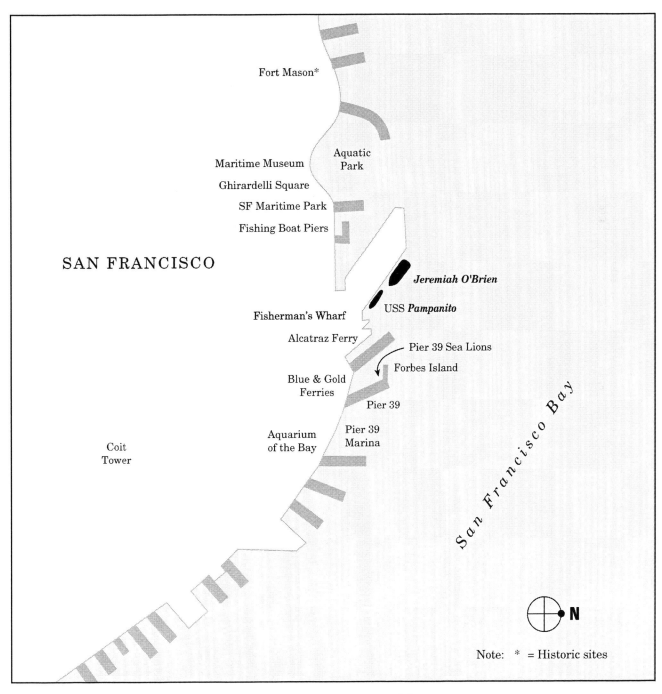

Figure 79 - **Fisherman's Wharf and Maritime Park Map**

Near Pier 39

Piers 27–31 are scheduled for a $100 million renovation to become a sports and recreation center.[1]

These old finger terminals are the types that were in use when FDR was president.

The "Welcome Home" on the pier was painted during World War II to honor returning veterans.[2]

Figure 80 - **Piers 27–31 planned sports recreation center**

Figure 81 - **The Aquarium of the Bay at Pier 39**

Aquarium of the Bay

The Aquarium of the Bay offers a view of what you would see under the piers and under the bridge. Moreover, you can see it without getting wet.

Pier 39 Marina

The small boat marina on the east side of Pier 39 has easy access to the waterfront activities and has not been invaded by the sea lions.

Figure 82 - **Pier 39 marina**

Figure 83 - **Sea lions at Pier 39**

Sea Lions at Pier 39

Bachelor sea lions hang out here at Pier 39 to nap when they are not feeding or breeding.

At one time the sea lions were all removed, but tourist objections allowed them to come back.

There are now fewer sea lions on Seal Rock near the Cliff House.

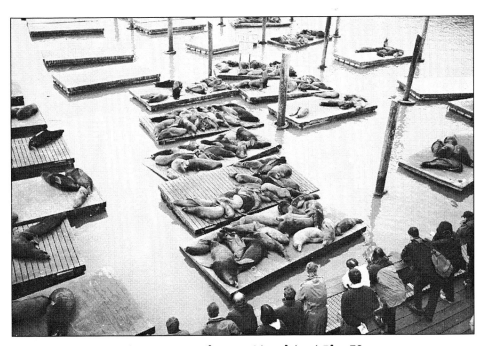
Figure 84 - **Sea lions and tourists at Pier 39**

Forbes Island

Forbes Island is that clump of trees and the tower. It is a very large floating home that now serves as a restaurant.

Figure 85 - *Forbes Island* **floating restaurant**

Fisherman's Wharf

The Pier 39 and Fisherman's Wharf area has lots of things to see and many restaurants. You can get there by ferry from Jack London Square or from Alameda.

Figure 86 - **Fisherman's Wharf sign**

Figure 87 - **Commercial fishing boats at Fisherman's Wharf**

Tour Boats

You can take both tour boats and ferries from this area.

Figure 88 - *Emerald Lady* **tour boat**

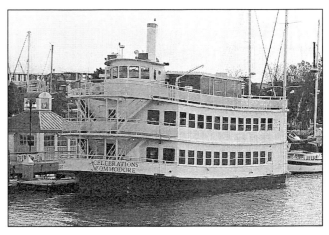

Figure 89 - **Hornblower tour boat**
Celebrations Commodore

1943 USS *Pampanito* (SS-383) Submarine

The first vessel we can see in the San Francisco National Maritime Historical Park is the 1943 USS *Pampanito* (SS-383) submarine.[3]

Figure 90 - **1943 USS *Pampanito* (SS-383) submarine at Pier 45**

She is a World War II Balao class fleet submarine. She made six patrols in the Pacific during World War II, sank six Japanese ships, and damaged four others. The *Pampanito*, restored to its 1943 condition, represents the height of World War II submarine development.

Located at Pier 45, Fisherman's Wharf, the *Pampanito* is open to the public seven days a week.[4]

1943 *Jeremiah O'Brien* Liberty Ship

The *Jeremiah O'Brien*, named after a Revolutionary War naval commander, is the last surviving unaltered Liberty ship.[5] During World War II, 2,700 Liberty ships were used in the massive sealift to every theater of the war.[6]

In 1978, she became part of the National Liberty Ship Memorial and has been a part of the National Maritime Museum since 1980. In 1995, she made the trip back to the D-day commemoration at Normandy, France.[7]

Pier 45 may be developed into a bay-themed learning center called "San Francisco at the Wharf."[8]

Figure 91 - **1943 *Jeremiah O'Brien* Liberty ship at Pier 45**

Maritime Historical Park

The San Francisco National Maritime Historical Park is on the Hyde Street Pier overlooking Aquatic Park and features historic ships and a museum.[9]

The Hyde Street Pier features six national landmark historic ships you can tour. All of them were built during FDR's lifetime.

1914 *Eppleton Hal* paddlewheel steam tugboat - see page 155.

1907 *Hercules* steam tugboat - see page 156.

1895 *C.A. Thayer* three-masted schooner - see page 157.

1891 *Alma* scow schooner - see page 157.

1890 *Eureka* Southern Pacific ferryboat - see page 158.

1886 *Balclutha* square-rigger ship - see page 159.

Other Historic Vessels

1951 *RELIEF* lightship at Jack London Square, Oakland - see page 8.

1943 USS *Hornet* aircraft carrier at Pier 3, Alameda - see page 151.

1945 *Red Oak Victory* at Richmond Point - see page 151.

1939 *ARTSHIP* at Ninth Avenue Terminal, Oakland - see page 149.

1934 *Potomac* at Jack London Square, Oakland - see pages 3, 148, 178 and 193.

1929 *Starfjord* private yacht at Jack London Square, Oakland - see page 150.

[1] "Envisioning a New Look for the Waterfront," *San Francisco Chronicle*, February 16, 2000, front page.

[2] Information from Howard Murray, a *Potomac* docent.

[3] The USS *Pampanito* (SS-283) submarine was commissioned November 6, 1943. From website [01/06/03] www.maritime.org/pamphist.htm.

[4] For more information see Historic Vessels *Pampanito* on page 153.

[5] "The *Jeremiah O'Brien* was named after the commander of the First American Naval Flying Squadron of the War of the Revolution." From website [01/06/03] http://pc-78-120.udac.se:8001/www/nautica/ships/jobrien.html.

[6] For more information see Historic Vessels *Jeremiah O'Brien* on page 154.

[7] Emery M. (1994) [photographs of the trip to Normandy].

[8] "Envisioning a new look for the Waterfront," *San Francisco Chronicle*, February 16, 2000, front page.

[9] For more information see San Francisco Maritime National Historical Park on page 153.

8 - The Golden Gate Area
The Golden Gate Area Map

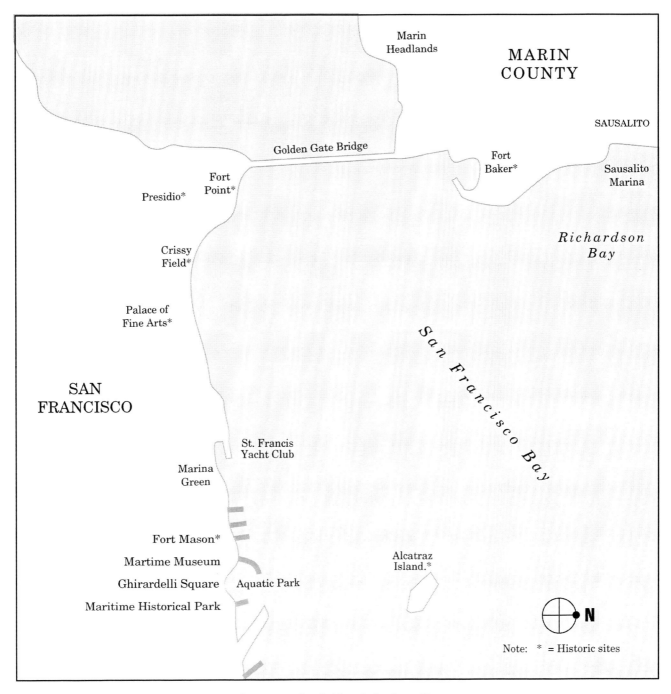

Figure 92 - **The Golden Gate Area Map**

Fort Mason

Fort Mason is just behind Aquatic Park. In 1797 the Spanish put a five-gun battery on the sand dunes here and called it *Bateria San Jose*.

Figure 93 - **Fort Mason, San Francisco**

Not much happened until the Civil War; then, in 1863 the U.S. Army put in a twelve-gun battery and called it Fort Mason, named after the first military governor of California.[2]

During World War II Fort Mason was an embarkation port, and over 1.5 million troops left here for the Pacific Theater.

In 1972, the area known as Fort Mason became part of the Golden Gate National Recreation Area.

Figure 94 - **Fort Mason, San Francisco** [1]

Palace of Fine Arts

San Francisco does things in a big way. Only nine years after the city lay in ruins after the 1906 earthquake and fire, it was rebuilt and hosted the 1915 Panama Pacific International Exposition for more than 19 million visitors.[4]

The Palace of Fine Arts is the only building left from the Exposition. It was designed by Berkeley's architect Bernard Maybeck.

Figure 95 - **San Francisco, 1906, Third and Market street area** [3]

Figure 96 - **1915 Exposition, Palace of Fine Arts**

Theodore Roosevelt was among those who visited the Exposition in 1915. That same year FDR was appointed to the Panama Pacific Commission.[5]

Though the Exposition was designed to celebrate the opening of the Panama Canal, it really celebrated the rebirth of a new international city by the Golden Gate.

Crissy Field

Crissy Field, as part of the Presidio, was also a Spanish military site. In the late 1800's there was a Coast Guard station here. It was also used in 1915 for part of the Panama Pacific International Exposition. In 1921 Crissy Field became an army airport and served through World War II.[8]

Crissy Field is now part of the Golden Gate National Recreation Area. The shoreline has been transformed into a recreation area and nature preserve. The park provides large parking lots, restrooms and public meeting rooms.[9]

Figure 97 - **Poster for Panama Pacific International Exposition, San Francisco, 1915** [6]

Figure 98 - **Crissy Field pre-1880** [7]

Figure 99 - **Crissy Field Park and Nature Preserve**

Presidio of San Francisco

The Golden Gate Bridge spans the bay's entrance, which was first fortified against invaders in 1794, when the Spanish put a thirteen-gun battery at the Presidio.[10] Part of that original building still stands and has been expanded to become the Officers Club. It is now flanked by eighteenth century cannons.[11]

The Presidio is the longest-lived army installation in the American West and has more than two hundred years of military history under three flags. There is an historical landmark at the Presidio.[13]

"Buffalo Soldiers" from the all-Black 9th Cavalry, garrisoned here in 1903, served as the nation's first African American Presidential Escort of Honor during Theodore Roosevelt's visit to the Presidio.[14]

Fort Point

Fort Point is under the arch at the west end of the bridge. Built in 1853 with a lighthouse and 126 massive cannons, it was ready for the Civil War.[15]

New weapons made the fort obsolete by 1886; however, the new lighthouse tower built in 1864 on top of Fort Point continued in operation until 1934.[16]

In World War II, a net was strung across the entrance to the bay, and searchlights and rapid-fire cannons were mounted atop the fort as defense against submarines. The antisubmarine nets were built at the Navy Net Depot in Tiburon.[17] In 1970, the fort became a National Historic Site.[18, 19]

Figure 100 - **Presidio of San Francisco, 1776** [12]

Figure 101 - **Presidio Officers Club**

Figure 102 - **1853 Fort Point, San Francisco, with lighthouse on top of fort**

Golden Gate Bridge

The Golden Gate Bridge is another Bay Area project partially funded by the FDR New Deal programs. Started in 1933 and completed in 1937,[21] the bridge took 25 million man-hours to build. It was the first major project to use safety nets. Though eleven men were killed on the job, that was the best safety record for any large project at that time.

Figure 103 - **The Golden Gate Bridge with classic gaff topsail schooner** *Ka'iulani* [20]

The bridge is 9,200 feet overall, and 4,028 feet separate the piers, with more than 200 feet of vertical clearance for the largest ships. The towers are 746 feet tall and the cables are 36 inches in diameter. The painters are continuously applying the 110,000 gallons of paint needed to cover the bridge.[22]

The bridge is independently owned and operated, whereas the other bay bridges are owned and operated by the State of California.

Point Bonita Lighthouse

Looking under the bridge on the Marin Headlands side, you can see Point Bonita Lighthouse, which has been in continuous use since 1855. The original light was moved from the cliff top to its present location in 1877, and the tower was rebuilt in 1907 after being damaged by the 1906 San Francisco earthquake. In 1981, it was the last California lighthouse to be automated. It is the only lighthouse in the world that is reached by a suspension bridge.[24, 25]

Figure 104 - **Point Bonita Lighthouse, Marin Headlands** [23]

Fort Baker

Fort Baker is at the north end of the bridge on the Marin shore. It was designated as a military site in 1850, and by 1870 it was a fine example of a seacoast fortification. New artillery batteries were added during World War II.

In 1990, it became part of the National Park Service.[26, 27]

Figure 105 - **Fort Baker at north end of Golden Gate Bridge**

Figure 106 - **1850 Fort Baker at north end of Golden Gate Bridge** [28]

Seacoast Fortifications

In addition to the forts inside the bay, the San Francisco and Marin headlands had more than fifty coastal defense fortifications constructed between 1870 and 1970.

During World War II, many of these sixteen-inch coastal defense guns were practice fired, lighting up the night sky. The sound could be heard all over the city.[29] There is an ongoing effort to preserve these coastal fortification sites.[30]

The following sites are open to the public. Battery Richmond Davis at Fort Funston was built in 1938.[31] Fort Cronkhite was constructed during 1940 to 1941 and used until the 1960s. It is the only restored mobilization barracks in the West.[32] The Nike Missile Site was built during the cold war and used from 1945 to 1974.[33] Battery East was built in the 1870's[34] and Battery Chamberlin near Baker beach was built in 1904.[35]

Figure 107 - **1938 Battery Richmond Davis, Fort Funston, San Francisco Headlands** [36]

[1] Photograph of Fort Mason from National Park Service website [01/06/03] www.nps.gov.

[2] Colonel Richard Mason (1847–1849) data from National Park Service website [01/06/03] www.nps.gov.

[3] Photograph of 1906 San Francisco earthquake damage from San Francisco Museum website [01/06/03] www.sfmuseum.org/1906/photos.html.

[4] Panama Pacific Iinternational Exposition data from San Francisco Museum website [01/06/03] www.sfmuseum.org/hist9/ppietxt1.html.

[5] See 1915 Time Line Reference on page 251.

[6] Poster from San Francisco Museum website [01/06/03] www.sfmuseum.org/history9/ppietxt1.html.

[7] Photograph of 1880 Crissy Field from National Park Service [01/07/03] www.nps.gov.

[8] Haller (1997) page 42.

[9] Guthrie (2001, May 5).

[10] Presidio data from National Park Service website [01/07/03] www.nps.gov.

[11] Haller (1997).

[12] Photograph of 1775 Presidio from National Park Service website [01/07/03] www.nps.gov.

[13] Historical Landmark No. 79 - Presidio of San Francisco, see page 231.

[14] *Golden Gate: Presidio of San Francisco Under Three Flags*, National Park Service Brochure.

[15] Haller (1997).

[16] Fort Point Lighthouse [01/07/03] http://www.nps.gov/fopo/exhibits/lighthouse/lite.htm.

[17] For information about the site see the Romberg Tiburon Center on page 213.

[18] Haller (1997) page 42.

[19] For more information on Fort Point see Local References on page 211.

[20] Photograph of schooner *Ka'iulani* courtesy of Captain Robert Michaan of the *Ka'iulani*.

[21] Started January 5, 1933 and completed May 27, 1937.

[22] Dupré, J. (1997) page 82.

[23] Photograph of Point Bonita Lighthouse from National Park Service website [01/07/03] www.nps.gov/goga/mahe/pobo/index.htm.

[24] Point Bonita Lighthouse first lit May 2, 1855. Photograph and data from National Park Service website [01/07/03] www.nps.gov/goga/mahe/pobo/index.htm.

[25] For more information on Point Bonita Lighthouse see Local References on page 213.

[26] Fort Baker data from National Park Service website [01/07/03] www.nps.gov/goga/mahe/foba.

[27] For more information on Fort Baker see Local References on page 211.

[28] Photograph of Fort Baker from National Park Service website [01/07/03] www.nps.gov/goga/mahe/foba.

[29] September 5, 1941 and May 9, 1941 are recorded dates for firing the costal 16-inch defense guns with 2,100 pound shells. Information from San Francisco Museum website [01/07/03] www.sfmuseum.org/war/40-41.html.

[30] Golden Gate National Recreation Area, *Seacoast Fortifications Preservation Manual*. From National Park Service website [01/07/03] www.nps.gov/goga/history/seaforts.

[31] Fort Funston data from National Park Service website [01/07/03] www.nps.gov/goga/fofu/index.htm.

[32] Fort Cronkhite data from National Park Service website [01/07/03] www.nps.gov/goga/mahe/focr.

[33] Nike Missile Site data from National Park Service website [01/07/03] www.nps.gov/goga/admin/feedemo/projects/project_nimi.htm.

[34] Battery East data from National Park Service website [01/07/03] www.nps.gov/prsf/places/bateast.htm.

[35] Battery Chamberlin data from National Park Service website [01/07/03] www.nps.gov/prsf/places/chamber.htm

[36] Photograph of 1936 Fort Funston Battery Richmond Davis from National Park Service website [01/07/03] www.nps.gov/goga/fofu/index.htm.

9 - Angel Island and Alcatraz
Angel Island and Alcatraz Map

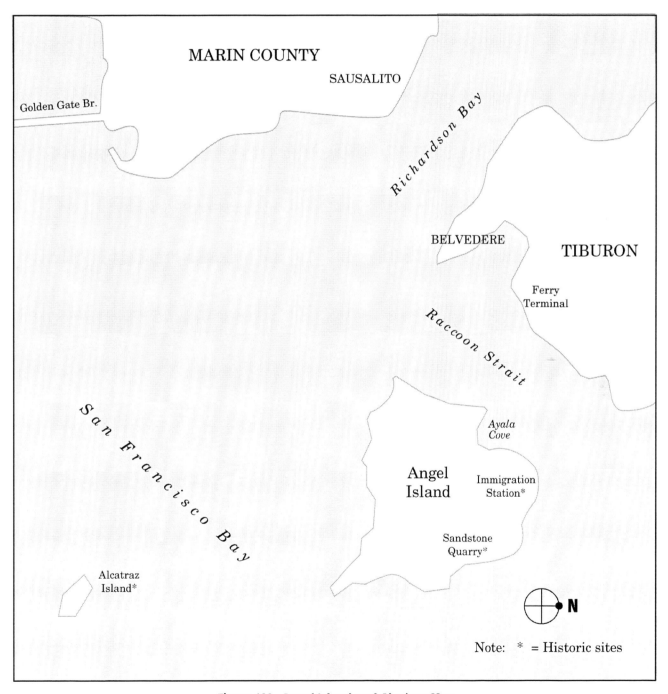

Figure 108 - **Angel Island and Alcatraz Map**

Figure 109 - **Angel Island**

Angel Island

Angel Island off the Marin shore looks like a small hill. It was named in 1775, when Lt. Juan Manuel de Ayala brought his sailing ship, the *San Carlos*, into San Francisco Bay and anchored in what is now Ayala Cove. Ayala christened the island *Isla de Los Angeles* (Island of the Angels).[2] The *San Carlos* was the first sailing ship to enter the bay.

The San Francisco Bay Area was explored during the time of the American Revolution while Captain James Cook was exploring the South Pacific.[3]

After 1808, Russian sea otter hunting expeditions visited the island and established a storehouse there.

Figure 110 - **Ayala Cove, Angel Island** [1]

In 1814, the British sixteen-gun sloop HMS *Racoon** was damaged off the coast of Oregon. She was able to reach San Francisco Bay and beached at Ayala Cove for repairs. In honor of the old ship, the channel between Angel Island and Tiburon is named Raccoon Strait.[4]

In the early 1850's, a quarry on the island's east side provided high-quality sandstone carved from the cliffs. This stone was used at Mare Island and to build San Francisco's original Bank of California. The quarry continued to operate into the 1920's.

In 1863, the government established Camp Reynolds at the west end of the island, with gun emplacements at Point Stuart, Point Knox, and Point Blunt.

---

* Note difference in spelling between HMS *Racoon* and Raccoon Strait.

By 1886, additional gun batteries were added to the southwest side of the island as Batteries Ledyard, Wallace, and Drew. The remains of these batteries are visible on a visit to the island. In 1892, a quarantine station opened at Ayala Cove, then known as Hospital Cove. In 1900, the army designated the entire island as Fort McDowell. Camp Reynolds became West Garrison, and what we know today as Fort McDowell was called East Garrison.

During the 1899 to 1905 Spanish-American War and Philippine Insurrection, Fort McDowell processed men going to the Philippines and also served as a detention camp.

In 1905, the year that FDR and Eleanor were married, construction of an immigration station began in the area known as North Garrison. It began partial operation in 1910. During the next thirty years this was the point of entry for most of approximately 175,000 immigrants. More than 97 percent of the immigrants processed were Chinese. In 1940 the immigration station was closed.

Then, in 1941, the immigration station was turned into a WW II prisoner-of-war processing facility. At the same time Fort McDowell itself served as a major point of embarkation for troops headed to the Pacific war zone. The army base closed in 1946.

From 1954 to 1962, the army maintained a Nike missile and control base on the island. In December 1963, Angel Island became part of the California park system.

Alcatraz

In 1775, the Spanish explorer Juan Manuel de Ayala entered the bay and saw a nearly barren rock island covered with pelicans. He named the island *Isla de Los Alcatraces* (Island of the Pelicans).

Though Alcatraz was a hazard to shipping, it had no lighthouse until 1854. This was the first lighthouse built on the Pacific coast. It was replaced by the current and taller lighthouse in 1909 and automated in 1963.

The island was a military fortification from 1859 to 1907. Fortress Alcatraz was the first United States permanent military fortification on the West Coast. During the Civil War, there were more than one hundred cannons and three hundred soldiers on Alcatraz.

Figure 111 - **Alcatraz Island**

During that time, the island took on an additional function; starting in 1861, Alcatraz was unofficially used as a military prison. When the fortification closed in 1907, Alcatraz became the Pacific Branch, United States Military Prison until 1933.

Figure 112 - **Alcatraz California State Park**

Alcatraz became a federal penitentiary in 1934. Alcatraz was to be a super prison to confine the worst of the federal offenders or "incorrigibles" who had been connected to organized crime, kidnapping, bank robbery, and bootlegging.

Included in this group were Al "Scarface" Capone, George "Machine Gun" Kelly, Alvin "Creepy" Karpis, and Robert "Birdman" Stroud.

A total of 1,576 convicts served time there. No one was ever executed or buried on Alcatraz. Five inmates committed suicide, eight were murdered, and two were killed in a shootout with guards.[5]

Several prisoners made escape attempts; those who reached the water and tried to swim were presumed drowned.

Two prisoners made a rubber raft, and although some of their belongings were found, the men were never found and were also presumed drowned. Another man did swim to shore. He was too weak to escape on land and was returned to Alcatraz.[6, 7]

Figure 113 - **Alcatraz Light**

Alcatraz closed as a prison in 1963 because it was deteriorating and becoming too expensive to operate. It cost three times as much per inmate to operate as any other federal penitentiary.

During World War II, the government assigned specific commercial operations to each of the federal prisons. All water had to be shipped to Alcatraz by barge. It was nevertheless designated as the laundry facility for all the military bases in the Bay Area.

After Alcatraz closed as a federal prison, a group called "Indians of All Tribes" offered unsuccessfully to buy Alcatraz and convert it into an American Indian study center. From 1969 until 1971 they occupied Alcatraz and tried to make it into a viable living and study area. The lack of water and power made this impractical.

Although the Native American group was unable to use Alcatraz, their occupation awakened the American public to the need to support Indian self-determination, and gave birth to a continuing political movement. The ensuing change in U.S. government policy helped establish Native American study centers.[8]

Alcatraz is now a California State Park, and tours are available from Fisherman's Wharf.[9]

Figure 114 - **Tour boat at Alcatraz Federal Penitentiary California State Park**

[1] Photograph of Angel Island Ayala Cove from Angel Island website [01/07/03] www.angelisland.org.
[2] Information from Angel Island website [01/07/03.] www.angelisland.org.
[3] Beaglehole, J. C. (1974) and from Captain James Cook website [01/07/03] www.jetcity.com/~kirok/cook.shtml.
[4] Note the variation in spelling between HMS *Racoon* and Raccoon Strait.
    Information from Angel Island website [01/07/03] www.angelisland.org.
[5] Lageson (1999).
[6] Duggleby (1990).
[7] Babyak (1988), Babyak (1994), Babyak (2001), Quillen (1992), Thompson (1994).
[8] Information from the National Park Service website [01/07/03] www.nps.gov/alcatraz/indian2.html.
[9] Information from the National Park Service website [01/07/03] www.nps.gov/alcatraz/faz2.html.

10 - Treasure Island and Yerba Buena Island (YBI)

Treasure Island and YBI Map

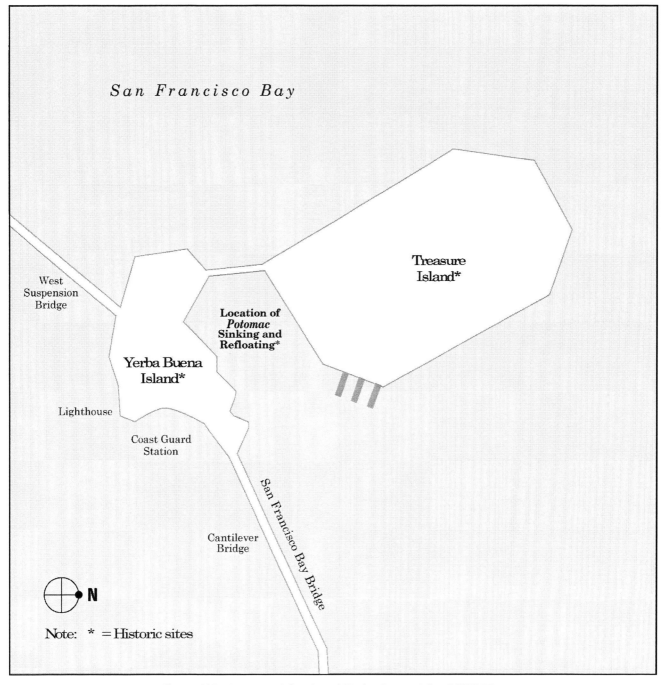

Figure 115 - **Treasure Island and Yerba Buena Island (YBI) Map**

Blossom Rock Buoy

The Blossom Rock buoy marks a submerged rock that was first put on a chart in 1826 and named Blossom Rock after the British man-of-war *Blossom* that discovered it. A number of vessels struck the rock before explosives were used to remove it in 1871.[1] There is only forty feet of clearance over the rock and the green/red quick-flash bell buoy marks the rock and the center of the inbound and outbound traffic lanes under the Bay Bridge.

Figure 116 - **Blossom Rock Buoy**

Building Treasure Island

Treasure Island is another FDR legacy built by the Army Corps of Engineers and partially funded by FDR's New Deal Work Projects Administration (WPA).[3] The WPA started work on the island in 1936 by building a three-mile-long perimeter rock wall on the shoal.[4] Other shoals were dredged and used as landfill. When completed, the area was covered with a thick layer of topsoil and planted with trees. The project was completed in eighteen months, on time and within budget.

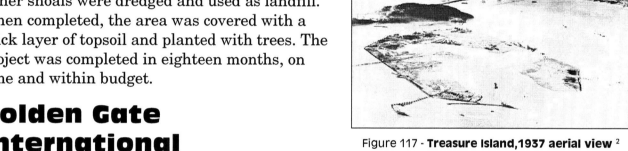

Figure 117 - **Treasure Island,1937 aerial view** [2]

Golden Gate International Exposition

If we had been sailing along here in 1939, we could have seen a new style of architecture designed by Californians. There were towers, tall windowless walls giving the effect of an ancient walled city. Massive statuary stood everywhere and long walkways surrounded shimmering pools. FDR and Eleanor each visited the 1939 Exposition on separate occasions.[6]

China Clippers

One of the highlights of the 1939 Exposition was the Pan American Clippers, the largest flying boats in the world. Though each had its own name, the airplanes were all known as China Clippers.

The first Martin M-130 made its maiden flight from Alameda to Manila in 1935. There is an historical landmark in Alameda commemorating the event.[7]

Figure 118 - **1939–40 Golden Gate International Exposition** [5]

In 1939, the new and larger Boeing B-314 planes were based at Treasure Island's new terminal.

On Treasure Island, you can see the original Pan American Clipper terminal and administration building and two original hangars behind it. During the 1939 Exposition the two hangars were used for the Palace of Fine and Decorative Art and the Hall of Air Transportation.[8]

Figure 119 - **Martin M-130 *China Clipper* over Bay Bridge, 1935** [9]

In 1934, Pan Am introduced the Clippers with two Sikorsky S-42 flying boats named the *Brazilian Clipper* and the *Pan American Clipper* .

However, these did not have enough flying range to make commercial transpacific or transatlantic flights. Pan Am bought ten of these planes for use in the Caribbean and South America; they were in service until 1946. In April 1935, one specially equipped Sikorsky S-42 made the first exploratory flight to Hawaii to test the feasibility of commercial service.

In October 1935, Pan Am started commercial operations. Three Martin M-130 airplanes flew across the Pacific with stops at Honolulu, Midway, Wake Island, Guam and finally Manila, after sixty

Figure 120 - **Pan Am Clipper administration building and hangar**

flying hours. Passengers stayed overnight in hotels on each of the islands.

From 1935 until 1939, the *China Clipper*, the *Hawaii Clipper*, and the *Philippine Clipper* were the only three airplanes in the world that were in commercial service carrying mail, cargo and passengers across either the Pacific or the Atlantic. The *Hawaii Clipper* was lost at sea in 1938;[10] the *Philippine Clipper* crashed in 1943; and the *China Clipper*, the last of these three Martin M-130 Clippers, crashed on landing in 1945.[11]

Figure 121 - **Pan Am Clipper hangar**

At the start of World War II in England in 1939, there were only eight production aircraft in the world that could carry passengers and cargo to England from the United States—two remaining Martin M-130's plus the six new Boeing B-314's. The final Pan Am commercial flight of a Clipper flying boat was on April 6, 1946. The Boeing B-314 *Anzac Clipper* was owned by several airlines and continued to fly until 1951.[12]

Figure 122 - **Short Solent 3 NJ203, Western Aerospace Museum, Oakland Airport**

Both FDR and Churchill flew to important meetings in Boeing B-314's with Pan Am crews.[13, 14] FDR flew from Miami, Florida to British Gambia, West Africa on January 11, 1943 on the Boeing B-314 *Dixie Clipper*. This was the first flight by a U.S. president. He celebrated his sixty-first birthday on this trip. At Bathurst, Gambia, FDR changed to a land-based aircraft, a TWA Douglas C-54 Skymaster, for the trip north to Casablanca, French Morocco, Africa, to meet with Winston Churchill to plan the European invasion.[15]

FDR made only one other flight, a roundtrip on the C-54 *Sacred Cow,* from Cairo, Egypt, to the Yalta Conference in February 1945.[16]

However, there were other flying boats. Starting in 1933, the U.S. Navy had the Consolidated P2Y seaplanes for long range patrols.[17]

During the War, the British built twenty-two Short-Solent flying boats. There are only two of these China Clipper type aircraft left in the world. Visitors can tour one at the Western Aerospace Museum at Oakland Airport's North Field. The other is in a museum in Polk City, Florida.[18]

With the start of World War II, the U.S. Navy ordered six new Martin Mars flying boats which were the largest ever commercially built. Two of these are currently used in British Columbia, Canada, for fire suppression service.[19, 20]

U.S. Navy and New Civilian Use

At the beginning of World War II, the U.S. Navy took over Treasure Island.[21] It served as a naval base until it closed in 1998.

The City of San Francisco now owns most of Treasure Island and is making plans for its future use.

Yerba Buena Island (YBI) Lighthouse

The Coast Guard maintains lighthouses along the Pacific Coast and in the San Francisco Bay. The YBI lighthouse was originally built in 1872.

In the past, the building above the lighthouse was the lighthouse keeper's home, but the Coast Guard Pacific Area commander now uses it for official functions.

Buoy Tender Station

Figure 123 - **Lighthouse On Yerba Buena Island (YBI) and Coast Guard Pacific Area commander's special function facility**

This Coast Guard station takes care of all of the buoys in the bay and delta area and part of the Pacific coast. The WLB 208 *Aspen* is the buoy tender now stationed here. The *Aspen* was launched April 21, 2001 and is painted black because it is a service vessel.[22]

The WLB 306 *Buttonwood* was launched in 1943 when FDR was president. She served on the central California coastal area from May 13, 1993 until May 13, 2001 when she was replaced by the *Aspen*. She is now serving in the Dominican Republic Navy.[23, 24]

The buoys on the dock are very large and painted different colors. The red buoys mark the right side of the channel when returning from the sea, and the green or black buoys mark

Figure 124 - *Aspen* at Coast Guard Buoy Tender Station, Yerba Buena Island (YBI)

the left side. Striped buoys mark a channel junction or an obstruction; yellow and orange are special purpose buoys, and blue buoys are for mooring.

The buoys are all numbered; green or black buoys are odd numbers and red buoys are even numbers. Many have lights, bells or whistles for guidance in the fog or at night.

Buoys and aids to navigation are shown on the mariner's charts.

Figure 125 – **Buoy tender WLB 208** *Aspen*

Container Cranes

As we come back up the estuary, we again go by the largest cranes in the world. These cranes can load a ship almost twice the size of the ship that is being loaded. For a comparison of this third generation container ship to the new sixth generation ships, see the container freighters size chart on page 98.

Figure 126 - **Largest container cranes in the world load a midsize ship**

Returning to Dock

As we return to dock and reluctantly go ashore, we can easily feel why this was FDR's "beloved" *Potomac*. We can visualize him sitting in his favorite chair on board the *Potomac*, happy and relaxed with his friends and colleagues. One of the pleasures of being a docent on the *Potomac* is to be able to frequently cruise on the

Figure 128 - *Potomac* **returning to FDR Pier at Jack London Square**

Potomac and vicariously share the day with President Franklin Delano Roosevelt.

When FDR was cruising on the *Potomac*, he may well have seen many of the same types of vessels that we now see in the San Francisco Bay. Though the size and design of some of these vessels have changed, the same types of vessels would have plied his home waters. FDR may have actually seen some of the historic vessels that are now preserved here in the San Francisco Bay Area.

The next section of the book, **What You Might See Afloat on San Francisco Bay,** has photographs of many of the different types of vessels that are often seen here on the bay or in the waters of any major port.

Figure 127 - **Going ashore**

If you have questions about what we have seen on our cruise, the answers may be in the last section of the book, **For More Information**. This section also includes a list of historical reference sources, websites, and bibliography.

[1] Hansen (1994). Blossom Rock blown up on April 23, 1871.

[2] Photograph of 1937 Treasure Island from San Francisco Museum website [01/07/03] www.sfmuseum.org.

[3] For more information, see "FDR's New Deal Agencies in the Bay Area" on page 169.

[4] Reinholt (1973) page 48. [February 11, 1936 started work on Treasure Island.]

[5] Photograph of 1939 Golden Gate International Exposition from San Francisco Museum website [01/07/03] www.sfmuseum.org.

[6] Reinholt (1973) page 58. [Both were visitors before the official opening.]

[7] Historical Landmark No. 440 - Alameda Terminal of the First Transcontinental Railroad. See page 225.

[8] Hunter (1940) pages 98–99.

[9] Photograph of Martin M-130 *China Clipper* from San Francisco Museum website [01/07/03] www.sfmuseum.org.

[10] Allen (2000) page 68.

[11] Allen (2000) page 103.

[12] Allen (2000) page 107.

[13] Allen (2000) page 100.

[14] Information from Pan Am Historical Foundation website [01/07/03] www.panam.org.

[15] Allen (2000) pages 102–103.

[16] Information on Yalta Conference from Camp David website [01/07/03] http://travel.to/campdavid.

[17] Information on Consolidated P2Y seaplanes from VP Navy website [01/14/01] www.vpnavy.com/webdocp2y.html.

[18] Information on the Short-Solent flying boats from the Western Aerospace Museum website [01/10/03] www.westernaerospacemuseum.org.

[19] Information on the Martin Mars aircraft from Flying Tankers website [01/07/03] www.martinmars.com/aircraft.html.

[20] For more information see China Clippers on page 205.

[21] The navy took over Treasure Island on April 17, 1942. Pan Am used its administration building and hangars for the Clippers until 1946. Information from Pan Am Historical Foundation website [01/07/03] www.panam.org.

[22] WLB 208 *Aspen* data from website [10/22/01] www.uscg.mil.

[23] PWLB 306 *Buttonwood* data from website [10/22/01] www.uscg.mil/pacarea *Aspen* news release 40-01, December 18, 2001 [03/20/02] www. uscg.mil/pacarea/pcp/newsreleases/2002/jan/0102.htm.

[24] For more information on the *Buttonwood* and *Aspen* see page 136.

What You Might See Afloat on San Francisco Bay

11 - Navigational Aids

There are two sets of Coast Guard rules for navigational aids: International Waters and Inland Waterways. On the bay and delta, the Inland Waterways rules are used.

Buoys

Buoys are anchored to the bottom at specific locations and are shown on charts by special symbols and lettering that indicate their shape, color, and visual and/or sound signals. They vary widely in size. The red buoys mark the right side of the channel when returning from the sea, and the green or black buoys mark the left side. Striped buoys mark a channel junction or an obstruction; yellow and orange are special purpose buoys, and blue buoys are for mooring.

Figure 129 - **Temporary racing buoy**

Some buoys are numbered; green or black buoys have odd numbers and red buoys have even numbers. Many have lights, bells, or whistles for guidance in the fog or at night.

Buoys and other aids to navigation are shown on the mariner's charts.

Yellow floating barricade anchor buoys and booms keep silt curtains in place around construction sites. Vessels traversing construction areas must maintain a speed that does not create a wake that could disturb the silt curtains.

Figure 131 - **Fixed position yellow racing buoy**

Figure 130 - **Yellow anchor buoy with floating barricade silt curtain**

History of Buoys

The first buoy ever used in the United States was a wooden spar type, moored in the Delaware River in 1767.[1] It was replaced by a lighthouse and a sturdy crew. Now, buoys made of steel are replacing early lighthouses. These buoys are shaped like a huge discus, and powered by onboard generators. They are designed to be left unmanned for one year on station.

These giant buoys have many uses, among them serving as sea-lane markers and control stations for sea traffic in heavily trafficked areas.

There are also special buoys used for the Worldwide Weather Watch. These buoys measure air speed and direction, temperature, barometric pressure, seawater temperature and salinity, as well as the speed and direction of the current. All data is sent to shore automatically.

Figure 132 - **Alcatraz red/green bell buoy**

However, what buoys do best is to alert mariners to dangers, obstructions, or changes in the bottom of the sea or waterways and to indicate navigable channels. The navigator can avoid dangers and plot a safe course by identifying a buoy and locating it on the charts.

Smaller buoys are identified by different shape, size, color, numbering, and the kind of signal they emit. Depending on their job, they may be lighted or unlighted, and signal with a bell, gong, whistle, or horn. Some may be equipped with light and sound. The sound may be caused by the rocking of the buoy, by gas, or by electricity from photocells.

Figure 133 - **Green bell buoy**

Figure 134 - **White speed limit Slow 5 MPH buoy**

Figure 135 - **White Slow No Wake buoy**

Buoys are painted red, black, white, green, yellow, blue, or a combination of colors.

All buoys, even the little tiny ones, are important!

Day Beacons

Day beacons are fixed markers such as this red day beacon on the estuary.

Figure 136 - **Red day beacons**

Lights

A variety of lights includes lighthouses, secondary lights, and minor-lights. Secondary lights mark harbors and are brighter than minor lights that are day beacons with a light.

Figure 139 - **Estuary entrance red light buoy #6**

Figure 137 - **Red secondary light #8 channel marker at the entrance to the estuary**

Figure 138 - **Green secondary light #7 channel marker at the entrance to the estuary**

Warning Signs

There are many types of signs warning boaters of hazards either to their vessels or to stationary facilities such as pipes or cables that are on the bottom.

Figure 140 - **Warning sign**

---

[1] From U.S. Coast Guard website [01/07/03] http: //152.121.2.2/d11/buttonwood/mission/histbuoy/txhitbu.htm.

---

12 - Commercial Ships

California Maritime Academy

The California Maritime Academy is a four-year state college of marine business, engineering, technology, and marine transportation, with a campus in Vallejo. It has an excellent reputation for its direct, hands-on approach. Cal Maritime is one of twenty-three campuses in the California State University system.

The mission of the California Maritime Academy is to provide each student with a quality college education combining intellectual learning, applied technology, leadership development, and global awareness. The college operates the training ship *Golden Bear*. She is 500 feet long with a displacement of 9,319 tons.[1]

Figure 141 - **California Maritime Academy's training ship** *Golden Bear*

Cruise Ships

Cruise ships frequent San Francisco, stopping at Pier 35, for travelers going to Asia, Alaska, Hawaii, Mexico, and through the Panama Canal.

Figure 142 - **Cruise ships at Pier 35**

Bulk Freighters

Bulk freighters may carry powdered materials, scrap iron, or large, heavy or bulky items that must be handled individually. Scrap iron is offloaded by magnetic cranes; powdered or small bulk

Figure 143 - **Dry bulk freighter**

items may be offloaded with built-in conveyor equipment.

Break-bulk freighters carry cargo that does not fit into standard containers and is handled either by shipboard cranes or terminal cranes.

Figure 144 - **Dry bulk freighter onboard unloading conveyor**

Figure 145 - **Ship with onboard heavy lift crane**

Figure 146 - **Ship with onboard heavy lift crane**

Figure 149 - **Break-bulk freighter with onboard cranes**

Figure 148 - **Ready Reserve with break-bulk onboard cranes**

Figure 147 - **Container or break-bulk freighter with onboard cranes**

Figure 150 - **Container freighter with onboard cranes**

Container Freighters

The Liberty and Victory ships used during World War II were about the size of the first generation ships shown on the chart below. For more information on ship sizes see World War II ships on page 147.

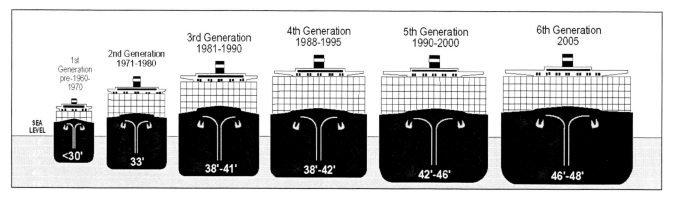

Figure 151 - **The growth of container ships** [2]

Figure 153 – **3rd generation container ship**

Figure 152 - **Container freighter mid-bridge**

Figure 154 - **Container freighter forward bridge**

Figure 155 - **Container freighter stern bridge**

Car Carriers

Car freighters are designed so that cars can be driven on and off on special ramps. Toyota combination car/container freighters give the company the option of delivering smaller loads of both cars and containers instead of using two ships.

Tankers

Super tankers do not enter San Francisco Bay. However, some large tankers do and have too deep a draft to go to the refineries fully loaded. Smaller lighter transfer tankers transfer the products between the refineries and the larger tankers in the anchorage areas between San Francisco and Oakland. These lighter transfer tankers unload the larger tankers until they are light enough so that their draft will allow them to go to the refineries. After the tanker leaves the shallow draft area, the lighter transfer tanker will fill the ship to capacity.

Figure 156 - **Car carrier** [3]

Figure 157 - **Combination car/container freighters**

Figure 158 - **Lighter transfer tanker used in the bay to lighten the load of large tankers**

Figure 159 - **Large tanker in anchorage**

Commercial Vessel Lifeboats

In the event of an emergency on the high seas where the crew must abandon ship, open lifeboats present a danger when being launched in heavy seas or when the vessel is listing. Open lifeboats are also difficult to handle safely in heavy seas. Most commercial ships use enclosed self-contained lifeboats that can be launched safely from a listing vessel in heavy seas.

Figure 160 - **Commercial freighter lifeboat**

These lifeboats are large enough for everyone on board. When the crew is strapped into its seats, the lifeboat is released, and it slides down its ramp and drops into the water. It will right itself and with its built-in motor and supplies, the crew can safely weather the most severe storms. They are bright orange so they can be more easily seen during rescue efforts.

Figure 161 - **Commercial freighter lifeboat**

[1] From the California Maritime Academy websites [01/07/03] www.csum.edu and www.maritime-education.com.
[2] Illustration of growth of container freighters from *Port of Oakland Vision 2000 Maritime Development Program*, used with permission.
[3] Photograph of car carrier docked at Benica by Captain Jan Tiura.

13 - Workboats

Special

The *Clean Bay* is a commercial oil spill clean-up vessel.

Figure 162 - **Workboat *Clean Bay***

Repair

The Caltrans work scow is used to move people and materials to bridges, towers, and other water access work areas.

Figure 163 - **Caltrans work scow**

Dive Boats

The dive boats have compressors and other special equipment needed by divers.

Figure 164 - **Dive boat**

Research

The Monterey Bay Aquarium Research Institute's (MBARI) *Western Flyer* is a stable platform research vessel. Under each of its hulls is a deep-water stabilizing float.[1]

Figure 165 - **MBARI stable platform research vessel *Western Flyer***

Tugboats

▪ Conventional Tugs

Conventional tugboats on the bay work ships and barges with ease, if not with elegance. They may be single or twin screw with one or two engines. These are the workhorses of the bay.

Figure 166 - **Conventional tugboat**

▪ Pusher Tugs

Pusher tugs are modified tugboats with "pusher knees" on the bow. These tugs are able to attach to barges when they are either loaded or light with the deck high above the water. The tug connects to the barge with steel cables and it becomes one unit.

Figure 167 - **Pusher tugboat**

▪ Tractor Tugs

Modern tugs are built with directional propulsion which allows the tug to exert thrust (push or pull) in any direction.

Figure 168 - **Tractor tugboat** *Delta Linda*

▪ Small Tugboats

Alert is an example of a small tugboat with a big agenda. Primarily a workboat, it has been lovingly maintained and is operated by a retired tugboat captain. It is a little tugboat with a big tugboat attitude. The *Alert* is shown next to the *Hercules*, the 1907 steam tugboat at the San Francisco Maritime Historical Park.

Figure 169 - **Small tugboat *Alert* next to the 1907 steam tugboat *Hercules*** [2]

▪ Small Craft Tugboat

There are a number of companies that have small tugboats to assist pleasure craft on the bay or the delta. Most are conventional power boats that can tow in pleasure craft. *Moses* was built to look like a miniature commercial conventional tugboat.

Figure 170 - **Small craft tugboat *Moses***

Water Taxi

Water taxis ferry crews, custom officers, agents, Coast Guard inspectors and other interested parties to and from anchored ships. These handy boats often carry pallets of supplies to and from ships. Pallets are lifted by the ship's stores crane. Some of these boats are owned by a company for its own use and others are available for hire.

Figure 171 - **Water taxi**

Figure 172 - **Water taxi** *Ailine Elizabeth*

Commercial Fishing Boats

Small commercial fishing vessels are abundant on the bay and at Fisherman's Wharf.

Figure 173 - **Boats at Fisherman's Wharf Pier 45**

Figure 174 - **Small commercial fishing vessel**

Barges

▪ Fuel Barges

Fuel barges are able to carry a number of petroleum products. Bargesare brought alongside ships while the vessel is at dock or anchored, and the fuel is transferred by hose.

Figure 175 - **Fuel barge with a pusher tug**

▪ Cargo Barge

Cargo barges are built in a number of sizes and are designed to carry anything from fireworks to construction materials. They have a flat deck and can be adapted to many types of payloads. Mud barges haul and dispose of dredged materials. They usually have the ability to dump dredged materials out the bottom at the dumping site.

Figure 176 - **Cargo barge with a load of rock**

Figure 177 - **Split-bottom barge for transferring and dumping dredged materials**

▪ Small Derrick Barge

There are many specially built barges plying the bay ranging in size from the very small to massive structures. The one pictured has a very small derrick mounted on deck.

▪ Derrick/Crane Barges

Barge-mounted derricks vary in size from little cranes, which can lift only a few hundred pounds, to massive derricks that can lift hundreds of tons. They can be very versatile.

Figure 178 - **Very small derrick barge**

For example, they can use a clamshell-bucket to dredge the channel bottom and then deposit the dredging in a split-bottom barge.

The same derrick barge may lift heavy or awkward cargo on or off a ship. It can also be rigged as a pile driver to construct bridges or docks. Barge cranes are used for construction in the same way that land-based cranes are used.

Figure 179 - **Barge crane used for construction**

Figure 180 - **Derrick barge rigged for dredging**

Figure 181 - **Auger hydraulic suction dredger**

Dredges

Several types of vessels can pick up materials off the bottom. Materials can include mud, sand and rock removed from the bottom to deepen the channel. Specific materials are "mined" from the bottom, such as commercial grade sand and oyster shells.

Figure 182 - **Auger on a hydraulic suction dredger**

Some dredgers use an auger at the end of a pipe that swings back and forth. The auger grinds up the bottom and a pump sucks the mud and water through a large pipe and deposits it on shore or in a mud barge. Hydraulic dredgers were first used on the estuary in 1886.

Figure 183 - **Barge sand dredger with pusher tugboat**

Other dredgers are built on a barge and use a series of digging buckets on a conveyor track. The moving buckets dig the material from the bottom and bring it up the conveyor and into the barge. This type of "mining dredger" may be used to recover sand or oyster shells from the bottom.

Some mining dredgers are also hydraulic dredges which suck the material off the bottom and pump it into the barge.

Ferries

There are now only a few ferry lines serving the bay. In the 1930's there were twenty-eight scheduled ferry routes crisscrossing the bay.

The first scheduled ferry started in 1850 when the steam sternwheeler *Kangaroo* went from San Francisco up San Antonio Creek to Oakland and Brooklyn.

Initially the sandbar at the mouth of the creek often stranded passengers until the tide came in. As a result, the City of Oakland started dredging the sandbar in 1859. Since 1864, the U.S. Army Corps of Engineers has been responsible for dredging the estuary and port facilities.

Figure 185 - **Ferry *Golden Gate***

Figure 184 - **Ferry *MV Zellinsky***

Tour Boats

▪ Party Boat *San Francisco Spirit*

There are many party boats available on the bay.

Figure 186 - **Party boat *San Francisco Spirit***

▪ Tour Boat

There is a wide range in size of tour boats on the bay.

Figure 187 - **Tour boat *Emerald Lady***

Figure 188 - **Tour boat *Chablis Commodore***

Fireboats

There are three main fireboats that operate in the San Francisco Bay; the Oakland fireboat *Seawolf* is the newest and is typical of new fireboats.

The *Seawolf* was new to Oakland in 1994, and replaced a modified 1939 navy yard tug, USS *Hoga*, which was the last vessel in active service from the December 7, 1941 attack at Pearl Harbor. The USS *Hoga* in now in the mothball fleet awaiting restoration.

The *Seawolf* is 65 feet long, 20 feet wide, and draws six feet of water. She has four Caterpillar diesel engines, each rated at 585 horsepower. Two are used for propulsion and two for pumping.

She has four turrets; the largest on the pilothouse can pump 3,500 gallon per minute. Total pumping capacity is 8,300 gallons per minute.

Figure 189 - **San Francisco fireboat *Phoenix***

Figure 192 - **San Francisco fireboat *Phoenix***

Figure 190 - **San Francisco fireboat *Guardian***

Figure 193 - **San Francisco fireboat *Guardian*** [3]

Figure 191 - **Oakland fireboat *Seawolf***

111

Police Boats

Most of the police departments in cities that border on the bay have their own boats.

Figure 194 - **Police rescue boat, SFPD**

Figure 196 - **Police boat, SFPD**

Figure 195 - **Police inflatable boats, SFPD**

Figure 197 - **Police boat, San Rafael**

Figure 198 - **Police boat, Oakland**

---

[1] Monterey Bay Aquarium Research Institute website [01/07/03] www.mbari.org.
[2] Photograph of *Alert* tugboat by Captain Jan Tiura.
[3] Photograph of *Guardian* fireboat honoring the USS *Missouri* by Captain Jan Tiura.

---

14 - Tall Ships

Topsail Schooner

Topsail schooners are sailing ships with two or more masts, all of which are rigged with fore-and-aft sails. They have one or more square sails or top staysails on the top of the fore mast. The stern mast is the taller and carries the main fore-and-aft sail. The topsail is typically used when running downwind and helps balance the main sail.

Topsail schooners are a popular design for charter boats. They are a majestic vessel and are good for local day charters or for long ocean voyages.

The topsail schooner *Californian* was built in 1984 and is a re-creation of the 1848 U.S. Revenue Marine Service cutter *C.W. Lawrence.* She is 94 feet on deck.

The *Californian* has been named the "Official Tallship Ambassador for the State of California" by the California legislature and governor.[3]

The 1984 gaff topsail schooner *Ka'iulani* is a charter yacht both on San Francisco Bay and

Figure 199 - **Tall Ship, topsail schooner** *Californian* [1]

Figure 200 - **Tall Ship, gaff topsail schooner** *Ka' iulani.* [2]

on long Pacific cruises. She is a modern, luxurious replica of a mid-nineteenth-century Pacific coast gaff-rigged topsail schooner. She is 65 feet on deck.

For information about sailing on these vessels, see Historic Data Sources on page 259.

Brig

A brig is a two-masted sailing ship that is square-rigged on both masts, carrying two or more headsails and a quadrilateral gaff sail or spanker aft of the mizzenmast.[5] The *Lady Washington*, known affectionately as *Lady Love*, was built in 1989 as a replica of the 1750 *Lady Washington*. She is 68 feet on deck. She frequently visits San Francisco Bay, often sailing with the *Hawaiian Chieftain*. The *Lady* carries the following sails: jib, foremast staysail, spritsail, several fore sails, fore course sail, fore top sail, fore top gallant sail, main staysail, main top staysail, main fore-and-aft sail, main top sail, main top gallant sail.

For information about sailing on the *Lady Washington*, see Historic Data Sources on page 259.

Figure 201 - **Tall Ship, brig** *Lady Washington* [4]

Brigantine

A brigantine is a two-masted sailing ship, with gaff-rigged fore-and-aft sails on one or both masts and full square-rigged on the foremast. The foremast carries the main sail which may be square alone or both square-rigged and have a fore-and-aft sail. This design is sometime called a gaff-rigged topsail ketch.

Figure 202 - **Tall Ship, brigantine** *Hawaiian Chieftain*

A fine example is the *Hawaiian Chieftain* out of Sausalito. She has a 1790's hull design, like vessels used by Captain Cook, with 1840's rigging.

She was built in 1988 and is 65 feet on deck.[6, 7] She carries three head sails, a fore course sail, fore top sail, fore top gallant sail, fore fore-and-aft, fore gaff topsail, mizzen fore-and-aft and a mizzen gaff topsail.

For information about sailing on the *Hawaiian Chieftain*, see Historic Data Sources on page 259.

Bark, Barque

A barque is a sailing ship of three or more masts with the foremast and mizzenmast square-rigged and the others fore-and-aft rigged. The U.S. Coast Guard barque *Eagle* is the largest of all Tall Ships flying the Stars and Stripes and the only square-rigger in the U.S. government service. She is a seagoing classroom for future officers of the U.S. Coast Guard.

The *Eagle* fully loaded is 1,816 tons. Her length is 295 feet overall, the main mast is 147.3 feet tall and her 23 sails have 22,227 square feet of sail area.[9,10]

Figure 203 - **Tall Ship, U.S. Coast Guard barque *Eagle*** [8]

The barque *Star of India,* which was part of the Alaska Packers fleet, is now at the Maritime Museum of San Diego. For more information and a photograph of the *Star of India*, see page 163.

Barkentine, Barquentine

A barkentine is a sailing ship with from three to five masts, of which only the foremast is square-rigged, the other masts being fore-and-aft rigged.

The barkentine *Dewaruci* is an Indonesian navy training ship that visited the Bay Area in April 2000.[11]

Figure 204 - **Tall Ship, barkentine *Dewaruci***

Ship

A sailing ship carries three or more masts with square-rigging on each mast, and may have a fore-and-aft sail on the mizzenmast as shown on the USS *Constitution*.[13]

The USS *Constitution*, the oldest commissioned warship afloat, was built in 1797 and is 204 feet on deck. She is on display in Boston Harbor.[14]

The *Balclutha* is a square-rigged Tall Ship that can be visited at San Francisco Maritime Historical Park. She was built in 1886 and is 257 feet on deck.[15]

Figure 205 - **Square-rigged ship, 1797 USS *Constitution***[12]

Figure 206 - **Square-rigged ship, 1887 _Balclutha_, photographed in Alameda near dry dock, March 24, 2001**

[1] Photograph of topsail schooner *Californian* by John Riise of the Nautical Heritage Society [04/01/01] www.californian.org.

[2] Photograph of *Ka'iulani* courtesy of Captain Robert Michaan of the *Ka'iulani*.

[3] The *Californian* was sold to the San Diego Maritime Museum on July 5, 2002. [07/22/02] www.sdmaritime.org.

[4] Photograph of *Lady Washington* by Robert Esposito, Panorama Designs, © 1992, used with permission.

[5] Parker (1994) page 8.

[6] Rogers (1985) page 25.

[7] Parker (1994) page 51.

[8] Photograph of barque *Eagle* from U.S. Coast Guard Academy brochure obtained on the barque *Eagle* when she visited San Francisco.

[9] Rogers (1985) page 11.

[10] Parker (1994) page 20.

[11] Lea Suzuki, "Sailing In for Opening Day," *San Francisco Chronicle*, April 28, 2000, page A24.

[12] U.S. Navy photograph of the 1797 USS *Constitution* by Photographer's Mate Second Class Gregg Pruitt, July 11, 2000 in Boston Harbor, from website [04/05/02] www.usnavy.mil.

[13] Rogers (1985) page 160.

[14] Parker (1994) page 12.

[15] Parker (1994) page 52.

15 - Pleasure Craft

Sailboats

- **Sails and Rigging Terms**

Rigging

boom: a spar extending from a mast to hold or extend the foot of a sail.

bowsprit: a spar extending forward of the bow to which foremast stays are fastened.

gaff: a spar supporting the top of a four-sided fore-and-aft sail.

halyard: a line used to raise sails, flags, yard or gaff.

sheet: a line used to control or "trim" a sail by adjusting its foot.

shroud: a line or cable providing athwartship support for a mast.

spar: a pole such as a boom, bowsprit, gaff, sprit or yard used to support sails and rigging.

sprit: a pole that extends diagonally across a sail from low on the mast to peak of the sail.

stay: a line or cable providing fore and aft support for a mast.

yard: a tapering spar slung to a mast to support and spread the head of a square sail, lugsail, or lateen sail.

yardarm: the part of a yard supporting a square sail from the center of the mast to the end.

Sails and Sail Terms

bend: to fasten one rope to another, a sail to its boom stay, or a cable to an anchor.

clew: lower corner of a sail where the sheet is secured.

foot: the lower edge of a sail.

gaff-rigged sail: a four-sided fore-and-aft sail with a gaff supporting the top of the sail.

genoa: a large jib with a low-cut foot and clew at deck level.

hank: a clip or ring to "hank on" jibs or staysails to their stays.

head: the top part or upper edge of a sail.

jib: a forward triangular headsail hanked on the forestay with a high-cut foot and a clew above deck level.

lateen sail: a triangular sail hung on a yard attached at an angle to the top of a short mast.

lugsail: a four-sided sail without a boom, with the foot larger than the head, bent to a yard hanging obliquely on the mast.

luff: leading edge of a fore-and-aft sail.

mainsail: a quadrilateral or triangular fore-and-aft sail with its luff secured to the mainmast.

marconi-rigged sail: a triangular fore-and-aft sail with the luff secured to a mast.

peak: upper aft corner of a gaff sail or spritsail.

spanker: a fore-and-aft sail set from the aft lower mast usually gaff-rigged.

spinnaker: a large ballooning triangular sail flown forward of the jib with a lower corner secured to a spinnaker pole, used when running before the wind and flown opposite the mainsail.

spritsail 1: a quadrilateral fore-and-aft sail extended by a spar running diagonally from the lower part of the mast to the sail's peak.

spritsail 2: a sail hung under the bowsprit from the spritsail yard.

square sail: a four-sided sail supported by a yard suspended horizontally across the mast.

staysail: a fore-and-aft sail hanked on a stay between a mast and the bow or between the masts, named for the stay to which it is hanked.

topsail: a square sail sometimes hung from a yard by a schooner.

For more information on sailing and sailing terms see *Royce's Sailing Illustrated*, Volumes I and II. Royce (1993) and (1997).

▪ Sloop

A sloop is a one-masted vessel fore-and-aft rigged and may have one or more jibs, a genoa, and a spinnaker. Typically, she will be seen with a mainsail and a headsail and be marconi-rigged.

Figure 207 - **Sloop with spinnaker**

Figure 208 - *America One*
12-meter high aspect sloop

Figure 209 - **Three close-hauled sloops racing on San Francisco Bay**

▪ Cutter

A cutter is a one-masted vessel fore-and-aft rigged, with a main, a jib, a staysail, a genoa, and sometimes a spinnaker. The mast is stepped further aft than on a sloop and generally carries two or more headsails.

Because there are more options, cutters distribute sail area among the main, the jib, and the staysail to balance the boat in different wind conditions.

Figure 210 - **Cutter**

Figure 211 - **MacGregor 26 motor sailboat** [1]

▪ Motor Sailboats

Some sailboats, such as this MacGregor 26, can use outboard motors with from 10 to 50 horsepower and are able to pull a water-skier. Others have large inboard motors. These motor sailboats are a balance between being an optimum sailboat and an optimum powerboat.[2] Many consider them to be the optimum family fun boat.

▪ Ketch

A ketch is a two-masted vessel fore-and-aft rigged on both masts. The after mast (called a mizzen or jigger) is shorter and stepped forward of the rudderpost. The vessel may have a jib, a staysail, a genoa, and a spinnaker. It may be either gaff- or marconi-rigged.

Figure 212 - **Classic gaff-rigged ketch with jib and staysail**

▪ Yawl

A yawl is a two-masted vessel fore-and-aft rigged on both masts; the after mast (called a mizzen or jigger) is often much shorter and is stepped aft of the rudderpost. The vessel may have a jib, a staysail, a genoa, and a spinnaker. It may be either gaff- or marconi-rigged.

This is the classic sailing yawl *Orion.* Constructed as a private ocean-going yacht in 1934, Orion is 64 feet of traditional grace and beauty.

For charter information on this vessel, see Historic Data Sources on page 259.

Figure 213 - **1934 classic sailing yawl** *Orion*

▪ Schooner

A schooner is a sailing vessel with two or more masts. The prevailing rig is fore-and-aft. The mainmast is on the aft mast and the vessel may use one or more jibs, a genoa, several staysails, and a spinnaker.

The 1932 staysail schooner *Barbara* has a flying jib, forestaysail, foresail, main topmast staysail, and main sail.

The *Ka'iulani* is a 1984 replica of a mid-nineteenth century Pacific coast gaff-rigged topsail schooner. As shown, she is carrying a flying jib, jib, staysail, foresail, foretopmast-staysail, main sail and, maintopmast-staysail.[3]

The *Gas Light* is a charter gaff-rigged scow schooner out of Sausalito. She was built in 1991 as a replica of the original *Gas Light* built in 1870. She is shown flying a boomed foresail, gaff-rigged fore and main sails, and a top staysail.

For charter information on these vessels, see Historic Data Sources on page 259.

The *Gold Star*, a wooden standard schooner[5] with a gaff-rigged foresail, is designed like the gill-netters used to fish the Grand Banks in the North Atlantic.

Figure 214 - **Staysail schooner *Barbara***

Figure 215 - **Gaff-rigged topsail schooner *Ka'iulani*** [4]

On long ocean voyages she can be rigged as a topsail schooner.

The *Gold Star* has sailed San Francisco Bay since the early 1960's and has also cruised to Mexico, Hawaii and Alaska. She is a private vessel out of the San Francisco marina.

The history of scow schooner *Alma* is included in the historic vessels section on page 157.

Figure 216 - **Gaff-rigged scow schooner *Gas Light*** [6]

Figure 218 – **1891 scow schooner *Alma***

Figure 217 - **Standard rigged schooner *Gold Star*** [7]

▪ Catboat

A catboat is a one-masted vessel with the mast well forward and with no jib.

A catboat does not use a boom on the sail; it uses a wishbone to hold the sail's foot.

A number of small catboats sail on the bay, such as the 13-foot Banshee and the 15-foot Laser.

For a real test of your sailing skills, try racing an 8-foot El Toro across the bay from Sausalito to the St. Francis Yacht Club. In fair weather and foul, the annual Bull Ship Race Association has been doing this for almost fifty years.

Figure 219 - **Catboat**

Figure 221 - **13-foot Banshee**

Figure 220 - **8-Foot El Toro** [8]

125

Figure 222 - **Catamaran**

▪ Catamaran

A catamaran is a two-hulled craft that may be ketch-, sloop-, cutter- or cat-rigged.

The catamaran is a stable, fast sailboat with a shallow draft.

▪ Trimaran

A trimaran is a three-hulled craft that may be ketch- sloop-, cutter-, cat- or hard-sail-rigged.

The trimaran is a fast and stable sailboat and generally has more room below decks than a catamaran.

Figure 223 - **Trimaran**

Figure 224 - **Hard-sail fixed-wing trimaran**

▪ Hard-Sail Fixed-Wing

A hard-sail fixed-wing sailboat has a fixed solid wing sail that rotates to control the craft. Generally, they are multi-hull vessels.

▪ Chinese Junk

A Chinese junk is a sailboat with an upturned square bow and stern. The sails often have many full-length stays running across the sails. The original Chinese junks had bamboo sails.

Figure 226 - **Hard-sail fixed-wing trimaran**

Figure 225 - **Chinese junk sailboat**

Power Boats

How vessels are described varies with different boat builders. Terms like yacht, motor yacht, cruiser, and trawler are all used to describe a vessel with an inboard motor, the bridge in a pilothouse, and an enclosed cabin. Some vessels will have a second bridge on top of the pilothouse to give the skipper a better view.

Figure 227 - **World's fastest motor yacht** *Gentry Eagle*

▪ Luxury Performance Yacht

Designed for maximum speed with luxury live-aboard facilities, luxury performance yachts can be used for long ocean voyages.

The *Gentry Eagle* is the world's fastest motor yacht at 63.5 knots. She is 114 feet long with 11,500 horsepower. She was built in 1988; in 1989 Ton Gentry set a world speed record in the *Gentry Eagle* by crossing the Atlantic from New York to London (3,446 nautical miles) in 62 hours and 7 minutes. Her top speed reached 69.6 knots.[9] She also made the fastest time crossing between San Francisco and Hawaii. In addition, she set many other speed records.

In 1992, *Gentry Eagle* was transformed into a beautiful and fast motor yacht. As a yacht, her top speed is 63.47 knots (73 mph).

▪ Hardtop Flybridge Yacht

The hardtop flybridge motor yacht gives the skipper protection from the weather and provides good visibility.

Figure 228 - **Aft cabin flying bridge motor yacht**

▪ Aft Cabin Motor Yacht

This vessel has an open fly bridge and the main cabin at the stern and does not have an open fantail.

Figure 229 - **Hardtop flybridge cruiser** [10]

Figure 230 - **Sport flybridge yacht** [11]

▪ Sport Flybridge Motor Yacht

This vessel has an open flybridge with a convertible canvas sunscreen. A flybridge allows the skipper to see over the levees in the delta area.

129

▪ Fantail Pilothouse Trawler

The cabin and pilothouse are one room with space behind the cabin on the fantail.

Figure 231 - **Fantail pilothouse trawler** [12]

Figure 232 - **Fantail pilothouse trawler with sail**

▪ Trawler

A good, easy to use vessel with live-aboard facilities.

▪ Sport Cruiser

This is a good general day cruiser for the bay.

.

Figure 233 - **Sport cruiser**

▪ Sun Sport Boats

These are fast smaller boats for a day of sport in the sun.

Figure 234 - **Sun sport boat**

▪ Sport Fishing Boats

These sport fishing boats have the power and speed to get to the fishing area plus the comfort for a day of fishing.

Figure 235 - **Sportfisher boat**

▪ Performance Boats

These vessels are designed for speed and have no live-aboard facilities.

Figure 236 - **Performance boat**

Figure 237 - **Performance boat**

Runabout Boats

Runabout boats are fun day boats for sport or fishing.

Figure 238 - **Runabout boat** *Boston Whaler*

Figure 239 - **Runabout boat**

▪ Inflatable Boats

Inflatable boats are lightweight, sturdy, stable workboats.

Figure 240 - **Inflatable boat with racing buoy**

Figure 241 - **U.S. Coast Guard rigid inflatable boat**

[1] Photograph of MacGregor 26 motor-sailboat courtesy of the MacGregor Yacht Corporation.

[2] Royce (1993) page 273 [illustrations of various motorsailer configurations].

[3] She is a charter vessel out of Sausalito, under Discovery Yacht Charters, www.sfyacht.com.

[4] Photograph of the *Ka'iulani* courtesy of the owner Captain Robert Michaan.

[5] Royce (1993) page 271 [illustration of the schooner family riggings].

[6] Photograph of *Gas Light* copyrighted by Mariah's Eyes Photography, used with permission. For information about Mariah's Eyes vessel photographs see Historic Data Sources on page 259.

[7] Photograph of the *Gold Star* courtesy of the owner Larry Cullen.

[8] Photograph of 8-Foot El Toro by Kimball Livingston of the Bull Ship race from Sausalito to St. Francis Yacht Club on April 22, 2001.

[9] Photograph of yacht at Jack London Square, Oakland; data from *Gentry Eagle* website [01/07/03] www.gentryeagle.com.

[10] Photograph of hardtop flybridge cruiser courtesy of Delta Pacific Yachts.

[11] Photograph of sport flybridge yacht courtesy of Richard Boland Yachts and Hatteras Inc.

[12] Photograph of fantail pilothouse trawler courtesy of Richard Boland Yachts and Trans World Boat Co.

16 - Military Vessels

Coast Guard

The Coast Guard uses hull color to identify the type of vessel. The rescue and enforcement vessels have white hulls, the service vessels have black hulls, and icebreakers have red hulls.

▪ High-Endurance Cutters

Four of these Hamilton class cutters are stationed at Alameda: WHEC 719 *Boutwell,* WHEC 720 *Sherman,* WHEC 722 *Morgenthau,* and the WHEC 724 *Munro.* They are 378 feet long, with a 42-foot beam and have a displacement of 3,300 tons fully loaded. They have a top speed of 29 knots and carry a complement of 167.

These cutters perform a variety of missions throughout the Pacific basin. Their foremost mission is protecting life and property at sea. The Coast Guard enforces maritime law and also works with the other branches of the armed forces in defense readiness.

The versatility of cutters provides a cost effective and non-redundant armed service. This capability allows the U.S. Coast Guard to be gainfully employed in peacetime and ready for immediate service in the nation's defense.[1]

Figure 242 - **Coast Guard cutter WHEC 719 *Boutwell***

▪ Seagoing Buoy Tenders

The WLB 306 *Buttonwood* was a Balsam class (180-foot) seagoing buoy tender which was stationed at Yerba Buena Island (YBI). The *Buttonwood* was commissioned on September 24, 1943, and decommissioned at YBI on June 28, 2001[2]. She is now serving in the Dominican Republic Navy where she will carry out the same mission she did for the U.S. Coast Guard.

She has been replaced by the WLB 208 *Aspen*, a 225-foot Juniper "B" class seagoing buoy tender. The *Aspen* was launched April 21, 2001. Along with smaller (45–65 feet) aids to navigation boats, they service the buoys and other navigational aids in the delta, bay, and along the California coast.[3]

Figure 243 - **Coast Guard seagoing buoy tender WLB 306 *Buttonwood*
(decommissioned June 28, 2001)**

Figure 244 - **Coast Guard seagoing buoy tender WLB 208 *Aspen***

• Polar Icebreakers

The *Polar Star* and the *Polar Sea* were commissioned in 1976. These two icebreakers were then the only polar icebreakers in the American fleet. They now have been joined by the WAGB 20 *Healy,* a scientific research icebreaker.[4] With a sturdy hull and high power, these icebreakers can ram their way through ice up to twenty-one feet thick and steam continuously through six feet of ice at three knots. These vessels are homeported in Seattle, Washington, and may be seen in the Bay Area on their way to or returning from the Antarctic. The *Polar Sea* visited the Bay Area in October 2000.[5]

Figure 245 - **Coast Guard icebreaker 10 *Polar Star***

• Patrol Boats

The primary missions of patrol boats are search and rescue (SAR), enforcement of laws and treaties, defense operations, port security and marine environmental response. The *Edisto* is 110 feet long and has a complement of 16.[6]

Figure 246 - **Coast Guard patrol boat *Edisto***

▪ Large Utility Boats

Large utility boats have maximum speed of 26 knots and a range of 280 miles. They have a crew of three enlisted personnel (one coxswain, one engineer and one crewman)[7].

Figure 247 - **Coast Guard large utility boat**

Figure 248 - **Coast Guard port security boat**

▪ Port Security Boats

All boats less than 65 feet in length are classified as small boats. The Coast Guard has approximately 1,400 small boats, including motor lifeboats, large utility boats, surf rescue boats, port security boats, port and waterways boats, aids to navigation boats, and a variety of smaller, non-standard boats. They operate near shore and on inland waters of the United States.

▪ Rigid Hull Inflatable (RHI)

Rigid hull inflatables (RHI) range in length from 13 to 25 feet.

Figure 249 - **Coast Guard rigid hull inflatable**

▪ Coast Guard Auxiliary

These are privately owned vessels that serve in the Coast Guard Auxiliary and assist the Coast Guard in a number of functions.

These boats have temporary "Patrol" signs on both sides.

Figure 250 - **Coast Guard Auxiliary patrol boat** *Tricia Belle*

Figure 251 - **Coast Guard Auxiliary patrol boat**

U.S. Navy

▪ Submarine

Submarine SSN 711
San Francisco docked
in Alameda next to the
historic USS *Hornet,*
October 11, 1999.

Figure 252 - **U.S. Navy submarine SSN 711** *San Francisco*

▪ Mine Hunter Carrier

U.S. Navy mine hunter carrier USN
M/V Blue Marlin with the USS
Raven (MHC 61) and the USS
Cardinal (HMC 60) on board to be
transported to the Arabian Gulf for
duty with the Fifth Fleet.

The *M/V Blue Marlin* can
temporarily sink enough for the
mine hunters to float aboard for
transport to assigned area of
operations.

Figure 253 - **U.S. Navy mine hunter carrier** [8]

▪ Guided Missile Destroyer

U.S. Navy guided missile destroyer
USN *O'Kane* (DDG 77) arriving at
Pearl Harbor, Hawaii.

Figure 254 - **U.S. Navy guided missile destroyer** [9]

▪ Fast Combat Support Ship

The USS *Arctic* (AOE 9) is a fast combat support ship and is the largest combat logistics ship able to rapidly resupply U.S. Navy combat forces.

Figure 255 - **U.S. Navy fast combat support ship** [10]

▪ Amphibious Assault Ship

The USS *Saipan* (LHA 2) is an amphibious assault ship shown steaming off the coast of South Carolina.

Figure 256 - **U.S. Navy amphibious assault ship** [11]

▪ Guided Missile Frigate

Guided missile frigate USS *Estocin* (FFG 15) is shown sailing off the coast of Puerto Rico, October 29, 1998.

Figure 257 - **U.S. Navy guided missile frigate** [12]

• Coastal Mine Hunter

The coastal mine hunter USS *Raven* (MHC 61) enters Baltimore's Inner Harbor, August 28, 1998.

Figure 258 - **U.S. Navy coastal mine hunter** [13]

• Amphibious Assault Ship

The amphibious assault ship USS *Bonhomme Richard* (LHD 6) was commissioned August 15, 1998, at Naval Air Station, Pensacola, Florida.

Figure 259 - **U.S. Navy amphibious assault ship USS *Bonhomme Richard* (LHD 6)** [14]

• Combat Stores Ship

The USNS *Spica* (T-AFS 9) is a combat stores ship shown here in the North Arabian Gulf, November 25, 1997.

Figure 260 - **U.S. Navy combat stores ship USNS *Spica*** [15]

▪ Hospital Ship

The U.S. Navy hospital ship USNS *Comfort* (T-AH 20) refuels at sea with the fleet oiler USNS *Laramie* (T-AO 203) near Norfolk, Virginia, August 11, 1998.

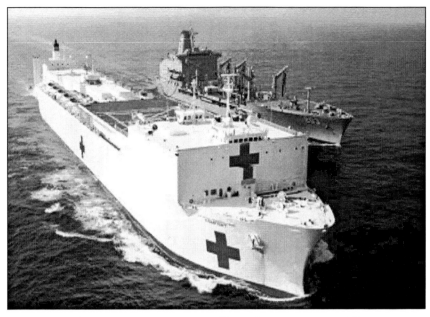

Figure 261 - **U.S. Navy hospital ship USNS *Comfort*** [16]

▪ Aircraft Carrier

USS *Kitty Hawk* (CV 63) departs Yokosuka, Japan, where she is forward-deployed, and gets underway for a scheduled two-month deployment to the western Pacific, April 11, 2000.

Figure 262 - **U.S. Navy aircraft carrier USS *Kitty Hawk*** [17]

▪ Landing Craft Unit

A landing craft unit (LCU) loaded with heavy equipment approaches the amphibious assault ship USS *Peleliu* (LHA-5) during Exercise Kernel Blitz in 1997 off the coast of Southern California.

Figure 263 - **U.S. Navy landing craft unit.**[18]

Ready Reserve

• Ro-Ro Ship

The Roll-on-Roll-off ship USS *Cape Henry* is a heavy equipment ferry.

The red-white-blue stripes around the superstructure indicate that it is maintained by a civilian crew in a ready-to-use condition. There are several of these ships in the Bay Area. They can carry military trucks, tanks and other heavy equipment.

Figure 264 - **Ro-Ro ship USS *Cape Henry***

• Alameda Pier 3, USS *Hornet* Area

Ready Reserve freighters at Pier 3 in Alameda, near the USS *Hornet*, are maintained by civilian crews and are in ready-to-use condition.

Figure 265 - **Ready Reserve fleet in Alameda at Pier 3 near the USS *Hornet***

Army Corps of Engineers

When a seaplane struck floating debris in 1942, the pilot was killed and Admiral Chester Nimitz was injured. After the accident, the U.S. Army Corps of Engineers was assigned to remove hazards to navigation from San Francisco Bay.[19]

Figure 266 - **U.S. Army Corps of Engineers patrol boat** *Wildcat*

▪ Patrol Boats

As a part of the San Francisco Bay Hazard Removal Program, the U.S. Army Corps of Engineers uses a number of small boats such as the *Wildcat* and the *Tiburon* to patrol the bay investigating hazards to navigation.

▪ Salvage Vessels

The San Francisco District's floating debris hazard collection boats *Coyote*, *Raccoon*, and *Grizzly* are based at the district's Sausalito base facility and remove about 90 tons of debris per month.

Some of the boats are converted WW II vintage aircraft recovery vessels modified for their new mission.[21]

Figure 267 - **U.S. Army Corps of Engineers patrol boat** *Tiburon*

Figure 268 - **Removing a hazard to navigation: U.S. Army Corps of Engineers** *Raccoon* [20]

Figure 269 - **U.S. Army Corps of Engineers vessel** *Grizzly*

[1] Information on *Munro* from visitor's booklet.

[2] Information on *Buttonwood* from website [10/22/01] www.uscg.mil/pacarea.

[3] Information on *Aspen* from website [04/05/01] www.uscg.mil/reserve/magazine.

[4] Information on *Healy* from website [11/27/01] www.uscg.mil.

[5] Information on *Polar Star* from visitor's booklet and website [04/05/01] www.uscg.mil/reserve/magazine.

[6] Information on *Edisto* from website [04/05/01] www.uscg.mil/reserve/magazine.

[7] Information on Coast Guard utility boats from website [04/05/01] www.uscg.mil/reserve/magazine.

[8] U.S. Navy photograph of *Blue Marlin* from website [04/05/01] www.navy.mil.

[9] U.S. Navy photograph of *O'Kane* by Photographer's Mate 2nd Class Arlo Abrahamson, on October 15, 1999 from website [04/05/01] www.navy.mil.

[10] U.S. Navy photograph of *Arctic* by Journalist 1st Class Andrew Thomas, June 18, 1999 from website [04/05/01] www.navy.mil.

[11] U.S. Navy photograph of *Saipan* by Photographer's Mate 1st Class Benjamin D. Olvey, January 17, 1999, from website [04/05/01] www.navy.mil.

[12] U.S. Navy photograph of *Estocin* by Journalist 2nd Class David Rush, October 29, 1998 from website [04/05/01] www.navy.mil.

[13] U.S. Navy photograph of *Raven* from website [04/05/01] www.navy.mil.

[14] U.S. Navy photograph of *Bonhomme Richard* by Litton Shipbuilding, from website [04/05/01] www.navy.mil.

[15] U.S. Navy photograph of *Spica* by Photographer's Mate 2nd Class Matthew J. Magee, November 25, 1997 from website [04/05/01] www.navy.mil.

[16] U.S. Navy photograph of *Comfort* by Photographer's Mate 1st Class J. Slaughenhaupt, Combat Camera Atlantic, August 11, 1998, from website [04/05/01] www.navy.mil.

[17] U.S. Navy photograph of *Kitty Hawk* by Photographer's Mate 3rd Class John Sullivan. April 11, 2000 from website [04/05/01] www.navy.mil.

[18] U.S. Navy photograph of landing craft unit by Sgt. Brook Kelsey, USMC, June 20, 1997 from website [04/05/01] www.navy.mil.

[19] The navy seaplane struck debris in San Francisco Bay on June 30, 1942.

[20] Photograph of *Raccoon* from website [04/05/01] www.spn.usace.army.mil/debris/fr.

[21] Salvage vessel data from website [04/05/01] www.spn.usace.army.mil/debris.

17 - Historic Vessels

World War II Ships

During FDR's lifetime, there were three major changes in cargo ships. Wooden ships were replaced by steel, but the last wooden commercial sailing ship was built in 1923.[1] Sailing ships were being phased out, although the last commercial sailing ships did not stop operating on the West Coast until 1950.[2] Liberty ships introduced a new way to make welded prefabricated ships.

Traditional shipbuilding changed little from the days of wooden ships through the start of World War II. Like wooden ships, steel ships were built from the keel up with hull plates riveted to closely-spaced frames. With this type of construction ships typically took twelve to fourteen months to build. Though construction was slow, Moore Dry Dock Company set a record in 1919 by launching six ships in a single high tide.

Most of the cargo ships built during World War II were of a turn-of-the century basic British tramp steamer[3] cargo ship design. With the start of war in Europe, the British ordered new cargo ships based on the standard design, and a number of San Francisco Bay Area shipyards were awarded contracts.

Recognizing the need for speed, the U.S. Maritime Commission authorized development and construction of prefabricated welded-section ships based on the design of WW I cargo ships. They were made in three sizes: C1, under 399 feet; C2, 400–449 feet; and C3, 450–499 feet. These were built to a number of specialized configurations, such as cargo, tanker, or troop ships. They used a three-cylinder reciprocating steam engine fed by two oil-burning boilers producing 2,500 hp and a speed of 11 knots, with a crew of 44.

Many of the prefabricated sections could be hauled to the shipyard by truck or rail. The first of 2,751 Liberty ships was launched on September 27, 1941. It took seventy days to build the first Liberty ship; the later speed record was four and a half days.

Because the Liberty ships were slow, a new Victory ship was designed with better hull design and a cross-compound steam turbine with double reduction gears producing over 6,000 hp. The first Victory ship was launched on February 28, 1944.[4, 5] Starting in 1944, some of the new C1 ships used diesel electric 2,200 hp propulsion.

Cargo ships built during World War II were used through the 1960's, when some were converted to carry new standardized containers. The second generation of container freighters were built specifically for efficient handling of containers. The older, smaller ships soon became obsolete. For a size comparison, see the chart on page 98.

Oakland and Alameda

Figure 270 - **1934 U.S. Coast Guard *Electra*, which became the *Potomac*, FDR's presidential yacht** [6]

▪ 1934 *Potomac*

Built as the Coast Guard patrol boat *Electra* in 1934, she was taken over by the navy to become the presidential yacht on March 10, 1936 and renamed the USS *Potomac*.

After President Roosevelt died on April 12, 1945, the USS *Potomac* stayed in service until the *Williamsburg* was available for President Truman. The USS *Potomac* was decommissioned in 1945 and served the state of Maryland as a fisheries vessel from 1946 to 1960.

In 1960 she was sold and used in inter-island ferry service in the Caribbean. Later she was a floating museum dedicated to Franklin D. Roosevelt. In 1964 she was purchased by Elvis Presley and donated to St. Jude's Hospital in Memphis, Tennessee.

A series of owners followed, and in 1980 the yacht was seized on suspicion of drug-running. Soon thereafter, she sank at her berth, was salvaged by the navy, and was purchased by the Port of Oakland, California. The *Potomac* is now owned by the Association for the Preservation of the Presidential Yacht *Potomac*. She has been completely rebuilt and restored, and is normally docked at FDR Pier, Jack London Square, Oakland, California.

For a pictorial tour of the *Potomac* as she is today, see page 178.

For the complete history of the *Potomac,* see Captain Walter Jaffee's book *The Presidential Yacht Potomac.*

▪ 1939 *ARTSHIP* (Retired California *Golden Bear*)

Historic eras of the ship include a romantic and commercial period, a period of war and triumph, a period of peace and education, and now a period of community creative potential.[7]

The Art Deco passenger/cargo ship was built in 1939 as the *del Orleans* to transport export and import goods between New Orleans and Rio de Janeiro; the ship brought bananas, beef, coffee and other goods to the United States from South and Central America. As a passenger-cargo vessel, the ship had twenty-six staterooms that accommodated fifty-two passengers, with dining and recreational saloons built in the Art Deco style of the age.[8]

During World War II she was commissioned by the United States and was renamed the USS *Crescent City* and served as a troop carrier, supply and hospital ship in the Pacific theater.

The vessel later became the student training ship *Golden Bear* at the California Maritime Academy in Vallejo, where students studied aboard the ship during the academic year and took cruises during summers to ports of call in Asia, the South Pacific, South America and the U.S. West Coast. She was decommissioned in 1995 and placed in the U.S. Reserve fleet in Suisun Bay, California.

Following legislation approved by Congress and President Clinton, the ARTSHIP Foundation received the vessel in August 1999, renaming it the *ARTSHIP* at a community-wide celebration attended by more than 5,000 people, with keynote speakers Mayor Jerry Brown, U.S. Representative Barbara Lee and Nobel Laureates Wole Soyinka and Mairead Corrigan MacGuire.

The ARTSHIP Foundation acquired the *Golden Bear* to serve as headquarters and primary program venue for the numerous community outreach and art programs run by the foundation and other art and cultural organizations.

The ARTSHIP Foundation is a nonprofit community committed to developing a creative arts and cultural education center at the Oakland waterfront. It has established programs

Figure 271 - **1939 *ARTSHIP*, retired California Maritime Academy TS *Golden Bear***

in an environment where creativity, personal growth, cultural sensitivity, and vocational skills can be developed and celebrated, and where the meaning and experience of the community can be realized through art, history, and education. ARTSHIP promotes and encourages artists and non-artists in all mediums to explore the indigenous roots of their cultural backgrounds.

An extensive renovation project is proposed to convert the ship into theaters, gallery space, classrooms, meeting space, studios, and other facilities necessary to support a major arts initiative.

It is envisioned that the *ARTSHIP* could be an integral part of the waterfront and a major waterfront attraction. The foundation hopes to obtain a permanent mooring in the vicinity of the Ninth Avenue Terminal. Landside facilities such as parking and servicing are also needed.[9]

For information about this vessel, see Historic Data Sources on page 259.

▪ 1929 *Starfjord*

The *Starfjord* is privately owned and berthed at Jack London Square. Built in 1929 as the *Acenca,* she was one of the finest luxury yachts of her day. Her registered owner was John Wheeler, a financier whose business actions reportedly gave rise to the expression "Wheeler Dealer." Although no documents exist, it is reported that the gangster Al Capone used the *Acenca* as if she were his own.

Over the years, she went through many owners, including a stint as an auxiliary miscellaneous naval vessel during World War II. With new engines and loving maintenance she has been restored to her original glory.[10, 11]

Figure 272 - **1929 *Starfjord*, private yacht at Jack London Square marina**

▪ 1943 USS *Hornet* (CV12)

The USS *Hornet* (CV12) is an Essex class aircraft carrier launched August 30, 1943. This eighth *Hornet* (CV-12) had a tremendous combat record in World War II, engaging the enemy in the Pacific in March 1944, just twenty-one months after the laying of her keel. Her shakedown cruise was the shortest in U.S. Navy history, lasting only two weeks. For eighteen months, she never touched land. She was constantly in the most forward areas of the Pacific war, sometimes within forty miles of the Japanese home islands. Her pilots

Figure 273 - **1943 USS *Hornet* (CV12), Alameda Pier 3**

destroyed 1,410 enemy aircraft and over one million tons of enemy shipping. Her planes attacked the Japanese super-battleship *Yamato* and played a major role in sinking her.

She launched the first strikes in the liberation of the Philippines, and in February 1945, the first strikes on Japan since the Doolittle raid in 1942. The "Grey Ghost" participated in virtually all of the assault landings in the Pacific from March 1944 until the end of World War II, earning nine battle stars and the Presidential Unit citation.

In 1969, *Hornet* recovered the Apollo 11 space capsule containing astronauts Neil Armstrong, Buzz Aldrin, and Michael Collins. A short time later, she recovered Apollo 12 with an all-navy crew of "moon walkers."[12] For information about this vessel, see Historic Data Sources on page 259.

Richmond

▪ *Red Oak Victory*

The SS *Red Oak Victory* (AK-235) is a VC2-AP3 class Victory ship built in the Kaiser Shipyard, Richmond, California, and launched November 9, 1944.

SS *Red Oak Victory* was acquired by the U.S. Navy from the U.S. Maritime Commission on December 5, 1944. Following a fitting-out period, she was loaded with cargo and departed San Francisco for Pearl Harbor on January 10, 1945. She then began her career as an ammunition ship and departed Hawaii loaded with munitions needed in the Marshall and Caroline Islands. She arrived in Ulithi on February 28, 1945, and commenced operating under Commander Service Squadron Ten.

From the Philippines, she delivered cargo ammunition to ships in the fleet until the end of the war in August 1945. During her hazardous tour of duty in the Pacific, USS *Red Oak Victory* handled many tons of ammunition, supplying the fleet without incurring a single casualty. She was returned to the U.S. Maritime Commission in June 1946.

USS *Red Oak Victory* operated in 1947, and again between 1950 and 1953, for the Luckenback Steamship Company. In 1957, and again from 1965 to 1968, she was operated by the Merchant Marine Administration. Between these years of operation, and until 1998, she was laid up in the Maritime Administration Reserve Fleet in Suisun Bay, California.

Red Oak Victory is one of the few remaining Victory ships and one of the last produced at the Kaiser Shipyard. She is named for the city of Red Oak, Iowa, which suffered the highest per capita casualty rate of all American communities during World War II. She was turned over to the Richmond Museum of History and returned to her new permanent home in Richmond on September 20, 1998.

For information about this vessel, see Historic Data Sources on page 259.

Figure 274 - **1944 *Red Oak Victory* moored at Richmond near where she was built at the Kaiser Shipyards** [13]

San Francisco

▪ San Francisco Maritime National Historical Park

San Francisco Maritime National Historical Park, a unit of the National Park Service, is located at the west end of Fisherman's Wharf, in San Francisco. This unique national park includes the historic fleet at Hyde Street Pier the Maritime Museum, and the Maritime Museum Library.

Each year more than a half million visitors experience the Hyde Street Pier and the Museum. Hundreds of Bay Area residents enroll in boat building and woodworking classes, and thousands of schoolchildren participate in educational overnight programs aboard the schooner *C.A. Thayer*. The park offers history, music and craft programs for all ages, and provides unique opportunities for docents, interns and volunteers to become part of history.[14]

For information about these vessels, see references in Historic Data Sources on page 259.

▪ 1943 SS-383 USS *Pampanito* Submarine

SS-383 USS *Pampanito* is a WW II Balao class fleet submarine; she was commissioned November 6, 1943 and decommissioned December 15, 1945. The *Pampanito* made six patrols in the Pacific during World War II, sank six Japanese ships, and damaged four others. The *Pampanito* is a National Historic Landmark, and is open to visitors daily at San Francisco's Fisherman's Wharf. Operated by the National Maritime Museum Association, the *Pampanito* hosts more than 250,000 visitors a year and is one of the most popular historic vessels in the country. In addition to daytime visitors, 3,000 school-age children a year participate in *Pampanito*'s educational overnight program.

Figure 275 - **1943 SS-383 USS *Pampanito* submarine at Pier 45**

The *Pampanito* is being restored to the specific period of late summer of 1945 to represent the height of WW II submarine development. The National Maritime Museum Association has scoured the country in search of missing equipment and spare parts. Almost all of the missing items have now been replaced, and much of the equipment on board is now restored operationally

This site offers an in-depth look at many issues involving a single ship, USS *Pampanito*. It includes a tour of the submarine, her history, lists of *Pampanito*'s wartime crew, descriptions of WW II submarine technology, and historic photographs. Also included are a WW II submarine memorial with the name of every submariner lost during the war, information about educational programs aboard *Pampanito*, and a description of *Pampanito*'s preservation and restoration programs.[15]

▪ 1943 *Jeremiah O'Brien* Liberty Ship

The *Jeremiah O'Brien*, a type EC2-S-C1 class Liberty ship, was launched on June 19, 1943.

 One of two surviving Liberty ships preserved in the United States, *Jeremiah O'Brien* is the last unaltered Liberty. The ship is a product of an emergency shipbuilding program during World War II that resulted in the construction of more than 2,700 Liberty ships. Designed as cheap and quickly built simple cargo steamers, the Liberty ships formed the backbone of a massive sealift of troops, material, and ordnance to every theater of the war. *Jeremiah O'Brien* made wartime voyages between the east coast, Canada, and the United Kingdom, to South America, Australia, and the Philippines. From June until December 1944, *Jeremiah O'Brien* made eleven trips between the United Kingdom and Normandy in support of the D-day invasion, including a trip from Belfast, Ireland, to Normandy with troops from Patton's Fifth Division.

Laid up in the National Defense Reserve Fleet in Suisun Bay in California, *Jeremiah O'Brien* was selected by the U.S. Maritime Administration in 1966 as the Liberty to be preserved for the future. In 1979, the ship was taken out of mothballs and restored to

Figure 276 - **1943 *Jeremiah O'Brien* Liberty ship at San Francisco Pier 45**

operating condition. She is open to the public 359 days a year at Pier 45 as a part of the National Maritime Museum and makes memorial cruises annually in May and October.

In 1994 *Jeremiah O'Brien* gained world attention when she steamed back to the Normandy invasion beaches to participate in ceremonies marking the fiftieth anniversary of D-day—the only U.S. veteran D-day ship present. She was operated by a number of WW II veterans who had experience with Liberty ships.

SS *Jeremiah O'Brien* is a National Historic Landmark and an American Society of Mechanical Engineers Landmark.[16] The *Jeremiah O'Brien* was named after a commander in the War of the Revolution. He was a naval officer, military commander and privateersman.

Put into the reserve fleet after the war, the *Jeremiah O'Brien* was transferred to the National Liberty Ship Memorial in 1978 to be reactivated. She was moved to her present location under her own steam on May 21, 1980.[17]

▪ 1914 *Eppleton Hall* Paddlewheel Steam Tugboat

Eppleton Hall is 100 feet long and was built in England in 1914.

The vessel, named after the Lambton family's ancestral home, was designed to tow ocean-going colliers (coal-carrying vessels) to and from the port of Newcastle on the River Tyne. Coal was a booming business, and towing the sailing vessels upriver to load saved days of transit time.

Figure 277 - **1914 *Eppleton Hall* paddlewheel steam tugboat**

Eppleton Hall, a steam side-wheeler with side-lever engines, is the only remaining intact example of a Tyne paddle tug. A direct descendent of the first craft to go into commercial service as harbor tugs, she worked on the Wear and Tyne rivers of northeast England from 1914 to 1967. In 1952 the tug was modified slightly to obtain a passenger certificate so that she could transport officials from newly launched steamers (after they had completed their sea trials).

She was sold for scrap in 1967, and while she sat on a mud bank, a fire destroyed her wooden afterdeck and interior. Subsequently refurbished, *Eppleton Hall* was a private yacht from 1969 to 1979. She was modified for an epic steam journey to San Francisco via the Panama Canal and passed through the Golden Gate in March of 1970.

She was donated to the National Park Service in 1979 and is now berthed at Hyde Street Pier.[18]

▪ 1907 *Hercules* Steam Tugboat

The *Hercules* was built in 1907 in New Jersey for the San Francisco Red Stack tugboat Company. When completed, *Hercules* towed her sister ship, the *Goliath*, through the Strait of Magellan to San Francisco. Both vessels were oil-burners; *Goliath* carried fuel, water and supplies for her sister ship.

Figure 278 - **1907 *Hercules* steam tugboat with tugboat *Alert* at her side**

The *Hercules* towed barges, sailing ships and log rafts between Pacific ports. Because prevailing northwest winds generally made travel up the coast by sail both difficult and circuitous, tugs often towed large sailing vessels to points north of San Francisco. In 1916, *Hercules* towed the *C.A. Thayer* (another one of San Francisco Maritime National Historical Park's historic fleet) to Port Townsend, Washington. The trip took six days. She also towed the *Falls of Clyde*, now a museum ship, to Hawaii. On trips back down the coast, *Hercules* often towed huge log rafts, laden with millions of board feet of Northwest timber, to Southern California mills. At other times, *Hercules* towed barges of bulk cargoes between other West Coast ports, and to Hawaii.

Hercules avoided the scrap yard but languished until the California State Park Foundation acquired her for the San Francisco Maritime State Historical Park in 1975. The National Park Service took over her restoration in 1977, and in 1986 she was designated a National Historic Landmark. *Hercules* has been documented as part of the Historic American Engineering Record's Maritime Project.

Today, after a thirty-year layup, she is operable again, and regularly steams the bay with a highly trained volunteer crew.[19]

• 1895 *C.A. Thayer* Three-Masted Schooner

The *C.A. Thayer* was built in 1895 and is 219 feet overall and 156 foot on deck. She is 36 feet wide and has a 105-foot tall main mast.

In the past, hundreds of sailing schooners carried lumber to San Francisco from Washington, Oregon, and the California redwood coast. *C.A. Thayer* was part of that mighty Pacific Coast fleet. Today, she is a rare survivor from the days when strong canvas sails billowed over tall deckloads of freshly milled fir, cedar and redwood.

After fifty-five years and a variety of careers, the *C.A. Thayer* made her final voyage in 1950. She was the last commercial sailing vessel on the West Coast.

The state of California purchased *C.A. Thayer* in 1957. After preliminary restoration in Seattle, Washington, an intrepid volunteer crew sailed her down the coast to San Francisco. The San Francisco Maritime Museum performed more extensive repairs and refitting and opened *C.A. Thayer* to the public in 1963. The vessel was transferred to the National Park Service in 1978 and designated a National Historic Landmark in 1984. After three full careers, lasting more than one hundred years, she remains—restored and maintained for future generations—to be experienced at the San Francisco Maritime Historical Park.[21]

Figure 279 - **1895 *C. A. Thayer* three-masted schooner with center mast removed** [20]

• 1891 *Alma* Scow Schooner

The *Alma* was built in 1891 and is 80 feet long overall with a 67-foot tall foremast.

Fred Siemer came to San Francisco from Germany in 1865 and started his own shipyard at Hunters Point. He constructed two scow schooners and named the first after his daughter, Adelia. After Adelia married, Siemer built the second scow for his son-in-law, James Peterson. That boat, constructed in Peterson's front yard in 1891, was named for Peterson's daughter, Alma.

Alma's construction was not unique, but it was unusual; her bottom planking was laid athwart-ship (side-to-side) instead of fore-and-aft. Called "log built" because the horizontally laid planks were quite thick, scows like *Alma* traded a bit of speed and ease of repair for economy and strength.

Like other scow schooners, *Alma* hauled a wide variety of cargoes during her career. Between 1850 and the early years of the twentieth century, the best highways around the

San Francisco Bay Area were the waterways, and the delivery trucks and tractor-trailer rigs of those days were flat-bottomed scow schooners.

Over 400 of these craft were constructed around the bay. Although similar vessels were found in New England and on the shores of the Great Lakes, the basic scow design was adapted to local conditions, and resulted in a craft uniquely suited to San Francisco Bay.

Figure 280 - **1891 *Alma* scow schooner**

Able to navigate the Sacramento/San Joaquin delta region's shallow creeks, sloughs and channels, the scows' strong, sturdy hulls could rest safely and securely on the bottom, providing a flat, stable platform for loading and unloading. Their squared bows and sterns not only maximized cargo space, but also made them cheap and easy to build. Typically constructed of inexpensive Douglas fir, their design was so simple that most scows were built "by eye," without plans of any kind.

However, progress, in the form of gasoline engines, doomed these hardy sailing vessels. The last sailing scow schooner was built in 1906, and by the 1920's most scows had been rigged down to one mast. Some continued to work as barges or oyster shell dredges. However, in 1957, improved highways and motorized trucks squeezed even *Alma*, the last survivor, out of profitability.[22]

▪ 1890 *Eureka* Southern Pacific Ferryboat

The *Eureka* was built in 1890, is 277 feet long, and carried 2,300 passengers and 120 automobiles. The *Eureka* is a side-wheel paddle steamboat. From the passenger deck up, she is nearly identical fore and aft. Her "double-end" design made disembarking quicker and easier. *Eureka*'s large "walking beam" steam engine remains intact and is maintained in working order

The *Eureka* was built in 1890 at Tiburon, California, for the San Francisco and North Pacific Railway and named *Ukiah* to commemorate SF&NPR's recent rail extension into that California city. A freight-car ferry, *Ukiah* was SF&NPR's "tracks across the bay," ferrying trains from Sausalito to San Francisco.

After World War I, *Ukiah* needed extensive repair, and shipwrights at the Southern Pacific yard labored for two years, eventually replacing all of her structure above the waterline. This kind of reconstruction was called "jacking up the whistle and sliding a new boat underneath."

Re-christened *Eureka*, she slid from the Southern Pacific yard as a passenger and automobile ferry (her present form) in 1923.

In 1941, *Eureka* had the dubious distinction of making the last Marin County run, and by the 1950's regular ferry service was limited to railroad connections.

Eureka kept working, but in 1957, when her crankpin snapped in mid-crossing, she was removed from service.

Figure 281 - **1890 *Eureka* Southern Pacific ferryboat**

Eureka's tall "walking beam" is the last working example of an engine type once common on America's waterways. It was manufactured by Fulton Iron Works of San Francisco. Coal (and later oil) was burned in boilers to produce the steam that drove a huge, vertical piston. Perched atop the engine, the walking beam changed this up-and-down motion into rotary motion via a connecting rod linked directly to the paddlewheel shaft.

The twin paddlewheels (each twenty-seven feet in diameter) made twenty-four revolutions per minute.

The vessel's last major shipyard repair was completed on May 19, 1954.

"As big as she was, she was about the fastest ferryboat on San Francisco Bay. She made the trip from the San Francisco Ferry Building to Sausalito in twenty-seven minutes," according to Captain A.R. Gustofson.

Eureka's last ferry run was in 1957 and she is now on display at the San Francisco Maritime Historical Park.[23]

• 1886 *Balclutha* Square-Rigger

The *Balclutha*, built in 1886, is 301 feet long overall with a 145-foot tall mainmast. On January 15, 1887, with a twenty-six man crew, *Balclutha* sailed under British registry from Cardiff, Wales on her maiden voyage, bound for San Francisco. The ship entered the Golden Gate after 140 days at sea, unloaded her cargo of 2,650 tons of coal, and took on sacks of California wheat. Because of the months-long ocean voyage, *Balclutha* made only one round-trip per year while engaged in the Europe to San Francisco grain trade. She arrived with a cargo three times, but also brought pottery, cutlery, Scotch whiskey (from Glasgow and Liverpool) and "Swansea general" (tinplate, coke and pig iron) to San Francisco.

After *Balclutha* ran aground in 1904, the Alaska Packers Association purchased her where she lay for the non-princely sum of $500. After extensive repairs, they renamed her *Star of Alaska*. All Packer iron and steel sailing vessels had the word "Star" in their names.

During her career, the *Star of Alaska* sailed up the West Coast from Alameda, California, carrying supplies and cannery workers. She anchored out in Chignik Bay, Alaska, in April. After

Figure 282 - **1896 *Balclutha* square-rigged ship, photographed in Alameda near dry dock, March 24, 2001**

supplies had been unloaded and the cannery workers had settled into the company's camp ashore, only a ship keeper or two would remain on board. In early September, her hold packed with cases of canned salmon, *Star of Alaska* would start the 2,400-mile voyage back to San Francisco Bay. She was considered a fast sailer, and averaged less than twenty-two days for the trip north and fifteen days when homeward bound.

During the winter, she was laid up with the rest of the Packers' fleet of thirty-odd vessels in Alameda, where shipwrights performed maintenance and renovation. In 1911, the poop deck was extended to house Italian and Scandinavian fishermen.

Later, additional bunks were added between decks for Chinese cannery workers. As a cargo ship, the *Balclutha* carried a crew of twenty-six. When she went north with the Alaska Packers as the *Star of Alaska*, she had her regular crews and more than two hundred men who would work in the canneries.

Star of Alaska was the only sailing ship the Packers sent north in 1930, and when she returned that September she, too, was retired.

Frank Kissinger purchased *Star of Alaska* in 1933 (for $5,000) and renamed her *Pacific Queen*. Kissinger took the ship south and, while anchored off Catalina Island, she appeared in the film *Mutiny on the Bounty* (Clark Gable and Charles Laughton also appeared in supporting roles). For a time thereafter, Kissinger towed her up and down the West Coast, usually exhibiting her as a "pirate ship." *Pacific Queen* slowly deteriorated, and she barely escaped WW II scrap metal drives.

In 1954, the San Francisco Maritime Museum purchased *Pacific Queen* for $25,000. Assisted by donations of cash, materials and labor from the local community, the museum restored the vessel and returned her original name. The ship was transferred to the National Park Service in 1978, and *Balclutha* was designated a National Historic Landmark in 1985. In the spring of 1998 *Balclutha* returned to Hyde Street Pier after $1.25 million in restoration work to her deck and rigging at a local shipyard.[24]

▪ Felucca Fishing Boat

In the late 1860's, Italian immigrant fishermen from the coastal villages near the city of Genoa came to San Francisco. Here they built their traditional fishing boats which became known as "San Francisco feluccas." The seaworthiness of these small, lateen-rigged boats worked well in San Francisco Bay.

At the San Francisco Maritime National Historical Park there is a 1985 replica of a late 1800's felucca with an inverted "V" mast, and a large triangular sail that hangs down from a long yard.

Figure 283 - **Felucca lateen-rigged fishing boat**

▪ 1927 *Santa Rosa* Ferryboat

The Southern Pacific Golden Gate Ferry *Santa Rosa* is now permanently berthed at Pier 3 and is used for commercial office space.

The following history of the *Santa Rosa* was written by Tom Lewis, who is a naval historian.[26, 27]

The *Santa Rosa* was one of six sister ships (boats) built for the flourishing automobile ferry business on San Francisco Bay during the 1920's. She was constructed in 1927 at the General Engineering and Dry Dock Company in Alameda, across the estuary from the *Potomac*'s berth. She was constructed for the Northwestern Pacific Railroad, a subsidiary of the Southern Pacific Company, for service between the Ferry Building and Tiburon or Sausalito. This assignment proved to be short-lived as the Southern Pacific bought the competing Golden Gate Ferry and consolidated the ferry systems on San Francisco Bay in 1929 as the Southern Pacific Golden Gate Ferries, Ltd. (SPGGF), becoming at the time the largest ferry system in the world. The *Santa Rosa* became a part of this fleet.

Figure 284 - **Circa 1900 felucca fishing boat on San Francisco Bay** [25]

However, the construction of the San Francisco–Oakland Bay Bridge in 1936 and the Golden Gate Bridge in 1939 doomed the existing ferry system. The *Santa Rosa* continued to serve on the Hyde Street to Sausalito route and the Ferry Building to Oakland Pier route until the bankruptcy of SPGGF in 1939.

The *Santa Rosa* was then sold for a nominal price to the Black Ball Ferry on Puget Sound, along with most of the serviceable SPGGF boats on the bay. She was towed at sea to Seattle in 1940.

However, the Puget Sound service had one important route from Seattle to Bremerton that demanded faster service and more passenger capacity. Accordingly, the *Santa Rosa* and sister ship *Fresno*, now named *Enetai* and *Willapa*, were re-engineered in 1941 and converted to single end operation for the long trip to Bremerton. The upper deck cabin was expanded to provide for more passengers and the two boats continued to serve until 1968 when they were replaced by new Washington State "super ferries."

The returned *Santa Rosa* that you see today is a partial reconstruction to the ferry's original configuration. As matter of interest, four of the *Santa Rosa*'s sister ships continue to operate on Puget Sound. These are the NWP boats *Redwood Empire* and *Mendocino* and the Southern Pacific boats *Stockton* and *Lake Tahoe*, all under new Northwest Indian names. These boats were first used in their original San Francisco Bay configuration until 1947. At that time, they were re-engineered with two General Motors diesels and war surplus generators. The original General Electric motors, driving the propellers at each end, were retained.

In the 1980's, these four boats were again re-engineered with Finnish diesels, still using the original GE propulsion motors, and at that time they were extensively rebuilt with wider sponsons, modern passenger cabins and modern pilothouses and controls. One can find these boats today, seventy-four years later, in good condition and operating on various routes in Puget Sound.

For the technically minded, the *Santa Rosa* is a steel hulled diesel electric. She measures 251 feet in length, was originally 46.3 feet in breadth and 19.1 feet in depth. She draws 15 feet of water. Her original engines were four war surplus (WWI) New London Shipbuilding Company submarine engines. As originally constructed for San Francisco Bay, she was to handle one hundred automobiles and a minor number of walk-on passengers.

Figure 285 - **1927** *Santa Rosa* **Southern Pacific Golden Gate Ferry**

Historic Vessel with New Home

▪ 1863 Barque *Star of India*

Although no longer in San Francisco, the *Star of India* was a sister ship to the *Balclutha*, known then as the *Alaska Star*, and was a part of the Alaska Packers fleet. She has been restored and is berthed at the Maritime Museum of San Diego, California.

The *Star of India* is the world's oldest active sailing ship. She was built on the stocks at Ramsey Shipyard on the Isle of Man in 1863. Iron ships were experimental then, and most vessels were still made of wood.

She was launched less than five months after her keel was laid. She bore the name *Euterpe*, after the Greek goddess of music. *Euterpe* was a full-rigged ship and would remain so until 1901, when the Alaska Packers Association rigged her down to a barque, her present rig.

She was sold to American owners in 1898 and in 1902 commenced sailing from Alameda, California, to the Bering Sea each spring with a load of fishermen, cannery hands, and supplies. She returned each fall laden with canned salmon. This went on until 1923, when she was laid up by her owners, the Alaska Packers. The Packers had changed her name in 1906, dubbing her *Star of India* in keeping with their company practice.

Figure 286 - **1863 Barque *Star of India* from the San Diego Maritime Museum, sailing on San Diego Bay** [28]

1 For more information see Stone Boat Yard in "China and Central Basin" on page 53.

2 For more information see Historic Vessels *C.A. Thayer* on page 157.

3 A tramp steamer is a commercial vessel that has no regular schedule but takes on and discharges cargo whenever hired to do so.

4 Information from U.S. Merchant Marine website [01/09/03] www.usmm.org.

5 Bonnett (1999).

6 The 1934 photograph of the USS *Potomac* from Franklin D. Roosevelt Presidential Library, courtesy of Potomac Association file 19504 #6.

7 The history of the *ARTSHIP* is from the ARTSHIP Foundation. See Historical Data Sources on page 259.

8 Goldberg, M. (1992) page 40, SS *del Orleans*.

9 Jack London Area Development Plan *OAK-4.4: Promote development of commercial-recreational uses in the vicinity of the Crescent Park and Clinton Basin.* From website [01/05/03] www.estuaryplan.com/jack_lon.htm.

10 Information on *Starfjord* from Miles Davis, who has owned the vessel since 1985.

11 Information on classic yachts from website [01/09/03] www.classicyacht.org.

12 Information on *Hornet* from website [01/09/03] www.maritime.org/hnsa-hornet.htm.

13 The 1999 photograph of *Red Oak Victory* by Tom Bottomley, Purser, SS *Red Oak Victory*.

14 Information on *C.A. Thayer* from website [01/09/03] www.maritime.org/safrhome.shtml and from website [01/09/03] www.nps.gov/safr/index.html.

15 Information on the *Pampanito* from website [01/08/03] www.maritime.org/pamphome.shtml.

16 Information on *Jeremiah O'Brien* from website [01/09/03] www.ssjeremiahobrien.org and from website [01/09/03] www.maritime.org/hnsa-job.htm.

17 Jackson (1991) pages 34–41, Sawyer (1985), Livingston (1984).

18 Information on *Eppleton Hall* from website [01/09/03] www.nps.gov/safr/local/eppie.html.

19 Information on *Hercules* from website [01/09/03] www.nps.gov/safr/local/herc.html.

20 Photograph of *C.A. Thayer* taken January 2001.

21 Information on *C.A. Thayer* from website [01/09/03] www.nps.gov/safr/local/thayer.html.

22 Information on *Alma* from website www.nps.gov/safr/local/alma.html.

23 Information on *Eureka* from website [01/09/03] www.nps.gov/safr/local/eureka.html.

24 Information on *Balclutha* from website [01/09/03] www.nps.gov/safr/local/balc.html.

25 Photograph and information on 1900 felucca fishing boats from website [01/09/03] www.nps.gov/safr/local/wharf.html.

26 Demoro (1971) Harlan (1967). Stories related by my grandfather, Hugh Ellison, Sup. SPGG Ferries Ltd. and my father, Arthur C. Lewis, Asst. Engineer, SPGG Ferries Ltd.

27 For more information on the *Santa Rosa* see page 161.

28 Photograph of barque *Star of India* courtesy of Capt. John Ruffino, Maritime Museum of San Diego.

For More Information

18 - Presidential References
List of all Presidents and Vice Presidents

Presidents
   Vice Presidents

1. George Washington (1789–1797)
   John Adams (1789–1797)
2. John Adams (1797–1801)
   Thomas Jefferson (1797–1801)
3. Thomas Jefferson (1801–1809)
   Aaron Burr (1801–1805)
   George Clinton (1805–1812)
4. James Madison (1809–1817)
   George Clinton (1805–1812)
   Elbridge Gerry, (1813–1814)
5. James Monroe (1817–1825)
   Daniel D. Tompkins, (1817–1825)
6. John Quincy Adams (1825–1829)
   John C. Calhoun, (1825–1832)
7. Andrew Jackson (1829–1837)
   John C. Calhoun, (1825–1832)
   Martin Van Buren (1833–1837)
8. Martin Van Buren (1837–1841)
   Richard M. Johnson (1837–1841)
9. William Henry Harrison (1841)
   John Tyler (1841)
10. John Tyler (1841–1845)
    None appointed (1841–1845)
11. James Polk (1845–1849)
    George M. Dallas (1845–1849)
12. Zachary Taylor (1849–1850)
    Millard Fillmore (1849–1850)
13. Millard Fillmore (1850–1853)
    None appointed (1850–1853)
14. Franklin Pierce (1853–1857)
    William R. King (1853)
    None appointed (1853–1857)
15. James Buchanan (1857–1861)
    John C. Breckinridge (1857–1861)

16. Abraham Lincoln (1861–1865)
    Hannibal Hamlin (1861–1865)
    Andrew Johnson (1865)
17. Andrew Johnson (1865–1869)
    None appointed (1865–1869)
18. Ulysses S. Grant (1869–1877)
    Schuyler Colfax (1869–1873)
    Henry Wilson (1873–1877)
19. Rutherford B. Hayes (1877–1881)
    William A. Wheeler (1877–1881)
20. James A. Garfield (1881)
    Chester A. Arthur (1881)
21. Chester A. Arthur (1881–1885)
    None appointed (1881–1885)
22. Grover Cleveland (1885–1889)
    Thomas A. Hendricks (1885)
    None appointed (1885–1889)
23. Benjamin Harrison (1889–1893)
    Levi P. Morton (1889–1893)
24. Grover Cleveland (1893–1897)
    Adlai E. Stevenson (1893–1897)
25. William McKinley (1897–1901)
    Garrett A. Hobart 1897–1899)
    Theodore Roosevelt (1901)
26. Theodore Roosevelt (1901–1909
    Charles W. Fairbanks (1905–1909)
27. William H. Taft (1909–1913)
    James S. Sherman (1909–1912)
    None appointed (1912–1913)
28. Woodrow Wilson (1913–1921)
    Thomas R. Marshall (1913–1921)
29. Warren Harding (1921–1923)
    Calvin Coolidge (1921–1923)
30. Calvin Coolidge (1923–1929)
    Charles G. Dawes (1925–1929)

31. Herbert Hoover (1929–1933)
    Charles Curtis (1929–1933)
32. Franklin D. Roosevelt (1933–1945)
    John N. Garner (1933–1941)
    Henry A. Wallace (1941–1945)
    Harry S Truman (1945)
33. Harry S Truman (1945–1953)
    None appointed (1945–1949)
    Alben W. Barkley (1949–1953)
34. Dwight D. Eisenhower (1953–1961)
    Richard M. Nixon (1953–1961)
35. John F. Kennedy (1961–1963)
    Lyndon B. Johnson (1961–1963)
36. Lyndon B. Johnson (1963–1969)
    None appointed (1963–1965)
    Hubert H. Humphrey (1965–1969)

37. Richard M. Nixon (1969–1974)
    Spiro T. Agnew (1969–1973)
    Gerald R. Ford (1973–1974)
38. Gerald R. Ford (1974–1977)
    Nelson A. Rockefeller (1974–1977)
39. Jimmy Carter (1977–1981)
    Walter F. Mondale (1977–1981)
40. Ronald W. Reagan (1981–1989)
    George H. W. Bush (1981–1989)
41. George Bush (1989–1993)
    J. Danforth Quayle (1989–1993)
42. William J. Clinton (1993–2001)
    Albert Gore, Jr. (1993–2001)
43. George Walker Bush (2001–Present)
    Richard B. Cheney (2001–Present)

FDR's Family

Franklin Delano Roosevelt
Born: January 30, 1882
Died: April 12, 1945

Anna Eleanor Roosevelt
Born: October 11, 1884
Died: November 17, 1962

Franklin and Eleanor married
March 17, 1905

Children:
Anna Eleanor Roosevelt (1906–1975)
James Roosevelt (1907–1991)
Elliott Roosevelt (1910–1990)
Franklin Delano Roosevelt, Jr. (1914–1988)
John Aspinwall Roosevelt (1916–1981)

Fala

Fala was FDR's faithful companion and lived at the White House from 1940 to 1945. He was the president's constant traveling companion, even accompanying him on several of his trips overseas. Fala spent many hours aboard the *Potomac*. An interesting note is that after FDR's death in 1945, Fala rode with Eleanor in the funeral procession, and she took care of Fala until his death. Fala is buried behind the graves of Franklin and Eleanor in the rose garden of the Roosevelt Hyde Park estate.

Figure 287 - **FDR's dog Fala** [1]

Figure 288 - **Fala is buried next to the birdbath near the graves of Franklin and Eleanor**

In addition, Fala is immortalized in bronze, sitting and looking up at his master at the Franklin Delano Roosevelt Memorial in Washington, D.C.[2]

FDR's New Deal Agencies in the Bay Area

The Agricultural Adjustment Agency (AAA) was created in 1933 to bring the farmers' share of the nation's income back to the level of 1909 to 1914. It sought to provide an "ever-normal granary" and was declared unconstitutional in 1936. Most of its duties were assumed by the Soil Conservation and Domestic Allotment Act that was reconstituted in 1938.

The Civilian Conservation Corps (CCC) was created in 1933 to succeed the agency known as Emergency Conservation Work. The mission was to provide employment and vocational training for needy young men through work in conservation and development of natural resources. It became part of the Federal Security Agency until it was abolished in 1942.

The Farm Security Administration (FSA) was created in 1937 to aid tenant farmers and to carry on rehabilitation work of the Resettlement Administration.

The Federal Emergency Administration of Public Works (better known as Public Works Administration) (PWA) was created in 1933 to reduce unemployment and to restore purchasing power through construction and long-range planning of public works. It was absorbed by Federal Works Agency (FWA) in 1943, which was created in 1939 to coordinate all public construction.

The Federal Emergency Relief Administration (FERA) was created in 1933 to relieve the hardships caused by unemployment and drought. It was abolished in 1938, and the Works Progress Administration (WPA) continued its work until 1942.

The Works Progress Administration (WPA) was created in 1935 to relieve unemployment; it was later called the Work Projects Administration. It was abolished in 1942.

The Maritime Labor Board (MLB) was created in 1938 to improve labor relations among seamen. It expired in 1942.

The National Labor Relations Board (NLRB) was created in 1935 to protect employees in their rights to self-organization and collective bargaining.

The US Maritime Commission was created in 1936 to develop a merchant marine to carry the domestic and foreign waterborne commerce of the United States on ships built, owned, and operated by United States citizens. It was originally the US Shipping Board and Merchant Fleet Corporation.

1945 Aircraft Carrier CVB-42
USS *FRANKLIN D. ROOSEVELT*

The Midway class carrier *Franklin D. Roosevelt* (CVB-42) was launched April 29, 1945 by New York Naval Shipyard as USS *Coral Sea* CVB-42, renamed USS *Franklin D. Roosevelt* May 8, 1945; she was reclassified CVA-42 on October 1, 1952.

In 1956 she was fitted with an angled flight deck, steam catapults and a hurricane bow. She was stricken from the navy list Sept. 30, 1977, and sold for scrap April 1, 1978.

Figure 289 - **1945 CVA-42 USS *FDR* after 1956 refitting** [3]

FDR's Travels on the *Potomac*

The presidential yacht used before the *Potomac* was the *Sequoia*.[4] The *Potomac* did not become the president's yacht until the spring of 1936. Like the *Potomac*, the *Sequoia* did not start as a presidential yacht. Originally a Department of Commerce inspection ship, she was used by President Hoover for two fishing trips during the very last months of his administration. Then, in March 1933 she was commissioned as a naval vessel to serve as President Roosevelt's yacht.

When it was announced in November 1935 that the president was to have a different yacht than the *Sequoia*, three reasons were given for the change. The *Sequoia* had a wooden hull that presented a fire hazard. There was always concern for the safety of the president and there was an understandable insistence that *Sequoia* be replaced by the *Potomac*, which had a steel hull.

The second reason for replacing the *Sequoia* was that it had gasoline engines. The *Potomac*, with its diesel engines, would be safer and more fuel efficient. The third reason offered was that because of its larger size, the *Potomac* would have room for Secret Service agents. (The *Potomac* is 165 feet long; the *Sequoia* was about 100 feet long.) When the president was using the *Sequoia*, the Secret Service agents, together with the press, would follow in another ship, the *Cuyahoga*. The most common cruise was the relatively short weekend cruise.

Whenever his schedule would permit it, president Roosevelt would get away for the weekend. The cruise would generally start early Saturday afternoon, although it would sometimes start on Friday. The ship would sail down the Potomac River into Chesapeake Bay until a small cove was found which promised good fishing. The ship would anchor and the fishing boats would be lowered over the side.

Because of his paralysis, several methods were used to get the president into his fishing boat. One way was simply to have him in the boat before it was hoisted out and lowered. Sometimes he was hoisted over the side in a boatswain's chair. The third method was to deploy the ship's gangway-ladder and have the president's boat brought alongside. After the president was wheeled to the gangway, two sailors would form a fireman's carry by locking their hands; he would put his arms around their shoulders and they would pick him up and walk down the gangway to the boat. The vessel would return to Washington on Sunday evening or Monday morning.

In addition to these short weekend cruises, there were longer fishing trips. The first fishing trip the president made on the *Potomac* was to the Bahamas and began at the end of March 1936, right after the commissioning of the *Potomac*.

The president rode a train from Washington to Florida, then boarded the *Potomac* to the Bahamas, and entertained the governor at a luncheon on board. Meeting or returning from the ship this way was typical on longer cruises. Until 1942, FDR ode in a standard private Pullman car when traveling by train. However, because of wartime security, the *Ferdinand Magellan*, one of six private Pullman cars made in 1928, was converted to an armor-plated presidential railcar and used by FDR.

One of the most notable trips on the *Potomac* took place in August of 1941, when President Roosevelt boarded the vessel for a secret meeting with Winston Churchill. When the *Potomac* sailed out of the harbor of New London on August 3, elaborate precautions were taken to have it appear that this was merely another fishing trip. In fact, the president would shortly transfer to the cruiser USS *Augusta* when they reached Martha's Vineyard, to be taken to Newfoundland where, on August 9, he would begin a series of meetings with the prime minister.

Today, our mental image of the meetings tends to be dominated by the scene of the joint religious service held Sunday morning, August 10, on the quarterdeck of the British battleship HMS *The Prince of Wales*. Most of the meetings actually took place on board the *Augusta* because of the difficulty of transferring the president to HMS *The Prince of Wales*.

At these meetings, the first between them, they outlined what came to be called the Atlantic Charter. The countries allied in the war against the Axis powers agreed to its principles. Later it became the basis for the creation of the United Nations. Interestingly, there never was an actual document, or a "charter" signed by the president and the prime minister. What does exist is the text of the official statement containing their joint declaration that was given to the media.

To conceal the fact that the president was participating in the secret meeting, the *Potomac* continued to cruise the coastal waters, with the chief of the White House Secret Service detail sitting on the fantail dressed in typical Roosevelt sea-faring clothes, such as the naval cloak Eleanor had given him and his slouch hat. At that time, the *Potomac* was equipped with an anti-aircraft gun located in the fantail. The restored ship does not have any armaments.

The *Ferdinand Magellan*, FDR's Railroad Car

The *Ferdinand Magellan* is unique among railroad cars in that it is the only car ever custom built for a president of the United States in the twentieth century. Originally built in 1928, the *Ferdinand Magellan* was one of six Pullman private railroad cars named after famous explorers.[6]

Until late 1942, the president used one of the private Pullman cars when he traveled by train. In early 1942, just after the United States became involved in World War II, White House aides Michael Reilly and Steven Early suggested that the president should have a custom built railroad car to afford him maximum protection when he traveled by rail. President Franklin Roosevelt approved of the idea after he was told that the car would be used for future presidents as well.

Figure 290 - **1928 *Ferdinand Magellan*, FDR's RR car**[5]

When the *Ferdinand Magellan* was chosen to be the presidential car, FDR's only request was to "make it a little more comfortable." The number of bedrooms was reduced from five to four to create more room for the dining room and the observation lounge. Nickel-steel armor plate five-eighths inch thick was riveted to the sides, floor, roof and ends of the car in a manner that made it undetectable when the car was viewed from any distance. Three-inch thick bullet-resistant glass, manufactured by laminating twelve sheets of one-fourth inch thick glass into one piece, was installed and sealed into the window frames, replacing conventional safety glass in the windows.

Two escape hatches were built into the car, one in the ceiling of the observation lounge and one on the side wall of the shower/bath in the presidential bathroom near the center of the car. Special trucks, wheels and roller bearings were installed to support the additional weight. A standard, heavyweight Pullman car of the *Magellan*'s era weighed about 160,000 pounds. The rebuilt *Ferdinand Magellan* weighed 285,000 pounds. At 142.5 tons, it is the heaviest passenger railcar in the United States.

The newly rebuilt *Ferdinand Magellan* was presented to President Roosevelt on December 18, 1942. During World War II, for security reasons, only the word "Pullman" appeared on the outside of the car so that from a distance, the rolling fortress looked like any other private rail car. Whenever it was part of a train, however, the train moved under the commodity code POTUS (the first letters of president of the United States). Every railroad official knew that POTUS had the right of way over all other rail traffic. To lessen the chance of sabotage during the war, the car did not have a permanent storage location in Washington, D.C. It was moved around when not in use and stored on various sidings.

At the Washington Navy Yard, a special elevator was installed on the observation platform at the rear of the car to aid the president in boarding the car while in a wheelchair. This elaborate device was removed from the railroad car after the death of President Roosevelt.

On January 9, 1943, a five car train was quietly assembled in Washington and the president's navy stewards were summoned from the presidential yacht *Potomac* to perform the duties ordinarily handled by Pullman porters. Officials preparing this special train were told not to issue any special instructions that might cause suspicion. The train left Washington, D.C. at 10:00 P.M. with President Roosevelt aboard, but only went as far north as Fort Meade, Maryland. An hour later, it was headed south, beginning President Roosevelt's journey to the now famous Casablanca summit meeting with Winston Churchill. In Florida, the president was transported by automobile to Pan American Airways where he boarded the seaplane *Dixie Clipper* for the flight to Africa via South America. This was the first time a seated U.S. president traveled by plane outside U.S. borders.

Franklin D. Roosevelt traveled about 50,000 miles in the *Ferdinand Magellan* during his presidency. He preferred to travel at 35 miles per hour. On March 29, 1945, he left Washington on the *Ferdinand Magellan* for a trip to the summer White House at Warm Springs, Georgia. A week later he died on April 12 of a stroke. On April 13, the funeral train bearing the president's body left Warm Springs for Hyde Park, New York. Mrs. Roosevelt was riding in the *Ferdinand Magellan*, which was the second car from the rear, for the first time since it was placed in presidential service. The casket containing the president's body was placed aboard the *Conneaut* (another Pullman private car), by removing a window to make an opening large enough to place the casket inside. This was done because the bullet resistant windows of the *Ferdinand Magellan* could not be removed. This car was then placed last in the train for the trip to Washington, D.C. and then on to Hyde Park, New York, where the president was buried in his rose garden on April 15, 1945.

The *Ferdinand Magellan* was taken out of service and arrived in Miami, Florida, at the Gold Coast Railroad Museum on January 15, 1959, where it is on exhibit. In 1978 the *Ferdinand Magellan* was listed in the National Register of Historic Places, and the next year the museum received permission to replace the Seal of the President of the United States on the rear platform of the car.

In August 1992, southern Florida was devastated by hurricane Andrew. The Gold Coast Railroad Museum was severely damaged by the fury of the storm. The train shed collapsed on the museum cars stored inside. All were heavily damaged and two were literally snapped in two. Although massive steel support beams crashed into the *Ferdinand Magellan*, the car sustained relatively little structural damage. The roof was dented and the paint was "sandblasted" from the sides, but the massively heavy construction of the car protected it from destruction. After a two-and-a-half year restoration, the car was placed back on public display in October 1996.

FDR's Shangri-La and the *Potomac*

During the months following America's entry into World War II, officials in Washington, following the urgings of President Franklin D. Roosevelt, searched the countryside surrounding Washington for an area that would be suitable for a presidential retreat.[8]

Figure 291 - **1942 Shangri-La / Camp David** [7]

The President's yacht, the USS *Potomac*, could not be utilized because of security problems; both the U.S. Secret Service and the U.S. Navy were fearful that German submarines might attempt to sink the ship if it were known that the president used it frequently for pleasure cruises. For reasons that dealt with the president's health, his physicians preferred some place that would remove the president from the oppressive heat of summertime Washington.

Thus, the criteria for the president's retreat were proximity to Washington, elevation to ensure coolness, and above all, a location where presidential security could be maintained.

The president liked the Catoctin Recreational Demonstration Area because it had an elevation of 1,800 feet. There was a group of cabins on the site and the existing buildings could be revamped to meet the requirements. At Catoctin on April 30, 1942, the president gave final approval to preliminary sketches for the lodge, and the National Park Service started to prepare the working drawings.

When reporters questioned the president about where Captain Doolittle and his Tokyo Raiders had taken off for their air raid on Japan, he smilingly told them "Shangri-La." [9]It followed as a matter of course to apply this name to the mountain retreat. On the president's first official visit, July 5, 1942, he wrote in his log book "USS *Shangri-La* launched at Catoctin, July 5, 1942."

Staff of the yacht *Potomac* also staffed and serviced the compound after construction. The president carried his seagoing theme further along these lines by referring to his visits as cruises.

As constructed, the lodge somewhat resembled the Warms Springs, Georgia, White House. Neither has front steps; both have a dining/living room located in the center which opens to a back porch/patio.

Furnishings throughout were simple. No particular style dominated, and all were obtained by combing the White House attic and navy storage. A conference table under a rustic wagon wheel chandelier dominated the living/dining room. Over the main door hung a replica of the presidential seal. The front entrance looked out upon a small pool that was stocked with trout. A rough-hewn log bench was provided for the president.

Figure 292 - **FDR fishing with Churchill** [10]

The communications cabin incorporated all communications equipment, including telegraph, a switchboard and two private telephone circuits. A special telephone trunk line connected the compound to the White House and was activated only when the president was in residence. An entirely separate system for inter-camp communications was also installed. The cabin had a full bathroom and an electric hot water supply.

On July 18, 1942, the president returned for his first overnight "cruise" and stayed for three days.

FDR Presidential Airplanes

In 1942 an aircraft was for the first time specifically outfitted for use by a U.S. president. However, it was never used by a president. It was a C-87A Liberator Express, an adaptation of the B-24 Liberator Bomber.

The C-87A was designed for passenger comfort and was fitted with sixteen Pullman-type upholstered seats that could be converted into five berths.

Figure 293 - **1942 *Guess Where 2* C-87A Liberator Express first designated presidential airplane** [11]

Only six of these planes were built, three for the U.S. Navy and three for the U.S. Air Force. One of these planes, designated as the presidential aircraft, underwent additional modification and was named the *Guess Where 2*. Eleanor Roosevelt used it for a trip to Central and South America; however, the president was never aboard. [12]

The first flight by a U.S. president in office was on January 11, 1943. FDR flew on the Boeing B-314 *Dixie Clipper* from Miami, Florida, to Bathurst, British Gambia, West

Africa.[13] He was on his way to the Casablanca conference to meet with Winston Churchill. For the trip to Casablanca, a double bed was installed for his use. FDR celebrated his sixty-first birthday, complete with birthday cake, on this flight.

The trip used a southern route in the hopes of avoiding German aircraft, and covered more than 17,000 miles and 90 hours flying time.[16] At Bathurst, FDR changed to a land based aircraft, a TWA Douglas for the trip north to Casablanca, French Morocco, Africa.

Figure 294 - **1942 Douglas C-54** *Sacred Cow*, **second presidential airplane** [14]

The second designated presidential airplane was the *Sacred Cow*. In 1942 Douglas Aircraft modified a C-54 Skymaster for FDR.

It had a crew of seven and could accommodate fifteen passengers. A conference room was provided that contained a large desk. An elevator behind the cockpit was used to lift the president in and out of the plane.

FDR preferred travel by ship or train and made only one trip aboard the C-54 *Sacred Cow*, to attend a conference in Yalta, U.S.S.R., with Winston Churchill and Joseph Stalin.

FDR traveled to Malta aboard the cruiser USS *Quincy*. From there on February 3, 1945, he flew aboard the *Sacred Cow* to Saki (near Yalta). On February 12, 1945, the *Sacred Cow* returned the president to the USS *Quincy* at Cairo, Egypt.

President Roosevelt never made another flight. However, General Douglas MacArthur, Winston Churchill, and President Truman all flew aboard the *Sacred Cow*.[17]

Figure 295 - **Pan Am Boeing's 314** *Dixie Clipper*, **first airplane to fly an American president, January 11, 1943** [15]

Table: Presidential Yachts and Small Craft

President, Years In Office	Presidential Use Dates	Vessel Name	Length (feet)	Notes
Rutherford B. Hayes (1877–1881)	1880–1891	Despatch	174	Originally the steamer America, it was purchased by U.S. Navy and commissioned in November 1873. Wrecked in gale October 10, 1891. 1873–1891 (Survived 18 years).
James A. Garfield (1881)				
Chester A. Arthur (1881–1885)				
Grover Cleveland (1885–1889)				
Benjamin Harrison (1889–1893)				
Grover Cleveland (1893–1897)	1891–1905	Dolphin	257	1885–1921 (Survived 36 years).
William McKinley (1897–1901)	1898–1905	Sylph	124	1898 – Used only a few times by McKinley.
Theodore Roosevelt (1901–1909)	1905–1929	Mayflower	273	Theodore Roosevelt used Dolphin and Sylph before the Mayflower.
William H. Taft (1909–1913)				
Woodrow Wilson (1913–1921)				
Warren Harding (1921–1923)				
Calvin Coolidge (1923–1929)				
Herbert Hoover (1929–1933)	1929–1936	Sequoia	100	President Hoover used the Sequoia only twice at the end of 1932; at that time it was a Commerce Department vessel.
Franklin D. Roosevelt (1933–1945)	1934–1936	Sequoia	100	The Sequoia was commissioned as a presidential yacht in 1933; when it was replaced by the Potomac in 1936, it became available for use by the Secretary of the Navy.
	1936–1945	Potomac	165	The Potomac was built for the Coast Guard in 1934 as the Electra. She was renamed and commissioned FDR's presidential yacht in March 1936. It was not actively used by FDR after 1941.
Harry S. Truman (1945–1953)	1945–1953 None	Williamsburg	244	Originally, Aras; built for private use in 1931. Bought by U.S. Navy 1941, converted to a gunboat. Navy sold it in 1962; in private use, it was damaged 1968 (37 years old).
Dwight D. Eisenhower (1953–1961)	1953–1961			
John F. Kennedy (1961–1963)	1961–1981	Sequoia	100	Sequoia served seven presidents for 44 years. She is afloat in private charter use and now 71 years old.
Lyndon B. Johnson (1963–1969)				
Richard M. Nixon (1969–1974)		Magie*		*The Magie, Lenora, and Guardian are listed as "small craft" and served several presidents under a variety of names. They are not considered by the Navy Historical Center as presidential yachts.
Gerald R. Ford (1974–1977)		Lenora*		
Jimmy Carter (1977–1981)		Guardian*		
Ronald W. Reagan (1981–1989)	None			
George H. Bush (1989–1993)				
William J. Clinton (1993–2000)				
George W. Bush (2001–Present)				

Touring Presidential Yacht *Potomac*

▪ Introduction

Figure 296 - **Potomac, November 1999**

It is convenient to think of the front, or forward, part of the *Potomac* as being the "business" part of the ship. That is, areas such as quarters for the ship's officers and crew, the radio room and the pilothouse are located here. It is also the part of the ship that was least changed when she was converted from a Coast Guard cutter to a presidential yacht.[18]

In contrast, major changes which involved constructing quarters and other facilities for the president and his guests are in the rear, or after, part of the ship.

When she was the presidential yacht, the USS *Potomac* was a commissioned naval vessel, and as such she would have been painted the familiar navy gray. Now she is white—a color which perhaps conforms more with our sense of what a presidential yacht should look like. We know the USS *Williamsburg*, President Truman's presidential yacht, was a commissioned naval vessel, and it was also painted white.

▪ The Main Dining Room or Saloon

The saloon provides a convenient and logical starting point, with the president's cabin and fantail as natural next stops.

A word about the terminology. Although saloon is perhaps most often used today to indicate a place serving liquor, it also has the more traditional meaning of a large public area and, particularly in connection with ships, to refer to the dining cabin. In the naval architect's drawing of the *Potomac* the main dining room is labeled "saloon."

The *Potomac* allowed President Roosevelt to get away from the daily pressures and routine of the White House. It also gave him the opportunity to take a cruise or a fishing trip and was something to look forward to. It was also a chance to get away from the routine (apparently unappetizing) cooking prepared under the direction of Mrs. Nesbitt, the Roosevelt's Hyde Park neighbor whom Mrs. Roosevelt had brought to the White House as housekeeper.

Figure 297 - **Potomac, main dining room or saloon; the center door is the elevator**

Except for the microwave, which obviously wasn't there when the *Potomac* was the presidential yacht, and the fact that the stove was oil fired, the galley is as it was then.

On the walls of the saloon are a number of small prints of sailing ships and sea battles. This is a direct reflection of the president's love of sailing and the sea. At the age of sixteen, Franklin Roosevelt acquired his own yacht, which he named the *New Moon*, and which he used throughout his years at Harvard University.

Later, when serving as assistant secretary of the navy during the administration of Woodrow Wilson, his love of the sea was emphasized by the strong attachment to the navy that he formed at the time and retained for the rest of his life. As assistant secretary of the navy, he had use of two ships, the *Dolphin* and the *Sylph*, each of which had earlier served as presidential yachts for Presidents Grover Cleveland, Benjamin Harrison and William McKinley.

Mobility was always a problem for President Roosevelt after he was stricken by polio in 1921. Because of his disability, getting him from the saloon and the fantail to the boat deck presented a problem for naval architects in designing the conversion of the *Electra* into the *Potomac*. Their solution, using the aft smokestack as a housing for a small elevator, was ingenious. When President Roosevelt was using it, it was more like a dumbwaiter; that is, a platform operated by ropes and pulleys. Today, behind its special door is a gated, electric elevator, as required by current regulations.

▪ The President's Cabin

The president's cabin required considerable restoration. One of the reasons that it took fourteen years from acquisition of the *Potomac* after its sinking in 1981 to its opening to the public in 1995 was its dedicated restoration for historical accuracy. This meant spending the time and effort necessary to acquire the plans, photographs, and documents that would assure accuracy, as well as finding the right people to do the job.

The cabin is quite small and narrow and the stainless steel bathtub is a sitz tub. Because of the strength in his upper body, the president could raise himself by pressing down and then swinging his body into the tub.

The most frequent comments of visitors to the *Potomac* are expressed when they see the president's cabin and

Figure 298 - *Potomac,* the president's cabin

react to its simplicity. Almost universally, whatever they may have conjured up in their mind's eye when hearing the term "presidential cabin" leads them to expect something bigger, more grand or more elegant.

Anyone who has visited the Roosevelt home in Hyde Park or, indeed, Theodore Roosevelt's Oyster Bay home, will have noticed that while these are large homes on estates, they demonstrate simplicity. Both of the Roosevelt branches were part of society and their family's roots went back to the earliest days of the country. Their sense of place and comfort did not require ostentatious display.

But there was, of course, another reason for simplicity. The *Potomac* was commissioned in March 1936, when the country was still in the midst of the Great Depression. It would have been bad policy to spend large sums of money furnishing a yacht for the president. The question of spending for presidential yachts has arisen several times in our history. So, for example, Presidents Hoover, Eisenhower and Carter, early in their administrations, decided that for reasons of economy they would not continue to have a presidential yacht.

▪ The Fantail

Entering the fantail, we come to one of President Roosevelt's favorite places on the ship. For the president, the social interchange of meeting, talking, getting reports, having a cocktail, exchanging stories or jokes, etc. was very important. President Roosevelt, perhaps more than any other president, relied on personal, face-to-face contacts to obtain the information he needed. His wife Eleanor was particularly important to him in this regard, serving as his eyes and legs and reporting to him the effects of a program or existing conditions in the places where she had traveled. She had learned to do this for him when he was governor of New York and continued while in the White House.

Also important to him, starting when he was governor and brought over to his presidency, was the formal cocktail hour. One can easily visualize him in the fantail of the *Potomac* acting as host and enjoying his martini.

A striking feature of the fantail is the curved settee. In the center, it is four feet deep. The President would often sit there in the center, using it as a chaise lounge. The sense of touching history comes easily here, as visitors sit on the settee or chairs and imagine themselves guests of the president, cruising down the Potomac River.

Just above the settee are glass windshields. When the *Potomac* was used as the presidential yacht, these were made of bulletproof glass.

Figure 299 - *Potomac*, **the fantail**

▪ The Guest Cabins

Originally, the *Potomac* had four guest cabins. However, in order to meet current regulations, one of the cabins had to be removed and the space used to put in the ladder to the fantail.

Visitors are free to enter and look around all of the cabins. They are not large and not elegant.

There is only a single bed in the president's cabin. Although Eleanor Roosevelt was on board to receive important guests, such as King George VI and Queen Elizabeth in 1939, and at least once celebrated her birthday with a party on board the vessel, she did not go on any overnight cruises. Eleanor Roosevelt was never comfortable on the sea. This can be traced back, at least in

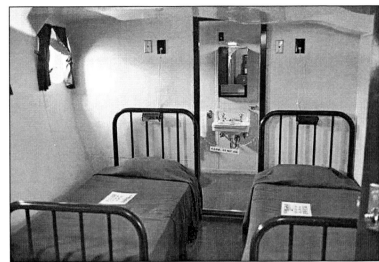

Figure 300 - **Potomac, the guest cabins**

part, to the fact that when she was about two and a half years old, she had a terrible experience at sea. She was aboard the *Britannic*, going to Europe with her family, when the ship was rammed in fog. After the collision, she had the frightening experience of being dropped over the side of the ship to her father who was standing in a lifeboat below.

Eleanor and Franklin had a complex relationship throughout the many years of their marriage. We do know that it changed significantly in 1918, when Eleanor found out that he was having an affair with Lucy Mercer, her social secretary.

In 1918, during the First World War, FDR, as assistant secretary of the navy, traveled overseas on an inspection trip. He became ill and returned home while still sick. Eleanor, in unpacking his bags, came across a packet of love letters.

Franklin turned down Eleanor's offer of divorce and the affair ended, both because Lucy Mercer was Catholic and because his mother told him that he would be disinherited.

However, years later, after Mercer's husband had died, she and Franklin reestablished contact, unbeknownst to Eleanor. Indeed, it was she who was in Warm Springs with the president in April 1945 when he died.

Although visitors will ask about famous people who have been on the vessel, Winston Churchill was not one of them. Although he was a good friend of the president, a visitor both at the White House and on President Truman's presidential yacht, the *Williamsburg*, he was never on the *Potomac*.

The visit of King George VI and Queen Elizabeth occurred on June 9, 1939. Their time on board was actually quite short. After being piped on board, the King and Queen went to the fantail where they were greeted by President and Mrs. Roosevelt. The vessel then sailed down the Potomac River to Mount Vernon. After seeing Washington's home and Arlington they returned to the White House by car.

Other royalty who were guests on the *Potomac* included Prince Karl of Sweden, Queen Wilhelmina of the Netherlands and Crown Princess Martha of Norway. Princess Martha was a particular favorite of the president. After Germany overran Norway, she and her family escaped to England and eventually Princess Martha and her children came to the United States for the duration of the war.

Important members of Congress and cabinet officers were among those who were guests aboard. The president could also use a cruise as an opportunity to talk in a private and relaxed atmosphere with someone who would be appointed to a crucial position.

▪ The Boat Deck Fantail

The fantail of the boat deck is the largest open area on the vessel. It's a marvelous place to enjoy the weather on a fine day and to observe and talk about the activities in the estuary. The boat deck was a major addition in converting the *Electra* into the *Potomac*.

Looking forward from the boat deck fantail is the door to the elevator that was built into the smoke stack.

Figure 301 - *Potomac*, **the boat deck and fantail with open elevator door in false stack**

Seeing the president suddenly appear from a smoke stack could have been quite surprising to guests on the fantail.

Forward on the boat deck are two Chris Craft motorboats donated to the Potomac Association. Although they are not the original boats that were on the *Potomac*, they are authentic 1930's craft just like the ones that were here. President Roosevelt himself insisted on having the Chris Craft motorboats so that he would not have to depend on the whaleboat that you see just forward of the Chris Craft.

Continuing forward, there are cylindrical containers on both sides of the vessel. These automatically inflatable life rafts, which can hold fifty people each, were not part of the equipment of the *Potomac* when she was the presidential yacht. Their presence reflects the fact that the *Potomac* today is a fully functioning vessel, meeting all current regulations.

▪ The Pilothouse

Although much of the *Potomac* consists of restoration, most of what is original can be seen in the pilothouse. These original parts include the teak doors, the binnacle (compass housing) and the steel balls on each side which neutralize magnetic interference, the steering stand (but not the steering wheel, which was somewhat larger than the current one) and the speaker tube.

Because the vessel is fully functional, there is also a good deal of modern navigational equipment here in the pilothouse.

Figure 302 - **Potomac, the pilothouse**

▪ The Engine Room

For reasons of safety, visitors normally are not permitted to enter the engine room. The twin six-cylinder diesel engines, which are not the *Potomac*'s original engines, can readily be seen from the entryway. The vessel generally travels at about ten to twelve knots. (Since a nautical mile is about 15 percent longer than a statute mile, that translates to about eleven and a half to fourteen miles per hour.)

Figure 303 - **Potomac, the engine room**

▪ The Radio Room

Opposite the engine room is a small radio room with little more in it than the radio and a typewriter which are from the 1940's. When at sea, the president communicated by means of an occasional mail pouch and the radio. The mail, after arriving by seaplane, was transferred to a small boat to be carried aboard.

The president was on a fishing trip when he made the radio address known as a "fireside chat" from the *Potomac* on March 29, 1941. She had pulled into the harbor at Fort Lauderdale, Florida, early in the day to allow him time to work on his speech. The

Figure 304 - *Potomac,* **the radio room**

next morning he returned to Washington by train. The Jackson Day dinners being held around the country provided the occasion for the speech.

The real purpose of the speech was to move the country toward a recognition of the threat that Germany and the Axis powers posed to the United States if Great Britain, which was standing alone, succumbed. There was still a significant isolationist feeling in the country, although most had already come together in support of the president. Congress had passed the Lend Lease Bill earlier in the month.

▪ Enlisted Men's Quarters

As one enters the compartment, it becomes obvious that it served multiple purposes for the enlisted crewmembers.

There are the bunks for sleeping, a pantry and the table for the crew's mess, and in the far corner, the combined office and stateroom. Food for the crew was cooked in the crew's galley located on the main deck on the port side.

Figure 305 - *Potomac*, forward enlisted men's quarters for stewards

The forward compartment was used by the twelve crew members who were stewards, all of whom were Filipino. Prior to President Truman's administration, the armed forces were not integrated and the navy was a rigidly segregated organization.

According to Jack Lynch[19], the crew consisted of the twelve stewards, sixteen seamen and twenty-six petty officers. If you count the number of bunks in this compartment and do the division, you'll see that the arithmetic doesn't work out. The answer, at least in part, is that the bunks were, in naval parlance, "hot bunks;" that is, they would be used by more than one person in a day.

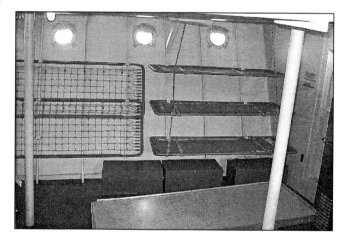

Figure 306 - *Potomac*, main enlisted men's quarters for crew

Just aft of the crew's quarters are cabins for the vessel's officers.

▪ Officers' Quarters

Two of the cabins, for the vessel's chief executive officer and for the engineering officer, are identified by the small plaques above their respective entrances. Like much else on the vessel, they are compact but comfortable. The third cabin, the double cabin, presents a question as to its use.

One of the stated reasons for the *Potomac* replacing the *Sequoia* was that there would be room on board the *Potomac* for the Secret Service agents. Some evidence suggests that, in fact, they were on board. On the other hand, Jack Lynch says that the Secret Service, together with the press, followed in the USS *Cuyahoga*,[20] as was the practice when the president was using the *Sequoia*.

Figure 308 – ***Potomac*, officers' quarters**

• Commanding Officer's Cabin

Ascending the ladder, the last tour stop is the commanding officer's cabin.

Situated directly below the pilothouse, it afforded the skipper of the vessel reasonably comfortable, although still simple, accommodations. Noteworthy is the absence of a telephone and other communication devices which one would see today, but there was always a sailor to run with a message.

Responsibility for a presidential yacht rested with a president's naval aide, generally a captain. The job of the naval aide aboard is undefined, except for attending the president at official functions and having technical command of the presidential yacht.

Normally, a lieutenant commander would be the actual skipper. When the naval aide was on board, he would have use of one of the guest cabins.

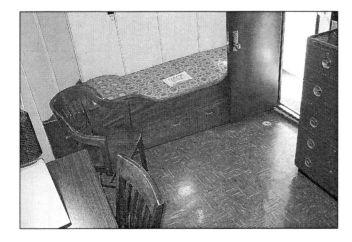

Figure 307 - ***Potomac*, commanding officer's cabin**

Figure 309 - ***Potomac*, commanding officer's cabin**

Summary of Presidential Yachts

When the Coast Guard cutter *Electra* was refitted and transferred to the navy for President Roosevelt's use as the *Potomac* in the spring of 1936, it joined a very small list of vessels that have served as presidential yachts.[21] A president, as head of state and as commander-in-chief of our armed forces, has always had the use of any vessel of the U.S. Navy. Normally such use would be in connection with official duties, although use for rest and relaxation was not excluded. It was not until the latter part of the nineteenth century, however, that specific naval vessels began to be used by presidents as a way to get brief escapes from the daily routine of the presidency.

The first such cruise by a president occurred on November 9, 1880, when President Rutherford B. Hayes, with members of his cabinet, went aboard the *Despatch* for a trip on the Potomac River. Originally the steamer *America*, she was purchased and commissioned by the navy in November 1873; after being commissioned, she was assigned to dispatch duty because of her speed (12.6 knots, maximum).

For most of the eleven years from 1880 through 1891; that is, through the administrations of Presidents Hayes, Garfield, Arthur, Cleveland and Harrison, the *Despatch* operated on the Potomac River, Chesapeake Bay and the coastal waters of the Atlantic from Virginia to Maine. During these years she was often used by the president, cabinet members, members of Congress and other government officials. She was wrecked in a gale off the coast of Virginia on October 10, 1891, and sold for salvage on November 12, 1891.

A commissioned ship of the U.S. Navy would not be given the specific role of presidential yacht until 1898, when the navy assigned the *Sylph* to the Washington Navy Yard. In the meantime, the *Dolphin*, an unarmored cruiser commissioned on December 8, 1885, was used from time to time by Presidents Cleveland, Harrison and McKinley, as well as by other dignitaries. Her service in the navy was long and illustrious; after thirty-six years of service, she was decommissioned on December 8, 1921.

President McKinley took only a few cruises during his term in office. Once the *Sylph*, which had been commissioned on August 18, 1898, became available, he used her as the presidential yacht. Although President Theodore Roosevelt took over another vessel as his presidential yacht, he used both the *Dolphin* and the *Sylph* on various occasions.

The next ship to be converted into a presidential yacht was the *Mayflower*. Built as a private yacht in Scotland in 1896, she was bought by the U.S. government in 1898 for use in the Spanish-American War as a dispatch vessel. The *Mayflower* subsequently became the flagship of the Caribbean squadron and was used as Admiral Dewey's flagship during a review of the fleet in 1905. On that occasion, Theodore Roosevelt saw her and decided to make her his presidential yacht.

The *Mayflower* had an illustrious career for twenty-four years, serving five presidents: Theodore Roosevelt, Taft, Wilson, Harding, and Coolidge. On board the *Mayflower* at Oyster Bay, President Theodore Roosevelt introduced the representatives of Japan and Russia to each other to begin the conferences which led to the treaty at Portsmouth, New Hampshire, that ended the Russo-Japanese War.

Although America had its millionaires in the nineteenth century, economy and Jeffersonian simplicity were taken to be virtues in the White House until the turn of the century. The acquisition of the *Mayflower*, the largest of the presidential yachts at 273 feet, represented this change in attitude.

As a presidential yacht, she was the last word in beauty and comfort, with an elegantly appointed dining saloon and a well-selected library, cabins for the president, his wife, and about a dozen guests, a reception room and a smoking room. For President Taft, the president's suite was modified to install an oversized marble bathtub. By the time of President Harding, the predominant color of the dining saloon was "Mrs. Harding's blue," a color emphasized by a number of blue vases and candlesticks added by Mrs. Coolidge.

In 1914, during President Wilson's term, the *Mayflower*'s service as a presidential yacht was briefly interrupted while she served as a patrol boat.

It was said of President Coolidge that it often seemed his main pleasure in life was the privilege of taking weekend cruises on the *Mayflower*. Although President Coolidge distrusted the sea, and on one famous occasion was photographed when he was seasick, the president used and enjoyed the yacht.

One of the first acts of President Hoover in 1929 was to give up use of the *Mayflower* for reasons of economy. During the Navy Department alterations that were to turn her into a survey vessel, an intense fire broke out. So much water was pumped into her that she sank at the dock.

President Hoover did not enjoy sailing. At such times as he did go on a cruise, he would either use available naval vessels or be the guest on yachts of friends. In 1932, at the end of his term as president, he took two fishing cruises. On both of these occasions he used a Department of Commerce inspection ship, the *Sequoia*.

When FDR became president, it was decided that the *Sequoia* would become his presidential yacht. Accordingly, she was commissioned as a naval vessel on March 25, 1933. While the *Sequoia* had a fairly good-sized cabin and bath on the main deck, there were two very small double cabins and three tiny single cabins on the deck below. The dining saloon could seat eight and there was a comfortable lounging deck aft. The small size and simple accommodations suited the president, particularly since he did not want a luxury yacht during the depression when so many people were in dire need.

Because the *Sequoia* had gasoline engines and a wooden hull and was not a good seagoing vessel, concern for the safety of President Roosevelt led to her replacement by the *Electra* as the presidential yacht. In announcing that the *Electra* had been chosen as the new presidential yacht, the president said that the change was being made because of insistence that he use a fireproof boat and because it would mean a saving of both manpower and fuel, since the *Electra* would accommodate Secret Service operatives, who previously had followed the *Sequoia* in the *Cuyahoga*, a smaller Coast Guard boat.

The *Sequoia*, once she was replaced by the *Potomac*, was no longer the presidential yacht during the remainder of FDR's term in office. However, she did remain in use as the official yacht of the secretary of the navy. Later, she would be used again as the presidential yacht by Presidents Kennedy, Johnson, Nixon, Ford, and Carter.

After the death of President Roosevelt, the Navy Department condemned the *Potomac* in the fall of 1945 as being top-heavy and unfit for duty in open waters. Accordingly, she was decommissioned and sold to the state of Maryland.

To replace the *Potomac*, President Truman accepted the *Williamsburg*, which formally became the presidential yacht on November 10, 1945. The 244-foot-long, steel-hulled, diesel-powered yacht, originally named the *Aras,* had been built in 1931 for private use.

A slim white ship with a crew of about a hundred, the *Williamsburg* was powered by diesel engines, air-conditioned, and equipped with radar and communications facilities. She had four guest staterooms in addition to the President's quarters. President Truman had the use of two pianos when on board. One was in the main dining room, the other in his private study.

In her last weeks of service as the presidential yacht under President Eisenhower, the *Williamsburg* was used to take wounded veterans on afternoon excursions on the Potomac River. She was decommissioned on June 30, 1953, and turned over to the Potomac River Naval Command for maintenance and preservation. From April 1, 1959, until being struck from the navy list on April 1, 1962, she was in "special status." During the remainder of President Eisenhower's term there was no presidential yacht.

President Kennedy brought *Sequoia* back into service. The *Sequoia* was finally sold in 1977 by President Carter. She was purchased by the Presidential Yacht Trust in 1981 and restored. The Trust planned to return the *Sequoia* to the government in 1988 after its restoration. However, President Reagan declined the offer. For several years thereafter, the *Sequoia* was sent to various parts of the country by the Trust for public tours and cruises. The *Sequoia* was later bought by a private individual and continues to be available for tours and cruises.

History of Specific Presidential Yachts

▪ Steamer River Queen

During the Civil War President Lincoln on several occasions used the *River Queen*, a steamer of 536 tons, leased by the quartermaster general and assigned to the War Department, at $241 per day. It was on this vessel that President Lincoln held his conference with the Confederate Peace Commissioners Alexander H. Stevens, R.M.T. Hunter, and John A. Campbell at Hampton Roads, Virginia, on February 3, 1865. On March 23, 1865, the president again made a trip from Washington, D.C. to Hampton Roads on board the *River Queen*.[22]

▪ 1873 Steamer *Despatch*

The steamer *Despatch* was a wooden-hulled steamer of 560 tons purchased in November 23, 1873. She was 174 feet in length; 25 feet, 6 inches in beam; with a draft of 12 feet, 4 inches. After being commissioned she was assigned to the North Atlantic station, and, in anticipation of war with Spain, sailed from Hampton Roads, Virginia, on November 30, 1873, joining the fleet at Key West on December 5, 1873. In the spring of

Figure 310 - **1873 steamer** *Despatch*, **first official presidential yacht**

1874 she returned north, arriving at the Washington Navy Yard on April 24, 1874. From 1874 to 1877, she was based in Washington.

It was not until 1877 that she was assigned special duty with the U.S. Embassy at Constantinople, Turkey.

Detached from this duty in 1879, she returned home and arrived at the Washington Navy Yard on June 30, 1879. She made her first cruise as a presidential yacht with President Hayes on a short trip on the Potomac River on November 9, 1880. She would be used as a yacht for Presidents Hayes, Garfield, Arthur, Cleveland and Harrison.

The *Despatch*, while returning to Washington, D.C. from a cruise along the New England coast with the secretary of the navy by way of Chesapeake Bay and the Potomac River, ran into a storm and sank on October 10, 1891. Everyone aboard survived. In 1997, Ben Benson, a salvage operator working with a magnetometer located the *Despatch* off Assateague Island, where she had been wrecked in 1891.[23]

▪ 1884 Gunboat *Dolphin*

The gunboat *Dolphin* was built as a small cruiser, dispatch boat or gunboat in 1884. From 1895, until the outbreak of World War I, she served as a "special dispatch boat," frequently carrying the secretary of the navy and the president. She was sold in 1922, but her final fate is unknown.[24]

Dolphin, a vessel of 1,486 tons displacement, was built by John Roach & Sons, Chester, Pennsylvania. Launched April 12, 1884, she was commissioned December 8, 1885. In addition to regular naval duties, this vessel at times cruised with the

Figure 311 - **1884 Gunboat** *Dolphin*, **second presidential yacht**

president, the secretary and assistant secretary of the navy, the Fleet Admiral of the navy, and various other high government officials and foreign dignitaries. President McKinley went from Washington, D.C. to New York for the ceremonies at Grant's Tomb on April 23, 1897, on the *Dolphin*.

She made a number of cruises with Presidents McKinley and Theodore Roosevelt, who assumed the presidency after the assassination of McKinley in 1901. The *Dolphin* was used until 1905, when the *Mayflower* became the presidential yacht.

The *Dolphin* continued in service until December 1921, and FDR, as assistant secretary of the navy, used the *Dolphin* during the entire Wilson administration (1913–1921).[25]

▪ 1898 Patrol Vessel *Sylph*

The patrol vessel *Sylph* was purchased during the 1898 war with Spain.[26] She had 152 tons of displacement, a length of 123 feet, 8 inches, and breadth of 20 feet. This vessel was commissioned at the Navy Yard, Norfolk, on August 18, 1898, and soon after was assigned to the Washington Navy Yard.

During her thirty-one years there, she was at the disposal of the

Figure 312 - **1898 patrol vessel *Sylph*, third presidential yacht**

president and the secretary and assistant secretary of the navy. In 1902, the *Sylph* began alternating with the *Mayflower* as the presidential yacht. McKinley was the first president to use the *Sylph*.

President Theodore Roosevelt made frequent cruises on her to his summer home at Oyster Bay, New York.

President Taft also used this vessel off the New England coast during the summers of his administration.

President Wilson was the last president to use the *Sylph*. After the *Mayflower* became the presidential yacht, the *Sylph* remained at the Washington Navy Yard for use by the secretary and assistant secretary of the navy.

• 1898 USS *Mayflower*

The USS *Mayflower* (WPG 183), at 2,690 tons displacement, was purchased March 19, 1898, from the Ogden Goelet estate. Her length was 275 feet, beam 36 feet, draft 17 feet. J. & C. Thompson built this vessel in Clydebank, Scotland in 1896. She was commissioned at New York on March 24, 1898, and served in the blockade of Cuba during the Spanish-American War and subsequently in Puerto Rican waters.[27, 28, 29]

In 1905, the *Mayflower* was assigned to duty as the presidential yacht.[30] Upon completion of this duty, she joined the North Atlantic Fleet. Later in the same year, she was employed as the flagship of Admiral Dewey and in 1903–1904 as flagship of the squadron in the Caribbean. From July to October 1904, she cruised in the Mediterranean. In 1905, President Theodore Roosevelt utilized this vessel in arranging terms of peace between Russia and Japan. She continued to be used as the presidential yacht by Presidents Theodore Roosevelt, Taft, Harding, and Coolidge until March 22, 1929. When Herbert Hoover became president, he ordered her to be laid up in the interest of economy. After being partially destroyed by fire on January 24, 1931, at the Philadelphia Navy Yard, *Mayflower* was stricken from the navy list and her hulk sold October 19, 1931, as junk. Raised and refitted, she would have a surprising end to her career.[31]

A wealthy financier subsequently restored the *Mayflower* to her original splendor. His fortunes turned, however, and he had to sell the yacht just before fleeing the country to escape prosecution and irate investors.

Then, with the start of World War II, she was bought by the War Shipping Administration in July 1942 and renamed the *Butte*; transferred to the Coast Guard in July 1943, she was recommissioned the *Mayflower* on October 19 and assigned patrol and escort duty along the Atlantic coast. Decommissioned in July 1946, she was sold in January 1947 to be used for seal hunting in the North Atlantic; however, she was damaged by fire early in March 1947. Resold early in 1948, she now sailed under Panamanian papers with a new name, the *Malia*. Ostensibly to be used in coastal Mediterranean trade, she actually sailed secretly to Haifa, carrying Jewish settlers from Europe to Palestine during the Exodus. Her subsequent fate is unknown.[32]

Figure 313 - **1898 USS *Mayflower* (WPG 183), fourth presidential yacht**

• 1925 USS *Sequoia*

The USS *Sequoia*[33] was classified as an auxiliary miscellaneous vessel and had 100 tons displacement, length on water line of 99 feet, extreme beam at water line of18 feet, 2 inches.[34] The Mathis Yacht Shipbuilding Company, Camden, New Jersey built her in 1925.

This vessel was taken over by the navy from the Department of Commerce on March 25, 1933, and commissioned on that date at Annapolis, Maryland. She was assigned to the Washington Navy Yard where she was fitted out as the presidential yacht. President Roosevelt made cruises on her from1933 to 1935.

Figure 314 - **1925 USS *Sequoia* (AG-23), fifth presidential yacht**

President Hoover used the *Sequoia* only twice and spent his last Christmas in office aboard the *Sequoia*. At that time it was a Commerce Department vessel.

The *Sequoia* was commissioned as a presidential yacht in 1933; when it was replaced by the *Potomac* in 1936 it became available for use by the secretary of the navy.

President Kennedy brought *Sequoia* back into service. The *Sequoia* was finally sold in 1977 by President Carter. She was purchased by the Presidential Yacht Trust in 1981 and restored. The Trust planned to return the *Sequoia* to the government in 1988 after its restoration. However, President Reagan declined the offer. For several years thereafter the *Sequoia* was sent to various parts of the country by the Trust for public tours and cruises. The *Sequoia* was later bought by a private individual and continues to be available for tours and cruises.

Because the *Sequoia* had served so many presidents and had been remodeled and refurbished so many times, her restoration produced a kind of "generic" presidential yacht, historically accurate in individual details, but representing a spectrum of forty-four years of the presidency.[35]

• 1934 USS *Potomac*

The USS *Potomac* (AG 25) was classified as an auxiliary miscellaneous vessel; she had 416 tons displacement, length of 165 feet, beam of 23 feet 9 inches, and mean draft of 8 feet, 1 inch.[36] She was built for $1.5 million by the Manitowoc Shipbuilding Company, Manitowoc, Wisconsin, and delivered to the U.S. Coast Guard as the patrol boat *Electra* in 1934.

Although FDR had used the *Sequoia* during his first term in office, he did not feel safe

aboard the all-wooden vessel. Afraid of a fire at sea and needing a larger vessel, he had the *Electra* refitted at the Navy Shipyard at Portsmouth, Virginia, and recommissioned by the U.S. Navy as the USS *Potomac*. The president, who led the country through the depression and most of

Figure 315 - **1934 USS *Potomac* (AG 25), sixth presidential yacht**

World War II, turned the yacht into a "Floating White House." He took weekend fishing trips to escape the oppressive Washington heat and humidity and to relieve his sinusitis and asthma.

Roosevelt had a small cabin with a single bunk, an adjoining bathroom and for his beloved dog Fala, a sleeping basket. FDR designed the bathtub himself. There is a saloon with a large table for dinner parties. To get from the main deck to the boat deck, an elevator was installed in a false smokestack. It was operated by the president using a rope and pulley. An electric motor could have been installed but FDR used the elevator as a form of exercise.

In 1939 the president hosted King George VI and Queen Elizabeth of England on board. Other guests during World War II included the exiled royal families of Norway and the Netherlands. Eleanor Roosevelt went on occasional cruises, but never slept aboard. She had been afraid of the water since she had to be rescued as a child after a collision at sea.

As America stood on the threshold of World War II, the *Potomac* played a vital role in a bit of nautical trickery.

Reportedly on a Cape Cod fishing trip, FDR departed the yacht for the cruiser USS *Augusta* at Nantucket Island. When the *Potomac* sailed from Buzzards Bay through the Cape Cod Canal to Cape Cod Bay, a White House Secret Service agent wearing the president's signature cape and waving the famous

Figure 316 - **USS *Potomac* False Stack FDR Memorial** [37]

cigarette holder doubled as the chief executive while FDR went to meet Winston Churchill off Newfoundland to negotiate and agree on the Atlantic Charter.

The navy staffed the yacht with three officers and a crew of fifty-four men, of whom twelve were Filipino stewards.

The weight of a gun added above the main deck had made the *Potomac* top-heavy and subject to capsizing. In 1945 she was condemned as unseaworthy. She did, however, continue as the presidential yacht until the USS *Williamsburg* was put into service. The U.S. Navy decommissioned the *Potomac* in 1945.

When the *Potomac* was modified, the elevator stack was removed and used as a FDR memorial at the Long Wharf on the Choptank River in Cambridge, Maryland.

She served the state of Maryland as a fisheries research vessel from 1946 until 1960. Later, she was used as a ferry in the Caribbean and then as a floating museum dedicated to FDR.

In 1964 Elvis Presley purchased her for $55,000. Elvis gave the vessel to Danny Thomas, who had it auctioned off for the benefit of St. Jude's Hospital. After having several other owners, she was seized in a drug raid and the United States took over ownership. By this time, the *Potomac* was in disrepair and everything of value had been removed. Put up for auction with a minimum bid of $20,000, she received no bids. Later, a bid was accepted for $15,000, and restoration began at a cost of $5 million, half a government grant and half matching funds from private sources. The latter were thanks in large part to efforts of FDR's son James and grandson Michael.[38]

• 1930 USS Williamsburg

The USS *Williamsburg* was originally the yacht *Aras*. She was constructed by the Bath Iron Works, Bath, Maine, for Hugh J. Chisholm, and was launched on December 8, 1930. The yacht *Aras* had her trial trip on January 10, 1931. She was 243 feet long, with a breadth of 36 feet. She was acquired by the U.S. government on April 24, 1941, and renamed the USS *Williamsburg* (PG-56).[39]

When President Truman assumed office, the USS *Potomac* had been condemned by the

Figure 317 - **1930 USS *Williamsburg* (AGC-369), seventh presidential yacht**

Navy Department as being unfit for duty in open waters; they recommended using the USS *Williamsburg* as the presidential yacht. President Truman accepted the recommendation, and on November 10, 1945, took the *Williamsburg* on her first cruise as a presidential yacht.

President Truman made several short cruises down the Potomac River. On August 16, 1946, the USS *Williamsburg* departed Washington, D.C., with President Truman on board, for a trip to Quonset Point, Rhode Island. On August 20, 1946, she got underway for Bermuda in company with the USS *Weiss*, returning to Washington September 2, 1946. President Truman entertained several foreign leaders aboard the yacht: May 1, 1947, President Miguel Aleman of Mexico; December 5, 1950, British Prime Minister Clement R. Attlee, and January 5, 1952, British Prime Minister Winston Churchill. The navy manned the *Williamsburg* with 8 officers, 130 enlisted men and 26 stewards.

On March 26, 1953, President Eisenhower and Prime Minister Rene Mayer, Republic of France, and their respective advisors had a conference and luncheon on board. They departed in the late afternoon after a cruise down the Potomac River. In mid-April, President Eisenhower announced that he no longer required the USS *Williamsburg* and ordered her decommissioned on July 1, 1953. In the interim two and one-half months, the president ordered that wounded hospitalized veterans of the Korean War be taken on afternoon trips down the Potomac River on the vessel.

Inactive after 1953, she was decommissioned at the Washington Naval Yard and turned over to the Potomac River Naval Command for maintenance and preservation. She was later transferred to Newport, Rhode Island, and on April 2, 1959, placed in "special status." She was struck from the navy list on April 1, 1962. She then served the National Science Foundation until she was damaged in a dry dock accident in 1968. Subsequently she was sold to become a hotel/museum in New Jersey, but was instead laid up. In 1993 she was sent to Genoa, Italy, for conversion to a cruise ship. Due to lack of interest and lack of funds, work on the *Williamsburg* has ceased, and it is now abandoned. She was later moved to LaSpezia, Italy, awaiting sale. In 1998, she had been gutted and faced with imminent scrapping, but an urgent appeal to the Italian government saved her. An organization was formed with the goal of returning her to the United States for restoration and preservation. No further information is available.[40, 41]

Small Craft Used by Presidents

The Naval Historical Center of the Department of the Navy lists the following vessels as small craft, and they are not included in the list of presidential yachts. They are included here because presidents used them as pleasure boats.

▪ 1931 *Lenore - Barbara Ann - Tricia - Honey Fitz*

This multi-named vessel of 94 tons displacement, length of 92 feet, beam of 16 feet and draft of 5 feet, was built in 1931 for Sewell Avery, chairman of Montgomery Ward, by the Defoe Boat Works of Bay City, Michigan. She was christened the *Lenore* after Avery's second daughter, who died at age four.

She originally cruised the waters of Lake Michigan near Avery's private estate at Iron Mountain. Serious infractions by Montgomery Ward over NRA wage and price provisions led to the purchase of the boat by the government in 1942.[42]

Figure 318 - **1931 *Lenore - Barbara Ann - Tricia - Honey Fitz***

The *Lenore* was used as a Coast Guard training ship and assigned to the Washington Navy Yard as a tender (escort) for the *Potomac*. Transferred to the navy on November 28, 1945, she was renamed the *Lenore II* and assigned as a tender (escort) to the presidential yacht *Williamsburg*. The *Lenore II* frequently carried the Secret Service agents who accompanied the president while he was aboard the *Potomac* or the *Williamsburg*.

In 1953, President Eisenhower retired the splendid but costly *Williamsburg* from active service, authorized the refurbishing and overhauling of *Lenore II* at a cost of $200,000, and rechristened her *Barbara Ann* in honor of his granddaughter. She was used for occasional cruises, and in the summers of 1957 and 1958, she sailed to Newport, Rhode Island, where she conveyed the president to and from his golfing excursions.

With the inauguration of President John F. Kennedy, the yacht was refitted and on March 7, 1961, was renamed the *Honey Fitz*, honoring JFK's grandfather.

President Johnson did not rename the *Honey Fitz* and preferred it to the larger *Sequoia*, which was still at the Washington Navy Yard.

President Nixon renamed the yacht *Tricia* after his daughter, and had the vessel auctioned off in December 1971 after a brief tour of duty providing cruises for hospitalized Vietnam veterans. The boat was subsequently purchased by Joe Keating, who named it *The Presidents*.

The yacht was again sold and completely restored and refitted as it had been during Kennedy's term and renamed *Honey Fitz*.[43]

▪ 1940 *Margie - The Susie-E. - Patrick J. - The Julie*

Built by the Fisher Boat Works in 1940 for L.P. Fisher, vice president of Fisher and Company, the craft was acquired by the War Shipping Administration in 1942 for the Coast Guard. She was transferred to the navy in 1945.

At a length of 64 feet, and beam of 14 feet, 6 inches, she has a main lounge, dining area and after-deck which can be used as a sundeck. She has three bunkrooms with eight bunks. Six to eight guests were accommodated comfortably. First named *Margie* in honor of President Truman's daughter, she was primarily a tender (escort) for the *Williamsburg*. Mrs. Truman often used her for trips on the Potomac River and to Chesapeake Bay.

President Eisenhower renamed her *The Susie-E* in honor of one of his granddaughters. President Kennedy renamed the yacht *Patrick J.* in honor of his paternal grandfather. In April 1963, the *Patrick J.* went to Hyannis Port with the *Guardian* for the president's use.

Figure 319 - **1940** *Margie - The Susie-E. - Patrick J - The Julie*

President Nixon renamed her *The Julie* in honor of his daughter and moved the yacht to Key Biscayne, where he retained his winter vacation retreat. Nixon sold *The Julie* at auction.[44]

• *Guardian*

The *Guardian* was built by the Electric Boat Works in June 1946, and has an overall length of 105 feet, beam of 22 feet and draft of 6 feet.

After serving as an experimental craft, she was assigned to the Potomac River Naval Command in November 1959 as a civil defense boat and escort for the presidential yacht *Williamsburg*. The *Guardian* carried two 16-foot fiberglass water jet boats. These boats were used to transport Secret Service agents on escort duty for the *Lenore II* and the *Barbara Ann*.

Figure 320 - **1946** *Guardian*

After the presidential yachts were decommissioned, the *Guardian* was released from presidential service and transferred to a naval aviation squadron in Norfolk, Virginia.

She was modified at Cambridge, Maryland, renamed DR-1 *Retriever*, and used to retrieve target practice drones in various ranges along the Atlantic coast.

Later she was assigned to the special boat unit in support of the Navy Seals. No further information is available.[45]

---

[1] Photograph of Fala by Percy T. Jones, used with permission from the Franklin D. Roosevelt Library.

[2] Rowan (1997) pages 102–111.

[3] Information on CVB-42 USS *FDR* from website [01/09/03] www.navy.mil, photograph from website [01/09/03] www.navsource.org/archives/02/42.htm.

[4] This history of presidential yachts was taken from docent training manual; *A Tour for Docents of the Presidential Yacht Potomac* written by *Potomac* docent and naval historian Les Dropkin.

[5] Information on the *Ferdinand Magellan* from the Gold Coast Railroad Museum from website [01/09/03]] www.goldcoast-railroad.org,used with permission.

[6] Photograph of the *Ferdinand Magellan* from the Gold Coast Railroad Museum from website [01/09/03] www.goldcoast-railroad.org, used with permission.

[7] Photograph of Shangri-La courtesy Franklin D. Roosevelt Library, used with permission.

[8] Information on Shangri-La used with permission from Camp David website [01/09/03] http://travel.to/campdavid.

[9] On April 18, 1942, Jimmy Doolittle and his Tokyo Raiders launched 16 B-25 bombers from the aircraft carrier USS *Hornet* and made an air raid over Tokyo. Of the 80 men involved, 64 returned to fight again and four others survived as prisoners of war.

[10] Photograph of FDR and Churchill fishing at Shangri-La courtesy Franklin D. Roosevelt Library.

[11] Information and photograph of *Guess Where 2* used with permission from Camp David website [01/09/03] http://travel.to/campdavid.

[12] In 1945 the *Guess Where 2* was scrapped.

[13] Bathurst, British Gambia is now Banjul, Gambia.

[14] Information and photograph of *Sacred Cow* from Camp David website [01/09/03] http: //travel.to/campdavid, used with permission.

[15] Photograph of *Dixie Clipper* courtesy Pan Am Historical Foundation website [01/09/03] www.panam.org, used with permission.

[16] Information on *Dixie Clipper* from Camp David website [01/09/03] http: //travel.to/campdavid, used with permission.

[17] The *Sacred Cow* was used until 1947. For more information see the Museum of Natural History website [01/09/03] www.airforce1.org.

[18] This pictorial tour of the presidential yacht *Potomac* was excerpted from the docent training manual *A Tour for Docents of the Presidential Yacht Potomac* written by *Potomac* docent and naval historian Les Dropkin.

[19] Jack Lynch was a *Potomac* docent who served on board the USS *Potomac* during FDR's use of the vessel; he is now deceased.

[20] Cannery (1995). [The U.S. Coast Guard patrol boat *Cuyahoga*, commissioned in 1927, was 125 feet long with two engines. Transferred to the U.S. Navy in 1933 for use as an escort for the presidential yacht and served in active duty until lost in a collision in 1978.]

[21] This history of presidential yachts was excerpted from the docent training manual *A Tour for Docents of the Presidential Yacht Potomac* written by *Potomac* docent and naval historian Les Dropkin.

[22] Information on *River Queen* used with permission from Camp David websites [01/09/03] http://travel.to/campdavid, and edited by *Potomac* docent Les Dropkin.

[23] Information on the *Despatch* used with permission from Camp David website [01/09/03] http://travel.to/campdavid, and edited by *Potomac* docent Les Dropkin.

[24] The U.S. Navy designation for the *Dolphin* was PG-24 gunboat.

[25] Information on *Sylph* used with permission from Camp David website [01/09/03] http://travel.to/campdavid, and edited by *Potomac* docent Les Dropkin.

[26] The U.S. Navy designation for the *Sylph* as of July 17, 1921, was PY-5 patrol vessel, converted yacht.

[27] The designation "USS" for naval vessels was first introduced in 1907 by President Theodore Roosevelt. The USS *Mayflower* would have been the first presidential yacht to use this designation.

[28] The U.S. Navy designation for the USS *Mayflower* was PY-1 patrol vessel, converted yacht.

[29] The USS *Mayfower* was decommissioned in New York, February 2, 1889, fitted out for special service in Puerto Rican waters and then recommissioned June 15, 1900.

[30] The USS. *Mayflower* was decommissioned in New York, November 1, 1904, for conversion to a presidential yacht and then recommissioned July 25, 1905.

[31] It was not so much the fire itself as the fact that so much water was pumped into her that she sank at the dock.

[32] Information on the USS *Mayflower* used with permission from Camp David website [01/09/03] http://travel.to/campdavid, and edited by *Potomac* docent Les Dropkin.

[33] Tegler (1997).

[34] Length of *Sequoia* overall is 104 feet.

[35] Information on *Sequoia* used with permission from Camp David website [01/09/03] http: //travel.to/campdavid, and edited by *Potomac* docent Les Dropkin.

[36] The *Potomac* waterline length is 160 feet.

[37] Photograph of USS *Potomac* FDR False Stack Memorial by Chad Malkus, September 2001.

---

[38] Information on USS *Potomac* used with permission from Camp David website [01/09/03] http: //travel.to/campdavid, and edited by *Potomac* docent Les Dropkin.

[39] The *Williamsburg* relieved the *Potomac* as presidential yacht on November 5, 1945; on November 10, she was re-designated AGE-369 9 general communications vessel.

[40] Information on USS *Williamsburg* used with permission from Camp David website [01/09/03] http: //travel.to/campdavid, and edited by *Potomac* docent Les Dropkin.

[41] The USS *Williamsburg* Preservation Society may be contacted at 262 McLaws Circle, Suite 203, Williamsburg, VA 23187; phone (757)220-5650. Information from Haze Gray website [01/09/03] www.hazegray.org/features/yachts.

[42] The 1931 *Lenore - Barbara Ann - Tricia - Honey Fitz* was acquired by the War Shipping Administration for the use of the Coast Guard and was ready for duty January 9, 1943 as (CG92004).

[43] Information and photograph of 1931 *Lenore - Barbara Ann -Tricia - Honey Fitz* used with permission from Camp David website [01/-0/03] http: //travel.to/campdavid, and edited by *Potomac* docent Les Dropkin.

[44] Information and photograph of *Margie - The Susie-E. - Patrick J. - The Julie* used with permission from Camp David website [01/09/03] http://travel.to/campdavid, and edited by *Potomac* docent Les Dropkin.

[45] Information and photograph of *Guardian* used with permission from Camp David website [01/09/03] http://travel.to/campdavid, and edited by *Potomac* docent Les Dropkin.

19 - Local References

First Europeans in San Francisco Area

The first Europeans in the area were Francis Drake and his crew on the *Golden Hind*, which had landed in Drake's Bay in 1579.[1,2]

Almost two hundred years later, in 1769, Captain Portola came overland from San Diego and saw the San Francisco Bay from a hill near Pacifica. In San Mateo, two historical landmarks denote where he saw the bay and where he camped.[3,4]

Only six years later, on July 4, 1776, the American Revolution started with the signing of the U.S. Declaration of Independence. Then, in September 1776, Spain established the San Francisco Presidio[5] and Mission Dolores.[6]

With numerous Spanish land grants, the Bay Area became a quiet ranching area. The Peralta[7] and Estudillo[8] homes still stand in San Leandro and the Sanchez Adobe, dating from 1842, is in Pacifica.[9] All are historical landmarks.

In 1821, the Mexican War for Independence ended and the focal point of government shifted from Spain to Mexico. This directly affected the Bay Area, since at the time there were about one thousand Europeans residing in the greater Bay Area.

John A. Sutter arrived in California in 1839 and set up a sawmill on the American River in what is now Coloma.[10] With the discovery of gold there in 1848, the East Bay started to grow, and by 1870 the railroad had come to town.[11]

Early Days in San Francisco Area

It is hard to visualize how the San Francisco Bay Area looked in the 1820's and even harder to realize what it was like for thousands of years before the Europeans arrived.

Early explorers said the bay abounded with fish and wildfowl, and the sky darkened when birds took flight. The hills were covered with massive redwoods and the valleys with giant oaks. The fish, wild game, acorns, and other plants supplied food for about forty Indian villages that lined the bay.[12]

The area around the San Francisco and Monterey Bays supported about ten thousand native peoples, representing about a dozen language groups. The native population were collectively called the Ohlone people. As practicing ecologists, they used only what they needed and there was plenty for all.[13]

California was so lush then that it supported more people per square mile than any other area in what is now the United States.[14]

Port of Oakland

The estuary gave access to the East Bay and it rapidly became a busy commercial and shipping area. The San Francisco Bay Area was the western terminus of the transcontinental railroad in 1869, the same year that the Suez Canal opened, giving shipping access to Europe without the long trip around Africa.

When the City of Oakland has made its mark on history, it often has been because of the Port of Oakland. Oakland was the first port on the West Coast to build terminals for the then-revolutionary container ships, thus becoming the second largest port in the world in container tonnage in the late 1960's and second only to New York in container terminal acreage.

The container era began in Oakland in 1962, when the S.S. *Elizabethport*, then the world's largest freighter, arrived at the Outer Harbor to inaugurate container ship operation by SeaLand Services, Inc.

To begin this new era, SeaLand modified four ships and invested in a fleet of five thousand trailers that "detach from their chassis to become giant shipping boxes." The Port of Oakland in turn spent $600,000 to upgrade piers to accommodate the line's revolutionary operations. "This marks a new milestone in low-cost ship transportation," SeaLand Chairman Malcolm P. McLean told six hundred dignitaries at opening ceremonies on September 27, 1962. "Through the use of sealed trailers, we are able to load and unload a vessel in one-sixth the time of conventional ships."[15]

Oakland International Airport's passenger terminal, completed in 1958 at a cost of $20 million, has shown the same historic spirit in accommodating new ventures and new technologies. It follows a tradition that began in 1927 when crews worked around the clock for twenty-three days to prepare what was then the world's largest runway, a 7,020-foot strip that served as takeoff point for the first flight across the 2,400 miles from the mainland to Hawaii. At the official dedication of the original airport the same year, Charles A. Lindberg arrived in his *Spirit of St. Louis* and declared, "You have here one of the finest airports I have ever seen. Oakland is setting the example for the cities of the country."[16]

The Port of Oakland gained prominence not only because of its natural advantages, but also because of a leadership that has known how to develop and market them to the benefit of both the global and local economies.

Oakland is almost three hundred nautical miles closer to Asia than southern California ports. This means reduced transit times, lower fuel and vessel costs, and faster turnaround for ocean carriers. It is served by two mainline railroads, the Union Pacific and the Santa Fe.

The port's Jack London Square is the only restaurant/retail center in the Bay Area where a diner can watch a giant container ship pass by less than fifty yards from the window. There are fifteen waterfront parks in Oakland, several of which afford close-up views of working marine terminals.

Jack London Square is a good place to reminisce about the port's colorful past. It is where the first ferry service to San Francisco began in 1850 and where Jack London borrowed his entrance fee for the University of California from the owner of Heinbold's First and Last Chance Saloon. The unusual name stems from the fact that it was the first and last chance to get a drink for residents of "dry" Alameda, who commuted to Oakland by ferry.[17]

The airport, too, has a rich history. It was the departure point for Amelia Earhart on her fateful round-the-world flight in 1937.

It was also the departure point for the Australian WW I ace Sir Charles Kingsford-Smith, who in 1928 made the first flight between North America and Australia. In addition, he made the first civilian flight to Hawaii. It was the West Coast terminus for United Airlines' newly introduced service to New York in 1937. The new DC-3's carried fourteen passengers in sleeping berths or twenty-four day passengers. It made the transcontinental flight in fifteen hours and twenty minutes, with three stops.[18]

Today the tradition of innovation continues—at the airport, seaport and in commercial real estate development. And when citizens of Oakland travel abroad to any of the commercial centers of the world, they often find that the port is Oakland's best-known feature.[19]

Figure 321 - **Posey Tube, Alameda Portal, as seen from Alameda**

Figure 322 - **Posey Tube, Alameda Portal, as seen from Brooklyn Basin**

Webster and Alice Street Bridges

To make travel a little easier for the fifteen hundred people living in Alameda, a drawbridge was built in 1871, extending from Webster Street in Alameda to Webster Street, Oakland. In 1873 a railroad bridge, starting from Alice Street in Oakland, connected to a rail line in Alameda.[20, 21] In 1893, it was demolished and replaced with a new railroad bridge at Harrison Street.[22]

Because of extensive shipping traffic on the estuary, the bridges were frequently raised, creating a problem for other traffic.

In 1927, the Posey Tube replaced the Webster Street Bridge.[23] The Webster Street Tube was completed in 1963.

Ironically, these tunnels are no longer deep enough to allow the largest container ships to pass overhead.[24]

L. J. Quinn's Lighthouse

Quinn's Lighthouse is now a restaurant and pub. It was constructed in 1903 by the U.S. Lighthouse Service as the Oakland Harbor Entrance Lighthouse. It cost $19,000 and replaced the original 1890 structure that had been badly damaged by marine worms that bored into its underwater structure. The lighthouse was located on the north side of the entrance to the Oakland estuary and served as a house for two lighthouse keepers and their families until the lighthouse service became part of the Coast Guard in 1939. From 1939 until the structure was moved to its present location in 1965 the families of the keepers lived ashore.[27]

Figure 324 - **Circa 1903 L. J. Quinn's Lighthouse** [26]

Figure 323 - **Circa 1950 L. J. Quinn's Lighthouse** [25]

The keepers of Oakland Harbor light did a lot of rowing, not just to go into town for supplies and mail, but also to tend the south jetty light across the Oakland estuary and at times the red lantern a mile to the east. When the keepers were not rowing to the other lights, they had to tend a white, fixed, fifth order lens in the lighthouse and rewind the weight that powered the mechanical striker on the station's 3,500-pound fog bell.

The fog bell was unforgettable. It hung less than a dozen feet on the other side of the wall from the bed of the keeper and his wife. Its

presence was unmistakable in thick weather. Given the fact that the lighthouse "oscillated" in high winds, it must have been something to be there on a stormy night with the fog bell pounding and the station shaking in the wind.

Eventually, the new light's setting began to change as the city extended out to engulf it.

The Western Pacific Railroad quite literally built its ferry landing around the lighthouse. Ferryboats and trains soon puffed about the little beacon, and keepers gained both compensation and distinction.

Figure 325 - **L. J. Quinn's Lighthouse and Pub**

The compensation factor was that they now could simply step off their porch onto the broad deck of the ferry slip and walk ashore. The rowboat remained, but its use was much diminished. The distinction was that they became the only lighthouse in California with direct transcontinental train connections.

It is not recorded how often, if ever, the lighthouse keepers took advantage of their unparalleled transportation facilities, but the finest passenger trains of the day were but a few steps away.

Today, the lovely old structure is a restaurant called Quinn's Lighthouse. It is located at 1951 Embarcadero Street, Oakland, and makes a pleasant stop in one of the nicest sections of the East Bay waterfront.

China Clippers

Pan American World Airways started its passenger Caribbean flying boat service in 1928 with the Sikorsky S-38. In 1931 Pan Am introduced the larger Sikorsky S-40 *American Clipper*—this was the first of the "Clippers." It was followed in 1934 by the larger Sikorsky S-42 with its 118-foot wingspan.

On April 16, 1935, Pan Am made its first exploratory flight from San Francisco (actually from Alameda) to Honolulu in a modified Sikorsky S-42; however, the Sikorsky S-42 was too small for commercial transpacific service.

Also in 1935, Pan Am introduced the larger Martin M-130 with a wingspan of 130 feet and named the first of the three flying boats the *China Clipper*. Pan Am inaugurated transpacific service with its first flight from Alameda to Honolulu on November 22, 1935.[28]

The Martin Company built only three of the planes, all for Pan Am: the *China Clipper*, the *Hawaii Clipper*, and the *Philippine Clipper*.

In 1939, the Boeing Company built twelve flying boats for Pan Am that were larger and more powerful than the three Martin Clippers. Designated the Boeing B-314, with a 152-foot wingspan, these craft extended service from Treasure Island to Hong Kong, Fiji, Samoa, and New Zealand. The public knew all of the Clippers as China Clippers in deference to the first and most famous of them all—despite each having its own name of *California Clipper, Pacific Clipper* and the like.

Figure 326 - **Pan Am Martin M-130 *China Clipper*, on first flight over Golden Gate Bridge during construction, November 22, 1935** [29]

Figure 327 - **Pan Am Martin M-130 *China Clipper*, loading for first flight from Alameda, November 22, 1935** [30, 31]

Half boat and half plane, the Clippers represented the transition from ships to aircraft as the world's primary mode of transportation. Because most cities across the globe, including San Francisco, possessed no sizeable airport, these first large transoceanic aircraft landed in water. As the Clippers approached their destination, high speed Pan Am boats cleared the water of small craft to make a safe "runway" for the "flying boats" to land.

After landing, the planes taxied to a pier to off-load the passengers and cargo; an underwater carriage on wheels could haul the plane out of the water, if necessary.

Throughout their careers, the Clippers were "ships," not "planes," to their crews. Each carried anchors, life rings, and rafts.

Interior appointments of the Clippers were luxurious. To attract passengers away from ocean liners, the planes were opulent. Sofas, easy chairs, tables, and lamps graced the cabins, and staterooms were available for those desiring complete privacy. In the dining saloon, passengers sat at linen-covered tables set with china, silver, and glassware. The fast and luxurious travel had its price; a round-trip ticket between San Francisco and Manila cost $1,710, enough to buy two new 1937 Ford cars.

When Clipper service began in 1935, the planes were berthed on the western shoreline of Alameda, near the Southern Pacific Ferry Mole. San Francisco planned an airport of its own, to be built on a man-made island in the center of the bay. The new Treasure Island was to house San Francisco's Golden Gate International Exposition of 1939–40 before it would open as the city's airport. But the Clippers, which did not need land for runways, were allowed to use the island as their base when the fair opened in February 1939.

Figure 328 - **Pan Am Sikorsky S-42, over Bay Bridge during construction, on first test flight from San Francisco (Alameda) to Honolulu, April 16, 1935** [32, 33]

Passengers arrived at the terminal building, then passed through the fair's Hall of Air Transportation before boarding the waiting Clipper in the Port of Trade Winds, the lagoon that separates Treasure Island from Yerba Buena Island. Fairgoers mobbed the fences around the pier, for the Clippers were a popular "exhibit." The loaded plane taxied into the bay opposite Berkeley, took off in a roar of engine exhaust and spray, and headed west over the Golden Gate Bridge. (Photographs of Pan Am's Treasure Island terminal and hangars are on page 83.)

Eighteen hours later, the Clipper landed at Honolulu. Continuing the next morning, the plane landed at Midway Island, Wake Island, and Guam before touching down at the final destination of Manila, sixty flying hours after leaving San Francisco. Passengers slept each night in island hotels while the crew fueled and serviced the planes. To accommodate the traffic, Pan Am had transformed the barren Pacific islands of Midway and Wake into suitable bases with hotels, restaurants, maintenance shops, and crew housing.

America's entry into World War II altered the fortunes of the Clippers. Japanese bombers caught the *Philippine Clipper* at Wake Island hours after the raid on Pearl Harbor on December 7, 1941. The attackers riddled the plane with bullets, all of which miraculously missed the fuel tanks, and the plane returned to Treasure Island crammed with as many evacuees from Wake Island as it could carry. The one Pan Am employee and several hundred U.S. Marines left on the island faced four years of internment in Japanese prisoner-of-war camps.

On the same day as the Japanese raid, the *California Clipper*, a Boeing B-314, lay at anchor at New Caledonia in the South Pacific. Its orders were to return to America via the safest route. The captain decided to return to San Francisco by avoiding the Pacific Ocean. This required going to Australia, the Dutch Indies, the Indian Ocean, Africa (landing in the Nile River), Rio de Janeiro, and the Caribbean. Back in the United States, the plane landed in New York, Florida, the Gulf of California, San Diego, and after 136 days, Treasure Island. When she finally reached home port, the *California Clipper* thereby unwittingly became the first commercial airliner to fly around the world! It was no easy feat to navigate across the continent of Africa in a seaplane that needed water to land in each night.

During the war, the Clippers flew for the navy as part of the Naval Air Transport Service (NATS). The planes avoided the battle zones of the Pacific by flying only between Treasure Island and Honolulu, but by the end of the war, all of the original three Clippers had been lost.

Figure 329 - **Pan Am Boeing B-314 *Yankee Clipper* leaving Treasure Island, 1939** [34]

207

For more information on the Pan Am Clippers, read Roy Allen's book *The Pan Am Clipper: The History of Pan American's Flying-Boats 1931 to 1949*.

Treasure Island

During the 1930's, the world's two largest bridges had been built across San Francisco Bay, and to celebrate their completion, the world's largest man-made island had risen from the waves.

Beneath the waters of the bay is an uneven terrain from 2 to 382 feet deep. Mariners long have avoided the treacherous shoals just north of Yerba Buena Island, where water is no deeper than 26 feet.

These watery acres were waste territory until it was decided to create upon them the site of the Golden Gate International Exposition, to be known as Treasure Island, during 1939, and thereafter to become an airport for the transpacific clipper ships.

Figure 330 - **Aerial view of Treasure Island under construction in 1935** [35]

Rock walls composed of 287,000 tons of quarried rock were sunk in the shoals. Twenty million cubic yards of sea bottom were dredged and piled within the walls. When the sand was thirteen feet above sea level, engineers "unsalted" it by a leaching process. Barges brought 50,000 cubic yards of loam from the mainland to enrich it.

Since the Works Projects Administration did not have the capacity at that time for this construction, it was turned over to the War Department, through which the Army Corps of Engineers was assigned the task. On February 11, 1936, the Corps started work on the project and subsequently issued plans and specifications for bidding. The Army Engineers hoped to engage several local dredging companies, but the dredgers sensed problems of risk and insufficient funds and refused to bid. In March the Corps finally took on the construction with its own plant and such rented equipment as conditions warranted. Five of the Corps' sea-going hopper dredges and three of its hydraulic pipeline dredges, as well as three rented hydraulic pipeline dredges, were utilized in the work.

A perimeter rock wall a little over three miles in length was built to provide containment and minimize erosion of the fill being placed on the shoals. The reclamation area on which the fill was to be placed varied from a minimum of two feet to a maximum of twenty-six feet below water. Sand and gravel from the Presidio shoals, Alcatraz shoals, and Point Knox shoals were either deposited directly by seagoing hopper dredges on the fill site or directly in front of hydraulic pipeline dredges for subsequent pumping into the fill area.

Hydraulic pipeline dredges also utilized areas immediately north, east, and south of the reclamation area. Final elevation of the island was thirteen feet above sea level. It measured 370 acres including the causeway to Yerba Buena. It took thirty million cubic yards of sand, gravel and mud to complete the fill.

Once the fill was completed, more than two hundred wells were drilled to leach the salt from the soil so that it would support vegetation. Eighty thousand cubic yards of rich peat topsoil were barged from the Sacramento and San Joaquin delta area and spread over the surface for gardens.

Work on the island was completed on August 24, 1937, eighteen months after start of work, on time and within budget.

When the engineers finished, a 400-acre island, one mile long and two-thirds of a mile wide, had appeared in the bay, connected by a 900-foot paved causeway to the Bay Bridge and equipped with ferry slips and landings for small craft and flying boats.

Figure 331 - **1939 World's Fair Gayway Ferris Wheels** [36]

Meanwhile botanists were hunting through all the continents for unusual trees and plants. For many months orchids, hibiscus, datura,[37] rare silver trees, orange trees, and palms were acclimated in a San Francisco plant hospital, then brought to bloom in electrically heated propagation beds. These plants composed the ever-changing floral patterns of the fairgrounds. Horticultural plans called for planting 4,000 trees, 70,000 shrubs, and 700,000 flowering plants. To water the plants—and quench the thirst of visitors—San Francisco water was piped over the San Francisco–Oakland Bay Bridge to a 3,000,000-gallon reservoir cut in the solid rock of Yerba Buena Island.

With federal aid, three permanent structures were built that later served the airport. They included the $800,000 administration building and the two $400,000 steel and concrete hangars, each 335 feet long and 78 feet high. These were used to temporarily house the $20,000,000 art exhibits and the foreign treasures loaned for the fair. Finally, around these structures began to rise a $50,000,000 fantasy—America's World's Fair on the Pacific.

The fairgrounds were designed as a walled city, enclosing a series of connected courts. Although a primary consideration was to plan step-saving routes across the 400 acres, the effect first noticed was the island's beauty—its vistas of pools, gardens, and lagoons, bordered with exotic buildings representing the Pacific nations. Cambodian, Mayan, and Incan motifs gave a charming strangeness to this modern exposition "city."

Early Railroad Depots

In 1863, a steam railroad took passengers and freight from Broadway along Seventh Street to Oakland Point and the ferry to San Francisco.[38, 39]

The first transcontinental rail service in the area was to the Woodstock wharf in Alameda, where the passengers took the ferry to San Francisco. Travel time between coasts was cut from over 120 days by ship around the Horn of South America to 6 days across the continent by rail. There is an historical landmark in Alameda commemorating this event.[40, 41, 42, 43]

The Woodstock terminal served for a few months until the Central Pacific started using its depot at Broadway and Seventh Street in Oakland and the Oakland Point ferry terminal. Then, starting in 1871, passengers used Oakland's new Seventh Street Long Wharf; passenger service was moved to the new Southern Pacific Mole in 1882, while the Long Wharf was used for freight until 1918.[44, 45, 46]

In 1903 the Western Pacific Railroad was founded. The first spike of the new railroad was driven in 1906, at Third and Union streets in Oakland.

Figure 332 - **1863 Central Pacific Railroad Depot on Seventh Street**

Figure 333 - **1903 Western Pacific Railroad Depot at Third and Washington**

To break the Southern Pacific monopoly, and with armed guards, the Western Pacific soon started laying track on the north estuary jetty. Southern Pacific lost the legal battle and both the Western Pacific and the City of Oakland gained control of a large portion of the waterfront, including all of the landfill areas.[47]

Western Pacific freight service started in 1909 and passenger service started in 1910 at the new Oakland Third and Washington Streets station, with passengers taking the ferry to San Francisco from the Western Pacific Oakland Mole.[48, 49] In 1911, ships started sailing directly from the Western Pacific Mole to Japan.

Western Pacific passenger ferry service from Oakland to San Francisco continued until 1917 when the U. S. government took over the railroads and Western Pacific was required to close its ferry and barge service.

All Western Pacific passenger trains then went to the Southern Pacific Oakland Mole. After World War I, Western Pacific ferry service resumed and continued until 1939.

The most memorable Western Pacific passenger train was the *California Zephyr*, which ran between Oakland and Chicago from 1949 to 1970. In 1983 Western Pacific merged with Union Pacific, thus ending eighty years of Western Pacific railroad service to Oakland. [50, 51]

Fort Point

The U.S. Army Corps of Engineers constructed Fort Point between 1853 and 1861 to prevent the entrance of a hostile fleet into San Francisco Bay. The fort was designed to mount 126 massive cannons. Rushed to completion at the beginning of the Civil War, Fort Point was first garrisoned in February of 1861 by Company I, 3rd U.S. Artillery Regiment. The fort was occupied throughout the Civil War, but the advent of faster, more powerful rifled cannons made brick forts such as Fort Point obsolete. In 1886, the troops were withdrawn, and the last cannons were removed about 1900.

The fort was then used for storage and training purposes for many years. Between 1933 and 1937, the fort was used as a base of operations for the construction of the Golden Gate Bridge. During World War II, Fort Point was occupied by about a hundred soldiers who manned searchlights and rapid-fire cannons mounted atop the fort and maintained a submarine net strung across the entrance to the bay. Fort Point is the only brick fort of its type on the West Coast.[52] It became a National Historic Site on October 16, 1970.[53] There is a photograph of Fort Point on page 70.

Fort Baker

Founded as an army post more than a hundred years ago, Fort Baker has begun a vital new chapter of public service. This picturesque site, the last military holding in the dramatic "post to park" conversion that has created much of the Golden Gate National Recreation Area, was transferred to the National Park Service in 2001. With its spectacular setting and significant history, Fort Baker adds a new dimension to an already remarkable collection of parklands at the Golden Gate.

The National Park Service, in partnership with the Golden Gate National Parks Association, is charting an exciting future for Fort Baker. This proposed plan, which describes the overall concepts for reuse of the site, calls for preserving the post's special historic and natural features while creating new opportunities for learning and enjoyment.

To many observers, Fort Baker is one of the gems of the national parklands at the Golden Gate. Its rich tapestry of historic structures, scenic views, natural features and recreational opportunities exemplifies the character of the Bay Area treasured by residents and visitors alike. The 35-acre site is nestled in a tranquil valley at the northern entrance to San Francisco Bay, near the north end of the Golden Gate Bridge.

An additional 183 acres of federally owned tidelands, a mile of pristine rocky bay shoreline and the picturesque harbor at Horseshoe Bay further enhance the site. A cluster of historic buildings arranged around a 10-acre parade ground lends it a campus-like appearance.

The land at Fort Baker was once used by the coastal Miwok, the indigenous inhabitants of present-day Marin County, who may have sought shelter from the wind here and gathered mussels, tule and cattails at the marsh. The earliest sailing vessel into San Francisco Bay anchored at Fort Baker's shores in 1775 and later, when the area was part of Rancho Sausalito, the fort was used for collecting spring water and grazing cattle.

When Congress established the Golden Gate National Recreation Area in 1972, Fort Baker was included within the park boundaries, to become part of the park when no longer needed by the army. The National Park Service (NPS) received more than 200 acres of the site, representing most of the open space, and opening portions of the fort to new tenants and recreational users.

In 1990, the NPS entered into partnerships at Fort Baker with the U.S. Coast Guard and the Bay Area Discovery Museum. The U.S. Coast Guard constructed a new facility at Fort Baker's Horseshoe Bay to replace a station that had operated near Fort Point. The Bay Area Discovery Museum rehabilitated some of Fort Baker's historic industrial buildings and transformed them into an exciting, hands-on learning center for children and families. Additional military-sponsored uses include a small yacht club and marina operated by the air force and army recruiting and reserve units.

The undeveloped areas of Fort Baker shelter a number of important habitats, including that of the Mission Blue Butterfly, a rare and endangered species.[54] Wildflowers, coastal scrub and grasslands cover the hillsides; an oak woodland graces its eastern edge; the steep cliffs below Battery Yates are home to nesting gulls, and a variety of water birds can be seen in the cove. Migratory wildlife pass through Fort Baker throughout the year, and certain seasons bring monarch butterflies, nesting cliff swallows and herring to the site.

Easily accessible from Marin County communities and San Francisco, Fort Baker offers a host of recreational opportunities and a gateway to the Marin Headlands and other national parklands north of the Golden Gate Bridge. It is one of the gems of the Golden Gate National Recreation Area, or as it is known today, the Golden Gate National Parks. There are photographs of Fort Baker on page 72.

Point Bonita Lighthouse

The half-mile walk to the Point Bonita lighthouse takes visitors along a narrow ridge, through a hand-chiseled tunnel and over a heart-stopping suspension footbridge to what seems like the end of the world. California's coastline stretches north and south; the Pacific rolls away to the west and San Francisco glitters on the bay. Heavy ship traffic created an urgent need for a lighthouse at the Golden Gate, which was known for its strong currents, summer fog, and winter storms. Because the early lighthouses on Alcatraz and at Fort Point could not be seen from all directions by approaching ships, in 1853 Congress funded construction of a lighthouse on a ridge three hundred feet above the water near Point Bonita. The lighthouse was equipped with one of the finest French Fresnel lenses and started operating in May 1855.

However, the builders were not familiar with the behavior of fog along the California coast. At its three-hundred-foot elevation, the light was frequently enveloped in fog, making it almost useless as a beacon to incoming ships. It was not long before it became clear that, to be effective, the lighthouse had to be relocated, and work began to prepare a site on a thin spine of rock at Land's End. By early 1877, the relocation was complete; the upper half of the 1855 lighthouse was placed on top of the newly constructed base, and in February, its three wicks were lit for the first time in the new location. The original fixed Fresnel lens is still in use; however, a 1,000-watt bulb replaces the original oil lamp and flashes on and off. A few years later, in 1898, Point Bonita Life-Saving Station was established nearby.

From this precipitous station, courageous "surf-men" rowed in 18-foot boats to rescue mariners in distress. The first lighthouse keepers fired a cannon every half hour in foggy weather, day and night. This western sentinel now operates automatically, sending a revolving beam of bright light out into the fog and issuing periodic booms. Apart from the lighthouse, sights along the trail include an historic Coast Guard rescue station, wildflowers and pillars of basalt rock formations.

Visitors can take a guided tour or explore the lighthouse on their own. The Coast Guard does not permit visitors above the first floor of the lighthouse since it is a real working lighthouse and not a museum. Coast Guard volunteers clean the lens and lantern room glass.[55] There is a photograph of Point Bonita lighthouse on page 71.

Romberg Tiburon Center

The Romberg Tiburon Center is an off-campus research and teaching facility operated year-round by San Francisco State University (SFSU). It was established in 1978 by the late Paul F. Romberg, president of SFSU, on a portion of a 42-acre parcel of land rich with history.

The site first came into use in 1877 when a packing plant to dry, process and ship codfish was constructed. At the turn of the century, the navy purchased the property for use as a navy ship coaling station. During construction of the Golden Gate Bridge in the 1930's, the north warehouse was used to reel cables for the bridge. The steel wire was wound and reeled, then barged to the Gate. Today, masses of tangled wire are still visible partially submerged off the north dock.

From 1931 to 1940, the navy lent the base to the state of California, which established its first nautical training school (later to become the California Maritime Academy). With the outbreak of World War II, the U.S. government re-appropriated the site for use by the navy, and the Maritime Academy relocated to its present site near Vallejo.

During World War II, the Tiburon facility was used for construction of anti-submarine and anti-torpedo nets. These nets were shipped to navy bases all along the West Coast and across the Pacific. The biggest job faced by Navy Net Depot personnel during this time was to lay an anti-submarine net seven miles long and 7,000 tons in weight across the entrance to San Francisco Bay.

The Navy Net Depot was active until 1958 when its operation was terminated and the property was transferred from the navy to the Department of Commerce. In the 1960's, the property became the National Marine Fisheries Service (NMFS), and in 1973, NMFS consolidated its operations on ten acres of the parcel. In 1977, the university submitted a proposal to develop a field station and marine laboratory dedicated to the study of San Francisco Bay. The Romberg Tiburon Center (RTC) was established on the remaining thirty-two acres. RTC strives to be a national and international center for significant, fundamental environmental research and education.[56]

Underside of the Bay Bridge

Originally, there was two-way traffic on the upper deck, three lanes in each direction. On the lower deck, there were three lanes of truck traffic and two Key System train tracks. On the underside of the bridge, the four larger girders on the south side supported each of the train tracks. On the north side, the six smaller girders supported the three lanes of truck traffic. In 1958, Key System service to San Francisco was discontinued. The train tracks were removed and the bridge reconfigured for one-way traffic on each deck.

Trucks

Trains

Figure 334 - **Underside of Bay Bridge, showing smaller truck and larger train support girders**

Retired Canadian Coast Guard Ships

Two retired Canadian Coast Guard ships, the *Vancouver* and the *Quadra*, were launched in 1966 and 1967. They were part of the Canadian weather service and stationed in the Pacific Ocean, designed to monitor the weather before the days of satellites.[57] The large structures on top of each ship supported weather radar antennas.

The ships were floating power plants that served to power the large radar and other weather station equipment. In the summer of 1999, they were being readied for service as a portable power plant[58] and were moved from Alameda in March 2000. As of early 2002 they were moored in Richmond near the *Red Oak Victory* and have reportedly been sold to China.

Figure 335 - **Retired Canadian Coast Guard ships, moored in Alameda, September 1999**

---

[1] Bean (1988) page 15.
[2] Kellecher (1997).
[3] Historical Landmark No. 47 - Anza Expedition Camp, San Mateo. See page 218.
[4] Historical Landmark No. 2 - Portola Journey's End, San Mateo County. See page 217.
[5] Historical Landmark No. 79 - Presidio of San Francisco, San Francisco. See page 231.
[6] Historical Landmark No. 327 - Mission Dolores, San Francisco. See page 237.
[7] Historical Landmark No. 285 - Peralta House 1860, San Leandro. See page 224.

[8] Historical Landmark No. 279 - Estudillo Home, San Leandro. See page 223.

[9] Historical Landmark No. 391 - Sanchez Adobe, San Mateo County. See page 219.

[10] Marshall Gold Discover State Historic Park in Coloma, California.

[11] See specific dates in the Time Line Reference Table on page 247.

[12] Margolin (1978) page 7.

[13] Margolin (1978) page 1.

[14] Bean (1988) page 3.

[15] Information from Port of Oakland website [01/20/03] www.portofoakland.com/aboutus/history.asp.

[16] Information from Port of Oakland website [01/20/03] www.portofoakland.com/aboutus/history.asp.

[17] Information from Port of Oakland website [01/20/03] www.portofoakland.com/aboutus/history.asp.

[18] Information on Douglas DC-3 from Chasing the Sun website [01/10/03] www.pbs.org/kcet/chasingthesun/planes/dc3.html.

[19] Materials excerpted with permission from brochure It's More Than a Port, Port of Oakland.

[20] Minor (1993) page 3.

[21] See 1870, 1873 Reference Time Line on page 248.

[22] Minor (1996) Bridges Become Tunnels.

[23] Sign on Alameda Portal of Posey Tube.

[24] Minor (1996) Bridges Become Tunnels.

[25] Photograph of Quinn Lighthouse from United States Lighthouse Society. See Historic Data Sources on page 259.

[26] Photograph of Quinn Lighthouse from United States Lighthouse Society. See Historic Data Sources on page 259.

[27] Extracted from materials written by Wayne Wheeler, president, United States Lighthouse Society. See Historic Data Sources on page 259.

[28] Historical Landmark No. 968 - Site of the China Clipper Flight Departure, Alameda. See page 229.

[29] Photograph of China Clipper courtesy Pan Am Historical Foundation from website [01/10/03] www.panam.org.

[30] Photograph of China Clipper courtesy Pan Am Historical Foundation from website [01/10/03] www.panam.org.

[31] Historical Landmark No. 968 - Site of the China Clipper Flight Departure, Alameda. See page 229.

[32] Photograph of Sikorsky S-42 courtesy Pan Am Historical Foundation from website [01/10/03 www.panam.org.

[33] Allen (2000) page 53.

[34] Photograph of Yankee Clipper courtesy Pan Am Historical Foundation from website [01/10/03] www.panam.org.

[35] Photograph of 1935 Treasure Island courtesy San Francisco Museum from website [01/10/03] www.sfmuseum.org.

[36] Photograph of Gayway courtesy San Francisco Museum from website [01/10/03] www.sfmuseum.org.

[37] Brugmansia pauciflora calycina is an evergreen shrub.

[38] Bagwell (1982) page 41.

[39] Cooper (1996) Birth on the Water.

[40] Cooper (1996) The Transcontinental Railroad Comes to Town.

[41] Historical Landmark No. 440 - Alameda Terminal of the First Transcontinental Railroad. See page 225.

[42] Bagwell (1982) page 52. [First Train arrived in Alameda Sept. 6, 1896. First train arrived in Oakland Nov. 8, 1869.]

[43] The Panama trans-isthmus railroad completed January 28, 1855. From website [01/10/03] www.trainweb.org/panama.

[44] Bagwell (1982) page 47. [In 1863, steam train went from Broadway down Seventh Street to new Oakland Point ferry.]

[45] Cooper (1996) The Transcontinental Railroad Comes to Town.

[46] Bagwell (1982) page 59. [Central Pacific opened the Long Wharf in 1871.]

[47] The courts ruled the Southern Pacific owned up to the 1852 low tide line and the City of Oakland owned all filled land.

[48] Bagwell (1982) page 59, map on pages 201–202. [Map at Oakland Public Main Library, Oakland Research Room.]

[49] Minor (2000) page 19.

[50] Information from Western Pacific Railroad Historical Society website [01/10/03] www.wprrhs.org/wphistory.html.

[51] The California Zephyr cars Silver Crescent and Silver Stag are in the Gold Coast Railroad Museum. See page 260.

[52] Third System Coastal Defense Forts were built after the War of 1812 when Congress realized the need for stronger fortifications. This type of fort design was used until 1867. Information on brick forts from American Coastal Defense Forts of the Third System 1816–1867 website [01/10/03] www.cdsg.org/brick.htm.

[53] Haller (1997) page 42. Additional information on Fort Point from websites [01/10/03] www.nps.gov/fopo and http://outdoors.myareaguide.com/fortpoint.

[54] Information on Mission Blue Butterfly (Icaricia icarioides missionensis) from California Endangered Insects website [01/09/03] www.mip.berkeley.edu/essig/endins/exhibit.htm.

[55] Point Bonita lighthouse first operated May 2, 1855. Information and photograph from National Park Service website [01/10/03] www.nps.gov, www.pigeonpointlighthouse.org/ptbonita.htm and [01/10/03] http://home.pacbell.net/leewaysf/marin.html.

[56] Information on Romberg Tiburon Center from History of the Tiburon Center website [01/10/03] http://rtc.sfsu.edu/history.htm.

[57] Jane's Fighting Ships 1976–77. [The Vancouver was launched July 1966 and the Quadra was launched March 1967.]

[58] Based on a discussion David Lee Woods had with the project engineer during the summer of 1999.

20 - Historical Landmarks

The numbers before the names of historical landmarks are those used by the state of California. The California Department of Parks and Recreation Office of Historic Preservation numbers each historical site sequentially when the site is approved. Site No. 1 is the Custom House in Monterey; there are currently nearly 1,100 sites. Site data and photographs used here are by Donald Laird; see photograph credits on page 283 and website references on page 263.

San Mateo County

▪ No. 2 - Portola Journey's End, San Mateo County

PORTOLA JOURNEY'S END

NOVEMBER 6–10, 1769
NEAR "EL PALO ALTO," THE TALL TREE, THE PORTOLA EXPEDITION OF 63 MEN AND 200 HORSES AND MULES CAMPED. THEY HAD TRAVELED FROM SAN DIEGO IN SEARCH OF MONTEREY, BUT DISCOVERED INSTEAD THE BAY OF SAN FRANCISCO. FINDING THE BAY TOO LARGE TO GO AROUND, AND DECIDING THAT MONTEREY HAD BEEN BY-PASSED, THEY ENDED THE SEARCH AND RETURNED TO SAN DIEGO.

Figure 336 - **Historical Landmark No. 2 - 1769 Portola Expedition Campsite**

Photographs taken 3/10/96

The plaque is located at the intersection of East Creek Drive and Alma Street in Menlo Park, but the site itself is actually in Palo Alto in Santa Clara County. It is across a footbridge on the other side of the creek that is the county line.

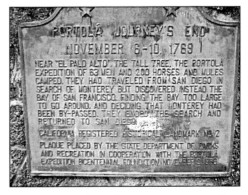

Figure 337 - **Historical Landmark No. 2 - 1769 Portola Expedition Campsite**

▪ No. 47 - Anza Expedition Camp, San Mateo

HISTORIC CAMP SITE

HERE ON THE BANKS OF SAN MATEO CREEK
CAPTAIN J. B. DE ANZA CAMPED,
MARCH 29, 1776, AFTER EXPLORING THE
PENINSULA AND SELECTING THE SITES FOR
THE MISSION AND PRESIDIO OF
SAN FRANCISCO. HERE ALSO THE PARTY OF
FAMILIES, SOLDIERS, AND PRIESTS, ON THE
WAY TO FOUND SAN FRANCISCO, CAMPED
FOR THREE DAYS, JUNE 24–27, 1776.

Figure 338 - **Historical Landmark No. 47 -
1776 Anza Expedition Camp**

Location: From El Camino Real (State Highway 82), go west one block on West 3rd Avenue, turn North on Arroyo Court, go 1/2 block and turn left; plaque is 300 feet west in San Mateo. Nothing remains of the original site.

Photograph taken 07/19/95

▪ No. 391 - Sanchez Adobe, San Mateo County

SANCHEZ ADOBE

THE HOME OF FRANCISCO SANCHEZ
(B. 1805, D. 1862), ALCALDE OF
SAN FRANCISCO AND COMMANDANTE OF
MILITIA UNDER THE MEXICAN REPUBLIC,
GRANTEE OF THE 8,926 ACRE RANCHO
SAN PEDRO, AND LATER A RESPECTED
AMERICAN CITIZEN. HIS HOUSE, BUILT
1842–6, AFTERWARDS WAS OWNED AND
REMODELED BY GENERAL EDWARD
KIRKPATRICK. IT WAS PURCHASED BY THE
COUNTY OF SAN MATEO IN 1947 TO BE
PRESERVED AS A PUBLIC MUSEUM.

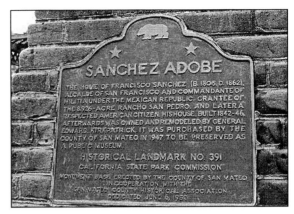

Figure 340 - **Historical Landmark No. 391 - 1842 Sanchez Adobe plaque, San Mateo**

Photographs taken 03/10/96

Location: Sanchez Adobe County Park, southwest corner of Linda Mar Boulevard and Seville Drive, Pacifica.

Figure 339 - **Historical Landmark No. 391 - 1842 Sanchez Adobe site, San Mateo**

Alameda County

▪ No. 45 - Site of Original Campus of University of California

SITE OF COLLEGE OF CALIFORNIA ORIGINAL CAMPUS OF UNIVERSITY OF CALIFORNIA

UNIVERSITY OF CALIFORNIA CHARTERED MARCH 23, 1868. LOCATED BETWEEN FRANKLIN AND HARRISON, 12TH AND 14TH STREETS, FROM 1869 TO 1873, USING BUILDINGS OF FORMER COLLEGE OF CALIFORNIA, SUCCESSOR TO CONTRA COSTA ACADEMY FOUNDED BY HENRY DURANT, JUNE 1853. HE WAS ELECTED FIRST UNIVERSITY PRESIDENT IN JUNE 1870. UNIVERSITY MOVED TO PRESENT BERKELEY SITE SEPTEMBER 1873.

Figure 341 - **Historical Landmark No. 45 - Site of College of California, original campus of University of California**

Photograph taken 3/11/96

Nothing remains of the original site, which was located at the northeast corner of 13th and Franklin Streets in Oakland.

No. 246 - Rancho San Antonio (Peralta Grant)

RANCHO SAN ANTONIO

GOVERNOR PABLO DE SOLA, LAST SPANISH GOVERNOR OF CALIFORNIA, AWARDED THE SAN ANTONIO GRANT TO DON LUIS MARIA PERALTA ON AUGUST 3, 1820, IN RECOGNITION OF FORTY YEARS OF SERVICE. FROM THIS POINT NORTHWARD, THE GRANT EMBRACED OVER 43,000 ACRES, NOW OCCUPIED BY THE CITIES OF SAN LEANDRO, OAKLAND, ALAMEDA, EMERYVILLE, PIEDMONT, BERKELEY, AND ALBANY.

Figure 342 - **Historical Landmark No. 246 - 1820 Rancho San Antonio**

Photograph taken 05/12/96

▪ No. 107 - Joaquin Miller Home, Oakland

"POET OF THE SIERRAS"

RESIDED ON THESE ACRES, NAMED BY HIM "THE HIGHTS," FROM 1886 TO 1918. IN THIS BUILDING, KNOWN AS THE ABBEY, HE WROTE "COLUMBUS" AND OTHER POEMS. THE SURROUNDING TREES WERE PLANTED BY HIM AND HE PERSONALLY BUILT, ON THE EMINENCE TO THE NORTH, THE FUNERAL PYRE AND THE MONUMENTS DEDICATED TO MOSES, GENERAL JOHN C. FREMONT, AND ROBERT BROWNING. "THE HIGHTS" WAS PURCHASED BY THE CITY OF OAKLAND IN 1919.

Figure 343 - **Historical Landmark No. 107 - 1889 Joaquin Miller Home plaque, Oakland**

Photographs taken 9/21/96

The home is located in Joaquin Miller Park, at the northwest corner of Joaquin Miller Road and Sanborn Drive in Oakland.

Figure 344 - **Historical Landmark No. 107 - 1889 Joaquin Miller Home site, Oakland**

• No. 279 - Estudillo Home, San Leandro

ESTUDILLO HOME

SITE OF THE LAST HOME OF JOSE JOAQUIN ESTUDILLO, GRANTEE OF RANCHO SAN LEANDRO AND HIS WIFE, JUANA MARTINEZ DE ESTUDILLO. IT WAS BUILT ABOUT 1850. THE FAMILY FOUNDED SAN LEANDRO, BUILT A HOTEL, AND DONATED SEVERAL LOTS, INCLUDING THE ORIGINAL SITE OF ST. LEANDER'S CHURCH.

Figure 345 - **Historical Landmark No. 279 - 1850 Estudillo Home plaque, San Leandro**

Photographs taken 05/12/96

The home is located at 550 West Estudillo, San Leandro, and is the rectory for St. Leander's Church.

Figure 346 - **Historical Landmark No. 279 - 1850 Estudillo Home site, San Leandro**

• No. 285 - Peralta House 1860, San Leandro

PERALTA HOUSE

FIRST BRICK HOUSE BUILT IN ALAMEDA COUNTY. CONSTRUCTED 1860 BY W.P. TOLER FOR IGNACIO PERALTA, EARLY SAN LEANDRO SPANISH SETTLER, WHOSE FATHER, DON LUIS MARIA PERALTA, RECEIVED LAND GRANT FROM SPANISH GOVERNOR DON PABLO VICENTE DE SOLA, OCTOBER 20, 1820.

Figure 347 - **Historical Landmark No. 285 - 1860 Peralta Home plaque, San Leandro**

Photographs taken 10/26/96

The home is located at 561 Lafayette at Leo Avenue, San Leandro.

Figure 348 - **Historical Landmark No. 285 - 1860 Peralta Home site, San Leandro**

▪ No. 440 - Alameda Terminal of the First Transcontinental Railroad

FIRST TRANSCONTINENTAL RAILROAD

ON SEPTEMBER 6, 1869
FIRST TRANSCONTINENTAL RAILROAD
TRAIN LINKING TWO GREAT OCEANS, AND
CONSISTING OF TWELVE CARS AND THREE
LOCOMOTIVES PASSED HERE ON WAY TO A
WHARF TERMINAL WEST OF HERE, A
LOCATION NOW COVERED BY LAGOON FOR
TAKE-OFF TRANS-PACIFIC PLANES,
AND WITHIN CONFINES, PRESENT
U.S. NAVAL AIR STATION.
ORIGINAL CELEBRATION
HELD NEAR THIS SPOT.

Figure 349 - **Historical Landmark No. 440 -
1869 Alameda Terminal of
First Transcontinental Railroad**

Photograph taken 3/11/96

The plaque is at the northwest corner of Lincoln Avenue and Webster Street, Alameda.

Nothing remains of the original site.

▪ No. 676 - Site of Saint Mary's College, Oakland

SITE OF SAINT MARY'S COLLEGE

"THE OLD BRICKPILE," 1889–1928
SAINT MARY'S COLLEGE ALUMNI
APRIL 25, 1959

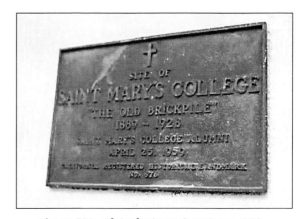

Figure 350 - **Historical Landmark No. 676 -
1889 Site of Saint Mary's College, Oakland**

Plaque photograph 03/11/96

The plaque is at 3093 Broadway and Hawthorne Avenue, Oakland.

Nothing remains of the original site.

• No. 694 - Church of St. James the Apostle, Oakland

CHURCH OF
ST. JAMES THE APOSTLE

THIS CHURCH FOUNDED UNDER
AUTHORITY OF BISHOP KIP,
FIRST EPISCOPAL BISHOP FOR
CALIFORNIA.
HAS GIVEN UNINTERRUPTED SERVICE
TO THIS COMMUNITY SINCE
JUNE 27, 1850.

Figure 351 - **Historical Landmark No. 694 - 1850 Church of St. James the Apostle**

Plaque photograph taken 03/11/96

Church photograph taken 01/31/98

The church is located at 1540 12th Avenue, at Foothill Boulevard, Oakland.

Figure 352 - **Historical Landmark No. 694 - 1850 Church of St. James the Apostle**

▪ No. 824 - San Leandro Oyster Beds, Alameda County

SAN LEANDRO OYSTER BEDS

OYSTERS WERE THE MAINSTAY OF THE CALIFORNIA FISHING INDUSTRY AT THE TURN OF THE CENTURY. ALONG THIS SITE (THE ORIGINAL MULFORD CANAL) THE SAN LEANDRO OYSTER BEDS FLOURISHED. IN 1892 WILLIAM ROBERTS FILED TITLE TO THE BEDS SOUTH ALONG SAN LORENZO CANAL AND IN 1895 THOMAS MULFORD FILED TITLE HERE AT MULFORD CANAL. THE BEDS WERE OFTEN PLAGUED BY "OYSTER PIRATES" SUCH AS JACK LONDON.

Figure 353 - **Historical Landmark No. 824 - San Leandro Oyster Beds.**

Photographs taken 03/11/96

The site is located at San Leandro Marina, south end of North Dike Road, San Leandro.

Due to pollution and other hazards, oysters are no longer commercially harvested in the San Leandro Marina area. However, the large shell mounds attest to the fact that oysters have been living in waters around the bay since prehistoric times. For many years oyster dredges "mined" the prehistoric beds for use as poultry feed and in human calcium supplement pills.

Figure 354 - **Historical Landmark No. 824 - San Leandro Oyster Beds**.

▪ No. 962 - Site of Blossom Rock Navigation Trees

SITE OF BLOSSOM ROCK

NAVIGATION TREES
UNTIL AT LEAST 1851, REDWOOD TREES ON THIS
SITE WERE USED AS LANDMARKS
TO AVOID STRIKING THE TREACHEROUS SUBMERGED
BLOSSOM ROCK IN SAN FRANCISCO BAY
WEST OF YERBA BUENA ISLAND.
ALTHOUGH BY 1855 THE ORIGINAL STEMS
HAD BEEN LOGGED,
TODAY'S TREES ARE SPROUTS FROM THEIR STUMPS.

Figure 355 - **Historical Landmark No. 962 -
Blossom Rock Navigation Trees, Redwood Park.**

Photograph taken 9/21/96

Site location at the Madrone Picnic Area, Thomas J. Roberts Recreation Area,

Redwood Regional Park, 11500 Skyline Boulevard, Oakland.

▪ No. 968 - Site of the China Clipper Flight Departure, Alameda

PAN AM CHINA CLIPPER

PAN AMERICAN WORLD AIRWAYS FABLED
CHINA CLIPPER (MARTIN M/130 FLYING BOAT)
LEFT ALAMEDA MARINA ON NOVEMBER 22, 1935.
UNDER THE COMMAND OF CAPTAIN EDWIN C. MUSICK.
THE FLIGHT WOULD REACH MANILA
VIA HONOLULU, MIDWAY, WAKE, AND GUAM.
THE INAUGURATION OF OCEAN
AIRMAIL SERVICE AND COMMERCIAL AIRFLIGHT
ACROSS THE PACIFIC WAS A SIGNIFICANT EVENT
FOR BOTH CALIFORNIA AND THE WORLD

Figure 356 - **Historical Landmark No. 968 - Site of the *China Clipper* flight departure, Alameda**

Photograph taken 10/26/96

Site location is in front of Building 77, northwest corner of 5th Street and Guam, Alameda Naval Air Station, now called Alameda Point.

▪ No. 970 - Rainbow Trout Species Identified, Alameda County

RAINBOW TROUT SPECIES IDENTIFIED

THE NAMING OF THE RAINBOW TROUT SPECIES WAS BASED ON FISH TAKEN FROM THE SAN LEANDRO CREEK DRAINAGE. IN 1855, DR. W.P. GIBBONS, FOUNDER OF THE CALIFORNIA ACADEMY OF SCIENCES, WAS GIVEN THREE SPECIMENS OBTAINED FROM THE CREEK. HE DESCRIBED AND ASSIGNED THEM THE SCIENTIFIC NAME SALMO IRIDIA. RAINBOW TROUT ARE NOW WORLDWIDE IN DISTRIBUTION AND ARE HIGHLY VALUED GAME FISH.

Figure 357 - **Historical Landmark No. 970 - Rainbow Trout Species Identified**

Photograph taken 9/21/96

Site located fifty yards past Redwood Gate entrance kiosk, Redwood Regional Park, Oakland.

San Francisco County

▪ No. 79 - Presidio of San Francisco, San Francisco

PRESIDIO OF SAN FRANCISCO

FORMALLY ESTABLISHED ON
SEPTEMBER 17, 1776,
THE SAN FRANCISCO PRESIDIO HAS BEEN
ADMINISTERED SUCCESSIVELY AS A
MILITARY HEADQUARTERS BY SPAIN,
MEXICO, AND THE UNITED STATES. A
MAJOR COMMAND POST DURING THE
MEXICAN WAR, CIVIL WAR, SPANISH-
AMERICAN WAR, WORLD WARS I AND II,
AND THE KOREAN WAR. IT REMAINS A
SYMBOL OF UNITED STATES AUTHORITY IN
THE PACIFIC.

Figure 358 - **Historical Landmark No. 79 - 1776 Presidio of San Francisco plaque**

Photographs taken 06/18/95

Located at the southwest corner of Funston Avenue and Lincoln Boulevard, San Francisco.

The Presidio is now operated by the National Park Service.

Figure 359 - **Historical Landmark No. 79 - Presidio of San Francisco Officers Club; original structure is part of this building**

▪ No. 80 - Montgomery Block, San Francisco

THE MONTGOMERY BLOCK

THIS, SAN FRANCISCO'S FIRST FIREPROOF BUILDING, ERECTED IN 1853 BY HENRY WAGER HALLECK, WAS THE HEADQUARTERS FOR MANY OUTSTANDING LAWYERS, FINANCIERS, WRITERS, ACTORS, AND ARTISTS. JAMES KING OF WILLIAM, EDITOR OF THE <u>BULLETIN</u> DIED HERE AFTER BEING SHOT BY JAMES CASEY, MAY 14, 1856. ESCAPING DESTRUCTION IN THE FIRE OF 1906, THE BUILDING IS PRESERVED IN MEMORY OF THOSE WHO LIVED AND WORKED IN IT

Figure 360 - **Historical Landmark No. 80 - 1853 Montgomery Block, San Francisco**

Photograph taken 08/24/95

Located at 600 Montgomery Street, San Francisco.

The plaque is located in the lobby of the Transamerica Pyramid.

No. 81 - Landing Place of Captain J. B. Montgomery, San Francisco

ON JULY 9, 1846, IN THE EARLY MORNING,
IN THE DAYS WHEN THE WATER CAME UP TO
MONTGOMERY STREET,
COMMANDER JOHN B. MONTGOMERY
FOR WHOM MONTGOMERY STREET WAS
NAMED LANDED NEAR THIS SPOT FROM THE
U.S. SLOOP-OF-WAR "PORTSMOUTH,"
TO RAISE THE STARS AND STRIPES
ON THE PLAZA, NOW PORTSMOUTH SQUARE,
ONE BLOCK TO THE WEST.

Figure 361 - **Historical Landmark No. 81 - 1846 Landing Place of Captain J.B. Montgomery**

Photograph taken 07/26/95

Located at 552 Montgomery Street, southeast corner of Montgomery and Clay, San Francisco.

▪ No. 83 - Shoreline Markers, San Francisco

THIS TABLET MARKS THE SHORE LINE OF
SAN FRANCISCO BAY
AT THE TIME OF THE DISCOVERY OF GOLD
IN CALIFORNIA, JANUARY 24, 1848.
MAP REPRODUCED ABOVE DELINEATES
OLD SHORE LINE.

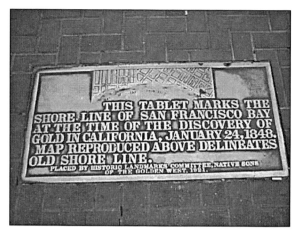

Figure 362 - **Historical Landmark No. 83 -
1848 San Francisco Shore Line**

Photograph taken 08/06/95

The map is visible in the photograph of the
plaque.

The plaque is in the sidewalk at the northeast
corner of Bush and Market Streets, San Francisco.

No. 236 - Entrance of the San Carlos into San Francisco Bay

FIRST SHIP INTO SAN FRANCISCO BAY

ON AUGUST 5, 1775, THE
SPANISH PACKET *SAN CARLOS*,
UNDER THE COMMAND OF
LIEUTENANT JUAN MANUEL DE AYALA,
BECAME THE FIRST SHIP TO ENTER
SAN FRANCISCO BAY.
A MONTH AND A HALF WAS SPENT IN
SURVEYING THE BAY FROM ITS SOUTHERN
MOST REACHES TO THE NORTHERN END
OF PRESENT-DAY SUISUN BAY.
THE SAN CARLOS DEPARTED
SEPTEMBER 18, 1775.

Figure 363 - **Historical Landmark No. 236 - 1775 Entrance of the San Carlos into San Francisco Bay**

Photograph taken 07/30/95

The plaque is located in Aquatic Park, at the northwest corner of Beach and Larkin Streets, San Francisco.

▪ No. 90 - Fort Gunny-Bags, San Francisco

Fort Gunny-Bags

WAS SITUATED ON THIS SPOT
HEADQUARTERS OF THE
VIGILANCE COMMITTEE
DURING THE YEAR 1856

Figure 364 - **Historical Landmark No. 90 - 1856 Fort Gunny-Bags, San Francisco**

Plaque photograph taken 08/28/96

Bell and painting photographs taken 1/31/98

The plaque is located on the south side of Sacramento between Davis and Front Streets, San Francisco.

Nothing remains of the site. The pictures show a painting of the fort in its prime and the original bell that was on the roof of the building. As of summer 1999, the plaque had been removed due to construction on the site.

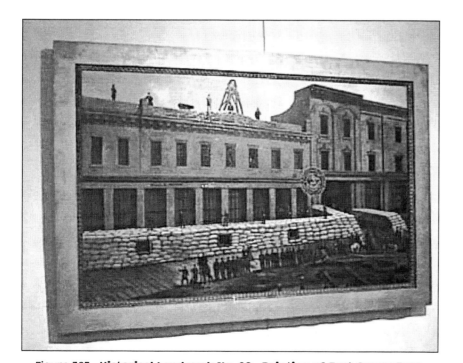

Figure 365 - **Historical Landmark No. 90 - Painting of Fort Gunny-Bags**

Figure 366 - **Historical Landmark No. 90 - Fort Gunny-Bags Bell**

▪ No. 327 - Mission Dolores, San Francisco

MISIÓN SAN FRANCISCO DE ASIS
MISSION DOLORES

THIS EDIFICE THE CONSTRUCTION OF
WHICH WAS STARTED IN 1788,
WAS DEDICATED AUGUST 2, 1791.
AN ADOBE STRUCTURE IN USE SINCE THAT
TIME, IT IS THE OLDEST BUILDING
IN SAN FRANCISCO.
ORIGINAL ADOBE BRICK WALLS AND
ROOF TILES ARE STILL IN PLACE.

Figure 367 - **Historical Landmark No. 327 - 1788 Mission Dolores plaque**

Photographs taken 08/24/95

The Mission is located on Dolores Street between 16th and 17th Streets, San Francisco.

Figure 368 - **Historical Landmark No. 327 - 1788 Mission Dolores**

▪ No. 587 - First Public School in California, San Francisco

```
THIS MARKS THE SITE
OF THE FIRST PUBLIC SCHOOL
IN CALIFORNIA
ERECTED IN 1847 —
OPENED APRIL 3, 1848
```

Plaque photograph 07/26/95

The plaque is located on Portsmouth Plaza, Clay Street and Brannan Place, San Francisco.

Figure 369 - **Historical Landmark No. 587 - 1847 First Public School in California, San Francisco**

• No. 650 - Site of the What Cheer House, San Francisco

SITE OF WHAT CHEER HOUSE

THIS IS THE SITE OF THE FAMOUS
WHAT CHEER HOUSE
A UNIQUE HOTEL OPENED IN 1852
BY R.B. WOODWARD
AND DESTROYED BY THE FIRE OF 1906.
THE WHAT CHEER HOUSE CATERED
TO MEN ONLY, PERMITTED NO LIQUOR
ON THE PREMISES, AND HOUSED
SAN FRANCISCO'S FIRST FREE LIBRARY
AND FIRST MUSEUM.

Figure 370 - **Historical Landmark No. 650 - 1852 Site of What Cheer House**

Plaque photograph taken 7/26/95

The plaque is located on the southwest corner of Sacramento and Leidesdorff Streets, San Francisco.

▪ No. 810 - Site of Old St. Mary's Church, San Francisco

SITE OF OLD ST. MARY'S

CORNERSTONE 1853—DEDICATED 1854
THE FIRST BUILDING ERECTED
AS A CATHEDRAL IN CALIFORNIA,
OLD ST. MARY'S SERVED THE ARCHDIOCESE
OF SAN FRANCISCO IN THAT CAPACITY
FROM 1854 TO 1891.
ONCE THE CITY'S MOST PROMINENT
BUILDING, MUCH OF ITS STONEWORK WAS
QUARRIED AND CUT IN CHINA AND ITS
BRICK BROUGHT "AROUND THE HORN" IN
SAILING SHIPS.

Figure 371 - **Historical Landmark No. 810 - 1853 Old St. Mary's Church, San Francisco**

Photographs taken 8/06/95

The church is located at the northeast corner of California Street and Grant Avenue. The plaque is on the Grant Avenue entrance to the church.

Figure 372 - **Historical Landmark No. 810 - 1853 Old St. Mary's Church, San Francisco**

▪ No. 861 - Site of First California State Fair, San Francisco

SITE OF FIRST CALIFORNIA STATE FAIR

CALIFORNIA'S FIRST STATE FAIR WAS HELD ON THIS SITE ON OCTOBER 4, 1854. SPONSORED BY THE CALIFORNIA STATE AGRICULTURAL SOCIETY, THE EXHIBITION OF "HORSES, CATTLE, MULES AND OTHER STOCK AND AGRICULTURAL, MECHANICAL AND DOMESTIC MANUFACTURE AND PRODUCTIONS" PROMOTED THE NEW STATE'S GROWING AGRICULTURAL INDUSTRY. A DIFFERENT CITY HELD THE FAIR EACH YEAR, UNTIL SACRAMENTO BECAME THE PERMANENT LOCATION IN 1861.

Figure 373 - **Historical Landmark No. 861 - Site of First California State Fair, San Francisco**

Photograph taken 08/06/95

The plaque is located at 269 Bush at Montgomery Street, San Francisco.

▪ No. 819 - Hudson's Bay Company Headquarters

HUDSON'S BAY COMPANY

ON THIS BLOCK, THEN ON YERBA BUENA'S WATERFRONT, STOOD THE CALIFORNIA HEADQUARTERS OF THE HUDSON'S BAY COMPANY. IN 1841, THEIR CHIEF TRADER, WILLIAM G. RAE, PURCHASED THE PROPERTY AND STARTED OPERATIONS. THIS VENTURE CAUSED WIDE SPECULATION ABOUT BRITISH INTENTIONS. INADEQUATE PROFITS, A DECLINING FUR CATCH, AND PRESSURE OF U.S. EXPANSION CAUSED HUDSON'S BAY COMPANY TO END CALIFORNIA OPERATIONS.

Figure 374 - **Historical Landmark No. 819 - 1841 Hudson's Bay Company Headquarters, San Francisco**

Photograph taken 7/26/95

The plaque is located at 505 Montgomery between Sacramento and Commercial Streets, San Francisco.

21 - Time Lines

USS *Potomac* Time Line

1934

June – UN Manitowoc Shipbuilding Co., Manitowoc, Wisconsin, launches the 18th "Thetis Class" U.S. Coast Guard patrol boat, named the *Electra*. The vessel is assigned to duty patrolling Atlantic coastal waters.

1935

November – The USCG *Electra* is dispatched to Norfolk Naval Shipyard, Virginia, for conversion to presidential service to replace the presidential yacht USS *Sequoia*.

1936

January – Conversion is completed. Additions include presidential and guest quarters, the boat deck, and a false aft smokestack to house FDR's elevator. The yacht is named USS *Potomac*.

March – Officially commissioned by the navy, the USS *Potomac* begins its service as FDR's "Floating White House."

1941

March 29 – FDR broadcasts a nationwide speech from the USS *Potomac* at Fort Lauderdale harbor in Florida.

August – An additional gun is added to the boat deck fantail in preparation for FDR's secret Atlantic Charter meeting with England's prime minister Winston Churchill.

November – Due to wartime concerns, FDR issues order for the USS *Potomac* to be confined to protected waters. Still officially the president's yacht, the USS *Potomac* is assigned to duty at the navy's Underwater Sound Testing Station.

1945

November – After FDR's death in April, the USS *Potomac* is decommissioned by the navy and returned to the U.S. Coast Guard.

1946

January – At Norfolk, Virginia, the *Potomac* is divested of fittings and furnishings, except for the president's custom stainless steel bathtub, and prepared for active duty by the U.S. Coast Guard. The dining saloon becomes the wardroom.

June – The *Potomac* is ordered to the Coast Guard Yard, Curtis Bay, Maryland, for permanent decommissioning from federal service.

June – The *Potomac* is turned over to the Maryland Tidewater Fisheries Commission and is used for fishery patrol and occasionally used by the governor of Maryland.

1960

April – Aging and expensive to operate, the *Potomac* is sold to W.G. Toone of Neptune Corporation for use as a ferry between San Juan, Puerto Rico, and the Virgin Islands.

1962

The *Potomac* is sold to Hydro-Capitol of Newport Beach, California. Plans to refurbish the vessel and use it as a traveling historical museum of the FDR era do not materialize.

1964

January – The *Potomac* is docked at Long Beach, California. Entertainer Elvis Presley buys the *Potomac* from Hydro-Capitol for $55,000. Presley offers it as a donation to the March of Dimes. His offer is refused due to the cost of refitting and maintaining the vessel.

April – Elvis Presley donates *Potomac* to St. Jude Hospital of Memphis, Tennessee.

May – Marie Pagliasso of Fresno, California, borrows $65,000 to buy the *Potomac* from St. Jude Hospital. She is an investment partner, along with Fresno businessman Carton Taylor, for a group called the Presidential Yacht *Potomac*, Inc. which intends to operate it as a floating disco in Long Beach, California. Her teak decks are torn up and replaced with concrete. The disco never opens.

1970

Carton Taylor becomes sole owner of the *Potomac* when the Pagliasso estate defaults on loan payments.

1971

Aubrey Phillips, a bail-bondsman and commercial fisherman, leases the *Potomac* from Carton Taylor.

1979

February – The *Potomac* is towed from Los Angeles to the Uptown Yacht Harbor in Stockton and opened to the public under the name "Presidential Yacht *Potomac*."

1980

August – The *Potomac* is towed 80 miles to Pier 26 in San Francisco, allegedly for repairs, and where Presidential Yacht *Potomac*, Inc. claims it will attract more support and will be open again for public viewing. The U.S. Department of the Interior considers her restoration and operation as a National Park Service floating museum. [9]

September 10 – The *Valkyure,* an eighty-five foot vessel, arrives at Pier 26 with a load of Colombian marijuana. Both *Valkyure* and the *Potomac* fly the flag of the bogus Crippled Children's Society organization. [9]

September 11 – The U.S. Customs authorities arrest everyone on the pier, and both the *Valkyure* and the *Potomac* are impounded at Treasure Island.

September – The *Potomac* is seized by U.S. Customs and the Drug Enforcement Agency (DEA), along with the illegal drug-laden yacht *Valkyure*. Investigators deem that the *Potomac* has been used as a "smugglers' command post" by a Long Beach drug ring using a fraudulent charity, The Crippled Children's Society, as a cover for its operations. Aubrey Phillips and the "Society" president are among those arrested and charged. [9]

October – The *Potomac* is towed to Clipper Cove Pier, Treasure Island Naval Base, to be held as evidence.

1981

March 18 – At 4: 00 a.m. the *Potomac's* hull is holed by a broken piling and she sinks at her berth in thirty-five feet of water.

March 30 – The Navy Reserve raises the vessel, patches its hull at a cost of $60,000 to the U.S. Customs Service, and tows the *Potomac* to Pacific Dry Dock in Oakland to be readied for auction. [9]

April 21 – The Port of Oakland, under Executive Director Walter Abernathy, makes the only bid at the U.S. Customs auction and buys the *Potomac* for $15,000. [9]

1982

September – The *Potomac* is placed ashore at Pacific Dry Dock in Oakland and stripped of all damaged equipment and fittings. [9]

1983

September 27 – The renovated and renamed Franklin D. Roosevelt Memorial Pier at the foot of Clay Street at Jack London Square is dedicated. [9]

1988

September – The *Potomac* is lifted onto a barge and towed to Colberg Shipyard in Stockton. [9]

1989

September – *Potomac* restoration at Colberg is completed, and she is towed to Jack London Square to complete finishing work.

1991

June 19 – The Port of Oakland announces that the *Potomac* has been designated a National Historic Landmark. [9]

July – All of the *Potomac's* heavy restoration work and sea trials are completed. [9]

1995

April 12 – 50th anniversary of FDR's death is commemorated at FDR Pier. [9]

April 12 – The *Potomac* is opened to the public after a cooperative effort, spearheaded by the Port of Oakland, organized labor, maritime corporations and dedicated volunteers.

May 20 – Maritime Day, the *Potomac* is opened to the public. [9]

June 28 – Dockside tours begin on the *Potomac*. [9]

Reference Time Line

1579

Francis Drake, on the *Golden Hind*, landed somewhere north of the bay, possibly in Drakes Bay. [2]

1595

November 30 – Sebastian Rodríquez Cermeño's ship, the *San Augustin*, was lost in a storm while anchored at Drakes Bay. He and his crew survived by sailing to Acapulco, Mexico, in a small open boat. [2]

1602

December 16 – Sebastián Vizcaíno entered and named Monterey Bay. [2]

1739

South Carolina is shaken by slave revolts. [4]

1740

Population of the thirteen colonies reaches 1.5 million, including 250,000 slaves; Boston and Philadelphia are the largest cities. [4]

1765

The Stamp Act is imposed on British colonies in the Americas. [4]

1769

April 11 – Captain Gaspar de Portolá in his ship the *San Antonio* arrived in San Diego and established a presidio. [2]

1769

November 1 – Captain Gaspar de Portolá, arriving overland, is the first to see San Francisco Bay from a hilltop near Pacifica and Millbrae. [2]

1770

April – Pedro Fages sees the Golden Gate while exploring the east shore of the bay. [2]

June 3 – A presidio and mission are established at Monterey bay. [2]

1773

December 16 – Boston Tea Party held by colonists in North America rebelling against British taxes. [4]

1775

April 19 – American Revolution breaks out in skirmish at Lexington, Massachusetts. [4]

1776

July 4 – U.S. Declaration of Independence. [4]

1781

October 19 – British Lord Cornwallis surrenders at Yorktown, Virginia, ending the American Revolution. [4]

1783

September 3 – United States independence recognized at the Treaty of Paris.

1787

September 17 – The delegates to the Constitutional Convention sign the U.S. Constitution.[4]

1789

April 30 – George Washington takes oath of office to become the first president of the United States and serves two terms until 1797.[4]

1803

With the Louisiana Purchase, the United States buys vast tracts of land from France.[4]

1804–1806

Lewis and Clark explore west of the Mississippi.[4]

1812–1814

United States is again at war with Britain; the White House is burned.[4]

1820

The U.S. Missouri Compromise ensures a balance between free and slave states.[4]

1822

Spanish rule ends in California; the United States recognizes Mexican independence.[2]

1828

July 16 – James Roosevelt (1828–1900) is born, father of Franklin Delano Roosevelt (1882–1945).[2]

1836

Texas wins independence from Mexico; Alamo is besieged. [4]

1838

The Trail of Tears: in the United States, thousands of eastern Native Americans are forced to move west. Many die on the trip.[4]

1839

Johann Augustus Sutter (1803–1880) arrives in California.[2]

1840

Richard Henry Dana's *Two Years Before the Mast* is published.

Lumber mills are established in the East Bay hills to log the redwoods.[7]

1842

October 19 – Commodore Thomas A. C. Jones of the U. S. Navy temporarily occupies Monterey.[2]

1845

The Irish Potato Famine begins.[2]

1846

Americans start arriving in Oakland in large numbers.[7]

1846–1848

After U.S. war against Mexico ends, California and New Mexico are ceded to the United States.[4]

1847

Survivors of the Donner Party are rescued.[2]

Yerba Buena is renamed San Francisco.[2]

1848

January 24 – Workers at John Sutter's mill on the American River discover gold.[7]

1849

The California gold rush starts.[2]

November 13 – California's first legislature is convened.

1850

Levi Strauss invents jeans in California.[4]

The U.S. Congress compromises over expansion of slavery and fails to resolve tension among the states.[4]

Union Iron and Brass Foundry, San Francisco, makes shaft bearings for the *John S. McKim*, the first propeller-driven commercial vessel built in the United States.[2]

A steam sawmill in the Oakland hills is the first power machinery in Oakland.[7]

September 9 – California is admitted to statehood.[2]

1850–1851

San Francisco is destroyed by fire six times in eighteen months.[7]

1851

June 9 – The San Francisco Committee of Vigilance is formed. It hangs 4, whips 1, deports 28, tries 15, releases 41.[2]

1852

May 4 – The California legislature establishes the town of Oakland.[7]

Steamboat landing is built at the foot of Broadway in Oakland.[7]

1853

The last time a person is mauled by a grizzly bear in the City of Oakland.[7]

In Oakland Henry Durant opens private academy with three pupils. It becomes the University of California.[7]

Oakland establishes regular police and fire service.[7]

1854

September 9 – FDR's mother, Sara Delano (1854–1914) is born.[2]

Sacramento becomes capital of California.[2]

March – Oakland establishes first newspaper, the *Alameda County Express*.[7]

1856

The anti-slavery Republican Party is formed in the United States.[4]

1860

Alameda has about 500 residents.[1]

Alameda's main train station is built on Park Street.[1]

Most of the redwood trees in the Oakland hills are logged off.[7]

1860's

The town of Alameda starts at east end of High Street, and the tiny village of Encinal at the north end of Grand Street.[1]

1861–1865

The United States in involved in the Civil War. Attempt by southern states to secede from the union is defeated.[4]

1864

Rail and ferry service is inaugurated by the San Francisco & Alameda Railroad (SF&A).[1]

1865

The Thirteenth Amendment to the U.S. Constitution outlaws slavery.[4]

1869

Suez Canal opens, increasing shipping opportunities for California.[8]

San Francisco & Alameda Railroad is absorbed by the Central Pacific (CP).[1]

1870

The town of Brooklyn is incorporated.[7]

First Webster Street bridge is opened.[1]

Alameda has 1,500 residents and its own newspaper.[1]

1872

Spring – The town of Alameda is incorporated, including the entire peninsula and western portion of Bay Farm Island.[1]

1873

Central Pacific builds a bridge over the estuary connecting Alice Street in Oakland to Alameda. [1]

Woodstock Station and the old San Francisco and Alameda Railroad pier are abandoned.[1]

1875

August – Gripped with panic, depositors descend upon the Bank of California to make withdrawals.[2]

The Alameda, Oakland and Piedmont Railroad begins running horse-cars between Alameda, Oakland and Piedmont.[1]

The Alameda, Oakland and Piedmont streetcar lines incorporate as the AO&P, later known as the Key System.

1876

Alexander Bell invents telephone.[4]

1877

U.S. inventor Thomas Edison invents the record player.[4]

1878

Alameda's second railroad, the South Pacific Coast (SPC), offers ferry service to San Francisco.[1]

1880

The population of Alameda reaches 5,700.[1]

In Alameda trains run every 30 minutes during the day and every 45 minutes until midnight. The commute from Alameda's East End [Fernside] to San Francisco Ferry Building takes 40 minutes.[1]

1882

The United States bans Chinese immigration.[6]

January 30 – Franklin Delano Roosevelt is born; he dies April 12, 1945.[2]

1883

Edison invents the light bulb. [4]

1884

October 11 – Anna Eleanor Roosevelt, wife of FDR, is born; she dies November 7, 1962.[2]

From Alameda, the South Pacific Coast Railroad builds a pier parallel to the estuary, which goes two and one-half miles out to deep water to a wharf and depot.[1]

With ten new stations in Alameda, the big new ferries make fifteen crossings daily to San Francisco.[1]

December 27 – The City of Alameda is organized.

1885

The Canadian Pacific railway opens.[4]

Central Pacific Railroad is reorganized as the Southern Pacific.[1]

Union Iron Works starts shipbuilding in San Francisco.[2]

1885–1895

FDR is tutored at home and abroad.[5]

1886

The Statue of Liberty is dedicated.[6]

1888

 Benjamin Harrison is elected president.[6]

1889

North Dakota, South Dakota, Washington and Montana become states.[6]

1890

Idaho and Wyoming become states.[6]

The population of Alameda reaches 11,000.[1]

1890's

Alameda's pier is filled in with rock and dredging materials and becomes known as the Alameda Mole.[1]

1892

Grover Cleveland is elected president.[6]

1893

Electric street cars replace horse-cars on the Alameda, Oakland and Piedmont Line.[1]

1896

Utah becomes a state.[6]

William McKinley is elected president.[6]

1896–1900

FDR attends Groton School. Headmaster Rev. Endicott Peabody says FDR possesses more than ordinary intelligence.[5]

1898

April 25 – United States declares war on Spain over Cuba.[6]

Spanish-American War: Spain gives Cuba independence; the United States takes Puerto Rico, Guam, and the Philippines as colonies.[4]

1900

Eastman Kodak introduces its one-dollar Brownie box camera, making photography accessible to everyone. [3]

FDR's father, James Roosevelt, dies. [5]

Guglielmo Marconi sends the first transatlantic wireless message from England to Newfoundland. [3]

Alameda population reaches 16,500.[1]

FDR enters Harvard University. [6]

President William McKinley is re-elected. [6]

1901

September 6 – President William McKinley is shot by anarchist Leon Czolgosz in Buffalo, New York, at the World's Fair.

September 14 – President William McKinley dies and Theodore Roosevelt becomes president at age 42.[3]

1901–1902

FDR writes for the *Harvard Crimson*. [5]

1902

The United States acquires control over the Panama Canal. [6]

Railroads reign for fast transportation; the *20th Century Ltd.* sets a record by traveling the rails from New York to Chicago in twenty hours. [3]

1903

June 24 – FDR graduates from Harvard.

FDR becomes engaged to Anna Eleanor Roosevelt.[5]

Henry Ford founds the Ford Motor Company, a key step forward in automobile history.[3]

Jack London publishes *The Call of the Wild*.[3]

The Alaskan frontier is settled.[6]

The Wright brothers make their first flight at Kitty Hawk, North Carolina.[3]

Western Pacific Railroad is founded in San Francisco.

1904

FDR is elected permanent chairman of the Harvard class of 1904.[5]

FDR enters Columbia Law School.[6]

President Theodore Roosevelt adds the Roosevelt Corollary to the Monroe Doctrine, asserting the United States' right to be an "international police power."[3]

The Russo-Japanese War marks Japan's emergence as a world military power; President Theodore Roosevelt brokers the peace agreement between the two powers in New Hampshire.[3]

Theodore Roosevelt wins presidential election.[6]

Work begins on the Panama Canal, signaling an important shift in U.S. and Caribbean relations. [3]

1905

March 17 – FDR marries Anna Eleanor Roosevelt, fifth cousin once removed. The couple tour Europe on their honeymoon trip.[5]

A new elegant Alameda Mole ferry depot opens. The last train was in 1939, and it was demolished in 1941.[1]

The National Audubon Society meets for the first time during the presidency of Theodore Roosevelt, champion of environmental conservation. [3]

1906

Theodore Roosevelt wins the Nobel Peace Prize for his role in negotiating an end to the Russo-Japanese War.[3]

Lawyer Mohandas K. Gandhi begins nonviolent resistance to protest the treatment of Indians in South Africa.[3]

U.S. troops occupy Cuba.[6]

April 18 at 5:12 A.M – A great earthquake hits San Francisco; 2,500 people die in the quake and the ensuing fires.[3]

1907

The first canned tuna is packed in San Pedro, California.[3]

FDR is admitted to New York bar.[6]

FDR is employed as junior clerk in law firm of Carter, Ledyard and Milburne, New York City.[6]

President Theodore Roosevelt bars all Japanese immigration to the United States.[6]

Oklahoma enters the Union and becomes the 46th state.[3]

1908

President Theodore Roosevelt visits Panama, the first U.S. president to travel abroad while in office.[3]

William Howard Taft is elected president.[6]

Henry Ford develops the first Model T automobile, which sells for $850.[3]

1909

FDR becomes a member of the Hudson-Fulton Celebration Commission.[6]

NAACP is founded under W.E.B. DuBois.[6]

Japanese forces begin a 36-year occupation of Korea, which they formally annex the following year.[3]

1910

November 8 – FDR is elected to the New York state senate (opposed by John F. Schlosser), with 52 percent of the vote.[5]

Alameda population reaches 25,000.

China abolishes slavery.[6]

Angel Island in San Francisco Bay opens as a quarantine station and point of entry for immigrants from Asia.[3]

1911

FDR declares his support for the Women's Suffrage Movement.[5]

The Chinese Revolution begins.[6]

November 28 – FDR receives degree of Master Mason conferred by Holland Lodge No. 8, New York City.[6]

Southern Pacific starts to use electric trains in place of the coal-fired steam trains.

1912

November 5 – FDR is re-elected to the New York state senate, (opposed by George A. Vossler), with 62 percent of vote.[5]

The *Titanic* sinks after hitting an iceberg in the North Atlantic; 1,513 passengers are lost, 711 are rescued.[3]

Theodore Roosevelt runs as the Progressive party candidate for the White House, drawing votes away from Republican incumbent William Howard Taft. Woodrow Wilson wins the election.[3]

New Mexico and Arizona become states, the last new states until 1959.[3]

1913

FDR is appointed Assistant Secretary of the Navy by President Woodrow Wilson.[5]

Federal income tax is introduced in the United States through the Sixteenth Amendment.[6]

1914

After ten years of work and 30,000 casualties during its construction, the Panama Canal opens to shipping traffic.[3]

James W. Gerard defeats FDR in the Democratic primary for the U.S. Senate.[5]

June 28 – World War I breaks out in Europe after the assassination of Archduke Franz Ferdinand of Austria.[3]

1915

May 17 – German U-boat sinks the passenger ship SS *Lusitania*, killing 1,198.[3]

Long-distance telephone service begins between New York and San Francisco.[3]

FDR becomes a member of the National Commission, Panama-Pacific Exposition.[6]

German U-boats blockade Britain, intensifying the hostilities of World War I.[3]

1916

In World War I, the Battle of the Somme rages for 140 days on a 20-mile front. Of three million soldiers engaged in battle, over 1.4 million soldiers are killed.

Germans intensify their air war on England with dirigibles and the first airplane raid on London.[3]

President Woodrow Wilson narrowly wins re-election with the campaign slogan, "He kept us out of war." [3]

1917

United States breaks diplomatic relations with Germany.[6]

The United States adopts FDR's plan to sow 70,000 mines in the North Sea as a barrier against German submarines.[5]

April 6 – The United States declares war on Germany, in response to her policy of unrestricted submarine warfare.[3]

America enters World War I and Congress authorizes emergency shipbuilding in San Francisco Bay Area.[2]

Czar Nicholas of Russia abdicates as revolution begins.[6]

1918

November 11 – Armistice is signed between Allies and Germany.[6]

Airmail service begins between Washington, D.C. and New York City. The price of a stamp is 24 cents.[3]

An influenza epidemic spreads across Asia and war-ravaged Europe to the Americas. The epidemic eventually kills 20 million people, including 500,000 Americans.[3]

FDR supports President Wilson's internationalism and endorses U.S. participation in a League of Nations international peacekeeping organization.[5]

FDR becomes overseer at Harvard University until 1924.[6]

1918

July–September – FDR tours European naval bases.[6]

President Wilson proclaims "Fourteen Points" as war aims.[6]

Germany's Kaiser Wilhelm II abdicates, leading to the end of hostilities in Europe. The combined death toll from the war passes six million. Another twenty million are wounded.[3]

1919

January 6 – Theodore Roosevelt dies in Oyster Bay, New York.[6]

FDR attends the Versailles Peace Conference with President Wilson.[5]

FDR travels to Europe to supervise the dismantling of the naval establishment.[5]

The Eighteenth Amendment prohibits sale and manufacture of intoxicating liquors.[6]

President Wilson presides over the first League of Nations and wins the Nobel Peace Prize.[6]

The Treaty of Versailles assigns most of the blame for World War I to Germany. The treaty requires Germany to cede territory to France, Belgium, and Poland, give up its colonies and pay extensive war reparations.[3]

1920

July 6 – FDR runs for vice president on the Democratic ticket with James N. Cox at the Democratic national convention in San Francisco.[5]

August 6 – FDR resigns as Assistant Secretary of Navy.[5]

In the presidential elections, Republican Warren Harding defeats James Cox and FDR to become the 29th president of the United States with Calvin Coolidge as vice president.[3]

Prohibition goes into effect; sales of coffee, soft drinks, and ice cream floats skyrocket.[3]

FDR returns to law practice in the firm of Emmet, Marvin and Roosevelt.[6]

The United States ratifies the Nineteenth Amendment, granting suffrage to American women. Carrie Chapman Catt founds the League of Women Voters to encourage women's participation in politics.[3]

1921

August – FDR is stricken with poliomyelitis (polio) at age 39, at Campobello, New Brunswick, Canada, [6] and spends much of the next seven years seeking to recover the use of his legs.[5]

Adolf Hitler's storm-troopers begin to terrorize political opponents.[6]

FDR becomes vice president of Fidelity and Deposit Company of Maryland in New York City.[6]

1922

Benito Mussolini forms a fascist government in Italy.[6]

The Irish Free State is established.[6]

Soviet states form the U.S.S.R.[6]

Due to heavy reparation payments from World War I, the German mark begins to devalue.[3]

1923

President Harding dies; he is succeeded by Vice President Calvin Coolidge.[6]

1924

June – FDR delivers "Happy Warrior" speech nominating Al Smith for president at the Democratic National Convention.[5]

FDR forms new law practice, Roosevelt and O'Connor.[5]

FDR manages Al Smith's presidential campaign, unsuccessfully.[5]

Republican President Calvin Coolidge is re-elected on a platform of "Coolidge Prosperity" and pro-business policies.[3]

In Russia, Vladimir Lenin dies, to be succeeded by a triumvirate headed by Joseph Stalin.[3]

1925

Hitler reorganizes the Nazi party and publishes the first volume of *Mein Kampf*.[6]

1926

After eliminating his competition, Josef Stalin establishes himself as a virtual dictator in the Communist Soviet Union, ushering in a 27-year reign.[3]

In Italy, Benito Mussolini makes fascism the state party.[3]

FDR's first book *Whither Bound* is published.[5]

Emperor Showa Tenno Hirohito comes to power in Japan after the death of his father; in ensuing years Japan's military branches grow in size and influence.[3]

Fascist youth organizations are founded in Germany and Italy.[6]

1927

FDR founds the Warm Springs Foundation in Georgia, a pioneering therapy center for polio victims.[5]

An economic conference in Geneva is attended by fifty-two nations.[6]

FDR's *The Happy Warrior, Alfred E. Smith* is published.[6]

Joseph Stalin becomes Soviet dictator.[6]

Cheers greet the *Spirit of St. Louis* when Charles Lindbergh lands in Paris. It is the first nonstop solo transatlantic flight in the history of aviation. Lindbergh flew 3,600 miles in 33 hours, forsaking a radio for additional gasoline.[3]

1928

November 6 – FDR is elected governor of New York (opposed by Albert Ottinger), with 50.3 percent of the vote.[5]

In the midst of Prohibition, physicians write prescriptions for whiskey as a therapeutic substance.[3]

Governor Alfred E. Smith places FDR in nomination for president at Democratic National Convention.[6]

The United States and many other nations sign Kellog-Brand pacts to outlaw war.[6]

Republican Herbert Hoover, Secretary of Commerce, is elected 31st president of the United States.[3]

1929

The first round-the-world flight is completed by the airship *Graf Zeppelin*, named for its inventor.[3]

October 29 – Stock prices in New York crash on "Black Thursday." The Great Depression begins.[6]

1930

November 4 – FDR is re-elected governor (opposed by Charles H. Tuttle), with 63 percent of the vote.[6]

Alameda population reaches 35,000.[1]

The Bank of U.S. and its many branches close, the most significant bank closing of the year.[6]

Over 1,300 American banks fail, and unemployment exceeds 4 million as the depression intensifies.[3]

1931

"The Star Spangled Banner," originally written in 1814 by Francis Scott Key, becomes the American national anthem by order of Congress.[3]

As worldwide depression deepens, Governor Roosevelt establishes the Temporary Emergency Relief Administration (TERA), making New York the first state government to assist in depression relief efforts.[5]

Japan occupies Manchuria, marking the rise of Japanese militarism and drawing a hard-line stance from Secretary of State Henry Stimson.[3]

Emigration from the United States exceeds immigration for the first time as depression deepens.[6]

Unemployed Americans march on the White House, demanding a national program of employment at a minimum wage. They are turned away.[3]

1932

April – FDR criticizes the Republican Party for its lack of concern for the "forgotten man" at the bottom of the economic pyramid.[5]

FDR's *Government-Not Politics* is published.[5]

In the United States, the Great Depression continues to take a heavy toll: in this year alone, 1,161 banks fail, nearly 20,000 businesses go bankrupt, and 21,000 people commit suicide.[3]

Wall Street's Dow Jones Industrial Average hits its depression-era low, 41.22.[3]

Franklin Delano Roosevelt, pledging a "New Deal," is elected president for the first of his four terms.[3]

1933

February 15 – Giuseppe Zangara fires a shot at FDR in assassination attempt in Miami, Florida.[5]

March 4 – FDR is inaugurated as the 32nd U.S. president. He reassures Americans that "The only thing we have to fear is fear itself."[5]

March 8 – FDR conducts the first of his 998 press conferences.[5]

March 9 – The Emergency Banking Relief Act is passed. FDR is granted sweeping powers to deal with the nation's shaky banking system.[5]

March 12 – FDR delivers the first of his many radio "fireside chats," focusing on the state of the banking system.[5]

FDR appoints Francis Perkins as Secretary of Labor, the first female cabinet member in U.S. history.[5]

FDR ensures that black Americans are included in federal jobs programs, but allows segregation.[5]

Frequency modulations (FM) permit radio reception without static.[3]

In the famous first 100 days, FDR creates the "alphabet agencies": CCC, TVA, AAA, FERA, NRA, CWA to help rebuild America's infrastructure and bring relief and jobs to millions of Americans.[5]

The Twenty-First Amendment repeals prohibition.[6]

The federal government passes a flurry of innovative social legislation, providing a New Deal for all Americans.[3]

FDR's *Looking Forward* is published.[6]

The United States recognizes the U.S.S.R. and resumes trade.[6]

Adolf Hitler becomes chancellor of crisis-ridden Germany. By the end of the year, Hitler has proclaimed the Third Reich, opened the first concentration camp at Dachau, eliminated all political parties other than National Socialism, and consolidated his dictatorial rule.[3]

1934

October 25 – The *Electra*, a 165B class Coast Guard sub-chaser, is launched by the Manitowoc Shipbuilding Corporation of Manitowoc, Wisconsin.[9]

In an effort to maintain the southern congressional vote for his New Deal legislation, FDR does not support anti-lynching laws.[5]

FDR's *On Our Way* is published.[5]

The Dust Bowl hits the U.S. west, blowing 300 million tons of topsoil away and devastating farmland in Kansas, Texas, Colorado, and Oklahoma.[3]

1935

May – FDR creates the Works Projects Administration (WPA), the federal government's largest job program for unemployed Americans.[5]

November 11 – *Electra* is transferred to the navy and reclassified as AG25 to designate it as auxiliary miscellaneous vessel.

Italy invades Ethiopia. Hitler publicly begins to re-arm Germany, creating the Luftwaffe in violation of the Versailles Treaty. Both Germany and Italy are beginning to test their strength.[3]

The Wagner Labor Relations Act is passed and prohibits employers from interfering with union organizing activities and creates the National Labor Relations Board to ends strikes.[5]

The Social Security Act, the most significant piece of New Deal legislation, passes Congress.[5]

Artists in the newly created Works Projects Administration are paid to decorate federal buildings.[3]

1936

FDR is re-elected president, defeating Alfred Landon, with 60.8 percent of the vote.[5]

Hitler and Mussolini form the Rome-Berlin Axis.[6]

Joseph Stalin begins a "great purge" to liquidate his enemies. By 1939, over 8 million are dead and perhaps 10 million imprisoned.[3]

Roosevelt signs the Neutrality Act.[6]

The Spanish Civil War begins, marking the growing rift between the fascist right and Marxist left in Europe. Hundreds of Americans volunteer for "Lincoln Brigades" to help fight Franco's fascism.[3]

1937

February 5 – FDR plans to reform the Supreme Court by adding one new justice for each current justice failing to retire by the age of 70 up to a maximum of six. Congress defeats the plan.[5]

Japan invades China.[3]

Italy withdraws from the League of Nations and joins a Germany-Japan pact.[3]

The Memorial Day Massacre leaves ten steel strikers dead in Chicago.[3]

Amelia Earhart and her aircraft disappear mysteriously over the Pacific.[3]

1938

FDR sends appeal to Hitler and Mussolini to settle European problems amicably.[6]

Launching military aggression that would later escalate, Hitler annexes Austria. British Prime Minister Neville Chamberlain and French leaders make the historic mistake of "appeasing" Germany at Munich.[3]

1939

Albert Einstein writes a letter to FDR regarding the possibility of using uranium to initiate a nuclear chain reaction, the fundamental process behind the atomic bomb.[3]

FDR begins correspondence with Winston Churchill, prime minister of Great Britain.[5]

FDR believes that a longer Christmas shopping season will boost the economy and proclaims that Thanksgiving will fall on the fourth Thursday of November every year. This shift is soon passed into law.[3]

Hitler's Germany invades Poland, which falls in a month. France and Great Britain declare war on Germany. Spain, exhausted from civil war, remains neutral.[3]

1940

November 5 – FDR is re-elected president, defeating Wendell L. Willkie, with 54.8 percent of the vote.[5]

December 29 – FDR delivers a fireside chat on national security and preparation. He says "There can be no appeasement of ruthlessness. We must be the great arsenal of democracy." [5]

FDR engineers the Lend-Lease Act giving military aid to Britain in exchange for long-term leases on air and naval bases.[5]

Germany launches a full-scale air war against England and extends persecution of the Jews into Poland, Romania, and the Netherlands.[3]

The United States adopts its first-ever peacetime military draft, anticipating the escalation of World War II in Europe.[3]

Winston Churchill succeeds Neville Chamberlain as Britain's prime minister.[3]

Shipbuilding in the San Francisco Bay Area increases with new orders for navy and cargo vessels.[2]

Nazi Germany successfully invades Denmark, the Netherlands, Belgium, and France in quick succession. France is divided into a northern occupied zone and the collaborative Vichy regime in the south.[3]

1941

February – FDR and Churchill confer at a series of secret meetings in Newfoundland and draft the Atlantic Charter, a declaration of principles which lay the basis for the United Nations.

May 27 – FDR appoints a Fair Employment Practices Committee (FEPC) to enforce his executive order banning discrimination in government and the defense industries.[5]

September 7 – FDR's mother, Sara Delano Roosevelt, dies.[5]

December 7 – Japan attacks Pearl Harbor, drawing the United States into war. Five battleships are sunk,

Nazi troops invade Soviet Russia, extending as far as Moscow, a move that will ultimately have drastic consequences for Germany.[3]

Admiral Chester Nimitz takes control of the Pacific fleet.[3]

The U.S. Treasury begins issuing Liberty Bonds to raise money for the WW II effort.[3]

The Lend-Lease Act permits President Roosevelt to send military supplies to Allies.[3]

1942

October – FDR announces a plan to try all Nazi war criminals.[5]

Americans tighten their belts in preparation for wartime shortages; coffee, sugar, and gasoline are rationed.[3]

President Franklin Roosevelt allocates more than 80 percent of his budget to the war effort and the production of planes, tanks, and military supplies. The ranks of the depression-era unemployed begin to flow into industry fueled by war.[3]

President Roosevelt issues Executive Order 9066, calling for the internment of 110,000 Japanese Americans.[3]

The U.S. government establishes the Manhattan Project, led by Robert Oppenheimer, to coordinate ongoing American efforts to design and build the atomic bomb.[3]

Allies agree not to make separate peace treaties with the enemies.[6]

Congress authorizes major shipbuilding in the San Francisco Bay Area.[2]

The U.S. government transfers more than 100,000 Nisei (Japanese Americans) from the West Coast to inland concentration camps.[6]

Nazi policy builds on its anti-Semitism to make Jewish extermination a systematic policy, the so-called "Final Solution."[3]

1943

January – At the Casablanca Conference, FDR and Churchill announce they will accept nothing less than an unconditional surrender from the Axis powers.[5]

November – FDR, Churchill and Russian leader Joseph Stalin meet in Teheran, the capital of Iran, for their first "Big Three" conference, to discuss the upcoming Allied invasion of Western Europe.[5]

Allied forces invade Italy, resulting in resignation by the Fascist Italian dictator Benito Mussolini and Italy's surrender to the Allies.[3]

Japan has its smallest rice harvest in fifty years.[3]

President Roosevelt repeals the Chinese Exclusion Acts of 1882 and 1902, making Chinese immigrants eligible for U.S. citizenship for the first time in more than fifty years.[3]

The Soviet army defeats German troops at Stalingrad.[3]

Allied bombings of Germany begin.[6]

Jews in Poland's Warsaw Ghetto heroically stand up against the Nazis, resisting the German army for six weeks.[3]

Despite early losses in the war, Allied forces rally and defeat German Field Marshal Erwin Rommel in North Africa.[3]

1944

January – FDR signs Executive Order 9417 establishing the War Refugee Board to aid in rescuing Jews and other victims of the war. [5]

June 6 – Allied troops storm the beaches at Normandy, France, on D-day under the command of General Dwight D. Eisenhower.[3]

November 7 – FDR is re-elected to a fourth term, defeating Thomas E. Dewey, with 53.5 percent of the vote.[5]

Congress passes the G.I. Bill of Rights, which finances the college education and home mortgages for many WW II veterans after the war.[3]

The Allies liberate France and Vichy falls.[3]

The U.S. Supreme Court upholds the constitutionality of Japanese-American internment.[3]

1945

January and February – FDR, Churchill and Stalin meet at the Yalta Conference to discuss the future of Europe, Asia and the United Nations.[5]

The Potsdam Conference outlines post-war policies toward Germany and Japan. The United Nations is established at a San Francisco conference and holds its first meeting the following year.[3]

April – Benito Mussolini, (1883–1945), Fascist dictator of Italy from 1922 to 1943, is executed.[6]

April 12 – FDR dies of a stroke in Warm Springs, Georgia. [5]

April 12 – Vice President Harry S. Truman becomes president in the closing days of World War II.[3]

April 15 – FDR is buried at Hyde Park, New York.

May 1 – Hitler commits suicide. [6]

May 8 – Germany surrenders.

July 16 – U.S. scientists test the first atomic bomb.[4]

August 6 – U.S. planes drop atomic bomb on Hiroshima.

August 9 – U.S. planes drop atomic bomb on Nagasaki.

August 14 – Japan surrenders.

January 27 – Soviet troops liberate prisoners in the concentration camp at Auschwitz.

An estimated 6 million people died in the German camps.[3]

World War II ends; the total human casualties from the war exceed 50 million people.[3]

---

[1] Minor (1993).
[2] Bean (1988).
[3] History Channel website [01/10/03] www.historychannel.com.
[4] History Channel website [01/10/03] www.historychannel.com.
[5] FDR Library website [01/10/03] www.fdrlibrary.marist.edu.
[6] FDR Life and Times. See FDR Library website [01/10/03] www.fdrlibrary.marist.edu.
[7] Bagwell (1996).
[8] Harrison (1971).
[9] Jaffee (1998).

22 - Historic Data Sources

The date [01/13/03] [mm/dd/yy] in a website reference indicates the date I last opened the website.

Vessel Photography

Mariah's Eyes Photography
Mariah Healey
2111 San Jose Ave.
Alameda CA 94501
Phone: 510-864-1144
Email: meyesphoto@mindspring.com

Panorama Designs
Robert Esposito
400 Beacon Hill Drive #10
Hoquiam WA 98550-2764
Phone: 360-533-6270
Email: panorama@olynet.com

Historic vessels
Glossary of Tall Ships Terms
See *Lady Washington* home page.
Website: [01/10/03] http://ladywashington.linsect.com

ARTSHIP
The ARTSHIP Foundation
103 10th Avenue
Oakland CA 96407
Phone: 510-268-4978 Fax: 510-238-5104
Website: [01/10/03] www.artship.org
Photograph on page 149.

Barque *Californian*
San Diego Maritime Museum,
Home of the World's Oldest Active Ship
1492 North Harbor Drive
San Diego CA 92101
Phone: 619-234-9153
Website: [01/10/03] www.sdmaritime.org
Photograph on page 113.

Gaff-rigged schooner *Gas Light*
Gas Light Charters
60c Liberty Ship Way
Sausalito CA 94965
Phone: 415-331-2769
Email: gaslightcharters @hotmail.com
Website: [01/10/03] www.gaslightcharters.com
Photograph on page 124.

Brigantine *Hawaiian Chieftain*
3020 Bridgeway, Suite 266
Sausalito CA 94965
Phone: 415-331-3214
Website: [01/10/03] www.hawaiianchieftain.com
Photograph on page 114.

USS *Hornet*
Aircraft Carrier Hornet Museum
Pier 3, Alameda Point
Alameda CA 94501
Phone: 510-521-8448 Fax: 510-521-8327
Email: hornetok@aol.com
Photograph on page 151.

Topsail schooner *Ka'iulani*
The *Ka'iulani* terminated commercial operations
effective July 23, 2001, and is for sale.
Discovery Yacht Charters
Website: [01/10/03] www.sfyacht.com
Photograph on page 113.

Liberty Ship *Jeremiah O'Brien*
National Liberty Ship Memorial, Inc.
Fort Mason, Building A
San Francisco CA 94123-1382
Phone: 415-441-3101
Fax: 415-441-3712
Email: liberty@ssjeremiahobrien.org
Website: [01/10/03] www.ssjeremiahobrien.org

Brig *Lady Washington*
Grays Harbor Historical Seaport
Phone: 1-800-200-LADY
Please, no email reservations.
Website: [01/10/03] http://ladywashington.linsect.com
Photograph on page 114.

Lightship *RELIEF*
United States Lighthouse Society
244 Kearny Street, 5th floor
San Francisco CA 94108
Phone: 415-362-7255 Fax: 415-362-7464
Website: [01/10/03] www.maine.com/lights/uslhs.htm
Photograph on page 8.

Classic yawl *Orion*
Orion Charters Inc.
Capt. Keith Korporaal
3842 Liggett Drive
San Diego CA 92106
Phone: 619-574-7504
Email: orionkeith@msn.com
Website: [01/10/03] www.orionsailing.com
Photograph on page 122.

Victory Ship *Red Oak Victory*
Richmond Museum of History
400 Nevin Avenue
PO Box 1267
Richmond CA 94802
Phone: 510-237-2933
Photograph on page 152.

Barque *Star of India*
San Diego Maritime Museum,
Home of the World's Oldest Active Ship
1492 North Harbor Drive
San Diego CA 92101
Phone: 619-234-9153
Website: [01/20/03] www.sdmaritime.org
Photograph on page 163.

Sequoia
Sequoia Presidential Yacht Foundation
P.O. Box 19106
Alexandria VA 22320
202-872-8228
USS Sequoia Presidential Yacht Official website:
[01/10/03] www.sequoiayacht.com

Museums & Libraries

California Maritime Academy
A California State University of Engineering,
Technology & Marine Transportation
200 Maritime Academy Drive
Vallejo CA 94590
Phone: 707-654-1000
Website: [01/10/03] www.csum.edu

Bancroft Library
University of California
Berkeley CA 94720-6000
Phone: 510-642-6481

Cable Car Museum
1201 Mason Street
San Francisco CA 94108
Phone: 415-474-1887
Website: [01/10/03] www.sfcablecar.com

California Military Museum
1119 Second Street
Sacramento CA 95814
Phone: 916-422-2883
Fax: 916-422-7532
Website: [01/10/03] www.militarymuseum.org

California State Railroad Museum
111 "I" Street
Sacramento CA 95814
Phone: 916-323-9280
Website: [01/10/03] www.csrmf.org

The Gold Coast Railroad Museum
Home of the Ferdinand Magellan
FDR's Rail Car.
12450 S.W. 152nd Street
Miami FL 33177-1402
Phone: 305-253-0063
Phone: 888-60-TRAIN (888-608-7246)
Fax: 305-233-4641
Website: [01/10/03]
www.goldcoast-railroad.org
Email: webmaster@goldcoastrailroad.org

Golden Gate National Recreation Area
Fort Mason, Building 201
San Francisco CA 94123-0022
Phone: 415-561-4700
Fax: 415-561-4750
Website: [01/10/03] www.nps.gov/goga
Email: George_Su@nps.gov

Alcatraz Island Visitor Center
Phone: 415-705-1042
Location: Alcatraz Island is located in the middle of
the San Francisco Bay; a ferry, located at Pier 41,
will take you to the island.

Cliff House Visitor Center
Phone: 415-556-8642
Location: Located below the street level where Point
Lobos Avenue meets the Great Highway, on the
western side of San Francisco.

Fort Point Bookstore
Phone: 415-556-1693
Location: The Fort Point Bookstore is located inside the fort, underneath the south anchorage of the Golden Gate Bridge, on the northernmost part of the Presidio.

Marin Headlands Visitor Center
Phone: 415-331-1540
Location: The Marin Headlands Visitor Center is located in the historic Fort Barry Chapel, at the intersection of Field and Bunker Roads.

Muir Woods Visitor Center
Phone: 415-388-7368
Location: Muir Woods Visitor Center is located at the entrance to Muir Woods, approximately 12 miles north of the Golden Gate Bridge.

Pacific West Regional Information Center
Phone: 415-561-4700
Location: The Pacific West Region Information Center is located on the first floor of Building 201 at Fort Mason.

William Penn Mott Jr. Visitor Center
Phone: 415-561-4323
Main post, 102 Montgomery & Lincoln Blvd.
Presidio of San Francisco.

The Maritime History Virtual Archives
Website: [01/10/03] http://pc-78-120.udac.se:8001/WWW/Nautica/Nautica.html.

Oakland Museum of California
1000 Oak Street
Oakland CA 94607
Phone: 510-238-2914
Website: [01/10/03] www.museumca.org
[Links to all major museums.]

Oakland Public Library
The Oakland History Room
125 14th Street
Oakland CA 94612

L. J. Quinn's Lighthouse
Historic Restaurant & Pub
51 Embarcadero Cove
Oakland CA 94606
Phone: 510-536-2050

Richmond Museum of History
400 Nevin Avenue
P.O. Box 1267
Richmond CA 94802
Phone: 510-235-7387
Fax: 510-235-4345

Museum of the City of San Francisco
PMB 423
945 Taraval Street
San Francisco CA 94116
Phone: 415-928-0289
Fax: 415-731-4204
Website: [01/10/03] www.sfmuseum.org
Exhibit at City Hall, South Light Court, Grove and Van Ness

San Francisco Maritime
National Park Association
P.O. Box 4703
900 Beach Street
San Francisco CA 94147-0310
Phone: 415-561-6662 ext. 28
Email: info@maritime.org
Website: [03/10/03] www.maritime.org

San Francisco Maritime
National Historical Park
Fort Mason, Building 204
San Francisco CA 94123
Phone: 415-561-7100
Small Boat Shop: 415-556-4031
State of California Office of Historic Preservation
Website: [01/10/03]
http://ohp.parks.ca.gov/default.asp

The Museum of the Franklin D. Roosevelt
Presidential Library
4079 Albany Post Road
Hyde Park NY 12538
Website: [01/10/03] www.fdrlibrary.marist.edu
Email: roosevelt.library@nara.gov
Phone: 845-229-5321

Sagamore Hill National Historic Site
20 Sagamore Hill Road
Oyster Bay NY 11771
Phone: 516-922-4271
Website: [01/10/03] www.nps.gov/sahi
Sagamore Hill was the home of Theodore Roosevelt, 26th president of the United States, from 1886 until his death in 1919.

Vallejo Naval and Historical Museum
Old Vallejo City Hall
734 Marin Street
Vallejo CA 94590
Phone: 707-643-0077
Website: [01/10/03] www.vallejomuseum.org

Historical Societies

American Aviation Historical Society
Northern California Chapter
P.O. Box 7081
San Carlos California 94070-7081
Phone: 650-631-4207
Website: [01/10/03]
www.norcalaahs.org/contact.htm

The Berkeley Historical Society
1931 Center Street
PO Box 1190
Berkeley CA 94701-1190
Phone: 510-848-0181
Website: [01/10/03] www.ci.berkeley.ca.us/histsoc
[Links to Bay Area Historical Societies.]

Chinese Historical Society
650 Commercial Street
San Francisco CA 94111
Phone: 415-391-1188

San Francisco History Center
San Francisco Public Library
100 Larkin Street, 6th Floor
San Francisco CA 94102
Phone: 415-557-4567
Website: [01/10/03] www.historyroom.com

San Francisco Maritime
National Park Association
P.O. Box 4703
900 Beach Street
San Francisco CA 94147-0310
Phone: 415-561-6662 ext. 28
Email: info@maritime.org
Website: [01/10/03] www.maritime.org

San Francisco Maritime
National Historical Park
Fort Mason, Building 204
San Francisco CA 94123
Phone: 415-561-7100
Small Boat Shop: 415-556-4031
Website: [01/10/03] http://ohp.parks.ca.gov

Western Aerospace Museum
8260 Boeing Street
Oakland CA 94614
Phone: 510-638-7100
Website: [01/10/03]
www.westernaerospacemuseum.org

Muwekma Ohlone Indian Tribe
Website: [01/10/03] www.muwekma.org

23 - Website References

Some of the information in the book came from websites; unfortunately, a number of these websites are no longer active. To assure accuracy I have tried to use only those websites where I felt the data was reliable and to cross check that data with data from other sources. The date [01/15/03] [mm/dd/yy] in a website reference indicated when I last opened a website.

Explorers

Captain James Cook [01/13/03]
    www.jetcity.com/~kirok/cook.shtml

Camp David

[01/13/03] http://travel.to/campdavid

FDR

Anna Eleanor Roosevelt [01/10/03]
    http://encarta.msn.com
Facts [01/10/03]
    http://gi.Grolier.com/presidents/nbk/quickfac/32fro
    os.html
Fireside Chat [01/10/03]
    http://www.mhrcc.org/fdr/fdr.html
Franklin D. Roosevelt Library, Museum, and Digital
    Archives, [01/10/03] www.fdrlibrary.marist.edu

Glossary

Washington home page [01/10/03]
    http://ladywashington.linsect.com
Glossary of U.S. Naval abbreviations [01/10/03]
http://www.history.navy.mil/books/OPNAV20-P1000
Maritime Terms and Definitions (circa 1944)
    [01/10/03] www.usmm.net/terms.html

Jack London

Digital Library [01/10/03]
    http://sunsite.Berkeley.edu/London
State Historic Park [01/10/03]
http://www.parks.sonoma.net/JLPark.html

Historic Aircraft

Presidential Aircraft
    [01/10/03] http://travel.to/campdavid
Amelia Earhart [01/10/03]
    http://ellensplace.net/eae_intr.html
Amelia Earhart [01/10/03]
    www.incwell.com/Biographies/Earhart.html
Boeing [01/10/03] www.boeing.com
Douglas DC-3 [01/10/03]
    www.pbs.org/kcet/chasingthesun/planes/dc3.html
Flying Tankers at [01/10/03]
    www.martinmars.com/aircraft.html
Martin [01/10/03] www.martinstateairport.com
Pan Am Clippers
[01/10/03] www.panam.org
[01/10/03] www.sfmuseum.org
Sikorsky [01/10/03] www.sikorsky.com
VP Navy - Consolidated P2Y Aircraft [01/10/03]
    www.vpnavy.com/webdocp2y.html

Historic Events

Mexican War [01/10/03]
    www.dmwv.org/mexwar/mexwar.htm
The Muwekma Ohlone [01/10/03] www.muwekma.org
Statue of Liberty [01/10/03] http://www.nps.gov/stli
Suez Canal [01/10/03]
    http://www.library.cornell.edu/colldev/mideast/sue
    z.htm

Historic Landmarks

Historic Landmarks [01/10/03]
   www.donaldlaird.com/landmarks
State of California Office of Historic Preservation
   [01/10/03]
   http://ohp.parks.ca.gov/default.asp?page_id=21381

Historic Port and Ship Lines

American President Lines [01/10/03] www.apl.com
Jack London Area Development [01/10/03]
   www.estuaryplan.com/jack_lon.htm
Matson Navigation [01/10/03] www.matson.com
P&O Lines [01/10/03] www.p-and-o.com
Port of Oakland [01/10/03] www.portofoakland.com
Seaports [01/10/03] www.seaportsinfo.com

Historic Shipyards

AGL [8/12/00]
   www.contracts.orc.doc.gov/fedcl/opinions/99opin/9
   7-160L.html
Mare Island Shipyards [01/10/03]
   www.vallejomuseum.org
Matson Navigation [8/12/00]
   www.contracts.orc.doc.gov/fedcl/opinions/99opin/9
   7-160L.html
Southern Pacific Co. United Engineering, Matson
   Navigation Todd, AGL [8/12/00]
   www.contracts.orc.doc.gov/fedcl/opinions/99opin/9
   7-160L.html
Todd Shipyards [8/12/00]
   www.contracts.orc.doc.gov/fedcl/opinions/99opin/9
   7-160L.html
United Engineering [8/12/00]
   www.contracts.orc.doc.gov/fedcl/opinions/99opin/9
   7-160L.html

Historic Vessels

Alma [01/10/03] www.nps.gov/safr/local/alma.html
ARTSHIP Foundation [6/5/01] www.artship.org
Balclutha [01/10/03]
   www.nps.gov/safr/local/balc.html
C.A. Thayer [01/10/03]
   www.nps.gov/safr/local/thayer.html

Eppleton Hall [01/10/03]
   www.nps.gov/safr/local/eppie.html
Dictionary of American Naval Fighting Ships
   [01/10/03] www.hazegray.org
Eureka [01/10/03]
   www.nps.gov/safr/local/eureka.html
Gold Rush Steamships [01/10/03]
   www.maritimeheritage.org/ships/ss.html
Hercules [01/10/03] www.nps.gov/safr/local/herc.html
MBARI Research Vessel [01/10/03] www.mbari.org
MNPH [01/10/03] www.maritime.org/safrhome.shtml
Naval Shipbuilding Museum [01/10/03]
   www.uss-salem.org
Navy FDR Aircraft Carrier [01/10/03]
   www.multied.com/navy/cvb42fdr.html
Portsmouth sloop-of-war [01/10/03]
   www.hazegray.org
Potomac [01/10/03] www.usspotomac.org
Presidential Yachts
   [01/10/03] http://travel.to/campdavid
Star of India San Diego Maritime Museum [10/14/01]
   www.sdmaritime.com/star.htm
USS *Hornet* [01/10/03] www.uss-hornet.org
USS *Pampanito* [01/10/03]
   www.maritime.org/pamphome.shtml
USS *Tuscaloosa* [01/10/03]
   www.hazegray.org/danfs/cruisers/ca37.txt

Japanese American Relocation

Japanese American Relocation [01/10/03]
   www.sfmuseum.org
Japanese Evacuation Order 1942 [01/10/03]
   www.sfmuseum.org/hist8/evac15.html

Merchant Marine

U.S. Merchant Ships Sunk or Damaged in World War
   II [01/10/03]
   www.usmm.org/shipsunkdamaged.html
U.S. Merchant Marine Casualties during World War
   II [01/10/03] www.usmm.org/casualty.html

Military

Alameda Naval Air Station [01/10/03]
   www.dtic.mil/envirodod/derpreport/alameda.html

Army [01/10/03] www.spn.usace.army.mil

Battery Chamberlin [01/10/03]
www.nps.gov/prsf/places/chamber.htm

Battery East [01/10/03]
www.nps.gov/prsf/places/bateast.htm

Coast Guard [01/10/03] www.uscg.mil

Fort Baker [01/10/03]
www.nps.gov/goga/mahe/foba/index.htm

Fort Cronkhite [01/10/03]
www.nps.gov/goga/mahe/focr/index.htm

Fort Funston [01/10/03]
www.nps.gov/goga/fofu/index.htm

Fort Mason [01/10/03] www.fortmason.org

Fort Point Historic Site [01/10/03]
www.nps.gov/fopo/home.htm

Fort Point Lighthouse [01/10/03]
www.nps.gov/fopo/exhibits/lighthouse/litekeepers.
htm

Fortifications Preservation Manual [01/10/03]
www.nps.gov/goga/history/seaforts

Marin Headlands [01/10/03]
www.nps.gov/goga/mahe/index.htm

Navy [01/10/03] www.navy.mil

Navy [01/10/03] www.mercy.navy.mil

Nike Missile Site [01/10/03]
www.nps.gov/goga/mahe/nimi/index.htm

Presidio of San Francisco [01/10/03]
www.nps.gov/prsf/home.htm

The Tiburon Center [01/10/03]
http://rtc.sfsu.edu/history.htm

Museums

Alcatraz [01/10/03] www.nps.gov/alcatraz/faz2.html

Angel Island [01/10/03] www.angelisland.org

California Maritime [01/10/03] www.csum.edu and
www.maritime-education.com

California Military Museum [01/10/03]
www.militarymuseum.org

California, State [01/10/03] www.ca.gov

National Park Service [01/10/03] www.nps.gov

Oakland Museum of California [Links to all major
museums.] [01/10/03] www.museumca.org

The Museum of the City of San Francisco [01/10/03]
www.sfmuseum.org

Places on the Bay

Alameda, City [01/10/03]
www.ci.alameda.ca.us/home/index.html

Alcatraz [01/10/03] www.nps.gov/alcatraz/faz2.html

Angel Island [01/10/03] www.angelisland.org

Berkeley, City [01/10/03] www.ci.berkeley.ca.us

Oakland, City [01/10/03] www.oaklandnet.com

San Francisco, City [01/10/03] www.ci.sf.ca.us

Presidential Travel

Presidential Yachts and Aircraft
[01/10/03] http://travel.to/campdavid
[01/10/03] www.airforce1.org

Railroads

California State Railroad Museum [01/10/03]
www.csrmf.org

Central Pacific [01/10/03] http://cprr.org

Golden Gate Railroad Museum [01/10/03]
www.ggrm.org

Panama Railroad [01/10/03]
www.trainweb.org/panama

Presidential Rail Car Ferdinand Magellan [01/10/03]
www.goldcoast-railroad.org

Railroad Museum [01/10/03]
www.goldcoast-railroad.org

Southern Pacific [01/10/03] www.sphts.org

Transcontinental Railroad[01/10/03]
http://www.mindspring.com/~jjlanham/trcc1.htm

Union Pacific [01/10/03] www.up.com

Western Pacific Railroad Historical Society [01/10/03]
www.wprrhs.org/wphistory.html

San Francisco

Cable Cars [01/10/03] www.sfcablecar.com

Emperor Norton [01/10/03]
www.zpub.com/sf/history/nort.html

California Historical Society [01/10/03]
www.calhist.org

Museum [01/10/03] www.sfmuseum.org

Timeline [01/10/03 www.historychannel.com

Acknowledgments

The author and the Potomac Association wish to acknowledge the time and effort of the many volunteers who contributed data, ideas, information, editing, and encouragement in the preparation of this narration and reference manual.

A special thanks goes to the staff at Oakland Room of the Oakland Public Library, Museum of the City of San Francisco, Oakland Museum of California, and the Franklin D. Roosevelt Presidential Library who gave generously of their time to help in my research.

Additional thanks goes to Donald Laird for the use of the historical landmarks text and photographs from his website and to Helen and Bill King for the text and photographs of the presidential airplanes and yachts from their website.

A special thanks to: Len Cardoza, Dredging Manager, and Janice Adam, Community Affairs Representative, Port of Oakland. They researched and wrote the narration for the Port of Oakland Harbor Tour. I have used their materials extensively throughout the text and in the reference section on the Port of Oakland. To Celia McCarthy, Cultural Resources Planner, Port of Oakland, for historical editing. To Ross Turner, Assistant Art Director, Port of Oakland for producing the maps and logo design.

To Judith M. Green, Fordham University, for editorial assistance and research help at the Franklin D. Roosevelt Presidential Library.

To Les Dropkin, *Potomac* docent and naval historian, for the Docent Training Manual materials, including the pictorial tour of the *Potomac*, and his editing for historical accuracy of the information on presidential vessels. To Tom Lewis for his article on the *Santa Rosa* ferryboat. To Douglas S. Brookes, Curator, Treasure Island Museum, for information on the China Clippers. To Roger Johnson from the *Red Oak Victory* for technical information on WWII historic vessels.

To historians Carl Prince, New York University; Kurt Lauridsen, University of California; Charles Wollenberg, Vista Community College; and Woodruff Minor for their careful reading for historical accuracy. To Frances Burress, Phyllis Chambers, Cy Donaldson, Angeline Papastefan, and Anne Ruffino for copyediting. A special thanks to Dorothy M. Frye for final copyediting.

In addition, to the board, staff, local historians, volunteers and committee members who reviewed this manual: Douglas Brooks, Linda Brewer, Donald R. Bonney, Gray Brechin, Richard Burress, Debra Cooper, Jeanne Day, Art Dreshfield, Oscar Erickson, Capt. Walter W. Jaffee, Bob Harmon, David McGraw, Howard Murray, Barbara Potter, Charles Priest, Lee Rink, Michael A. Roosevelt, Syrell Sapoznick, Harry M. Short, Capt. Jan Tiura, Margaret Thomas, John Underhill, Shirley Vayson-Smith, and Mary Whitehead.

Potomac Association
About the Presidential Yacht *Potomac*

The presidential yacht *Potomac* is the only memorial to FDR in the western United States and is owned and operated by the Association for the Preservation of the Presidential Yacht *Potomac* (Potomac Association). The Potomac Association is a 501(c)(3) educational organization dedicated to remembering Franklin D. Roosevelt and his era, in partnership with the Port of Oakland. The Association's tax ID is 93-0830589.

**The Association for the Preservation
of the Presidential Yacht *Potomac***
(Potomac Association)

P.O. 2064
540 Water Street
Oakland, California 94604

24-hour Information Line: 510-627-1502
Office: 510-627-1215
Fax: 510-839-4729
Email: info@usspotomac.org
Website: www.usspotomac.org

Potomac Association Statement of Purpose

The specific purpose of the Potomac Association is to organize, direct, and sustain the community effort necessary to restore, operate and preserve the presidential yacht *Potomac*, an historic vessel of national significance, in order to provide continual educational opportunities for members of the public.

The educational programs of the Potomac Association will primarily focus on Franklin D. Roosevelt and his era, utilizing to the best advantage President Roosevelt's yacht, the *Potomac*. Emphasis will be placed on the leadership of President Roosevelt in the economic recovery from the depression, the development of historic social legislation, and the Allied victory in World War II.

(From Potomac Association Articles of Incorporation, 1983.)

Potomac Association Mission Statement

"To preserve and operate the presidential yacht *Potomac* for use as a classroom and museum dedicated to imparting to present and future generations the continuing impact of Franklin Delano Roosevelt's era." (From minutes of the Potomac Association meeting, April 8, 2002.)

Potomac Association Volunteer Program Goals

To attract individuals from the community to volunteer positions within the Association.

To offer volunteers important, meaningful, and satisfying work that matches their interests, skills, talents, and time availability, and the opportunity to participate in perpetuating an understanding and appreciation of President Franklin D. Roosevelt and his era.

To promote a mutually productive work relationship between volunteers and employed staff.

To value and recognize the contribution of each volunteer.

Potomac Financial Support

The *Potomac* is an important cultural and educational resource for the Bay Area's many communities, and with public support will continue to be available for a diverse and ever expanding audience. The *Potomac's* small size, unique history and design combine to create a rare museum setting. It offers small-scale, yet intimate and scholarly lectures; in-depth educational curricula designed to forge long-term relationships with visitors of all ages; and community outreach that targets local communities.

Funding provided by dedicated patrons has been critical to its success. By making the vessel accessible and relevant to ever-increasing and diverse constituencies, the *Potomac* is making a valuable contribution to its immediate community and beyond.

You may help support these efforts by becoming a member of **Friends of the *Potomac*.**

Finding the *Potomac* Map

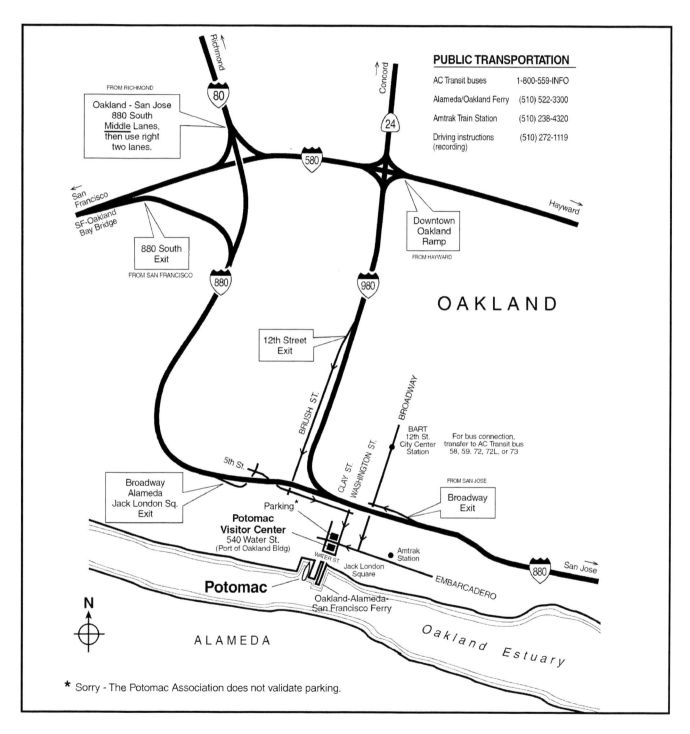

Figure 375 - **Finding the *Potomac* Map**

Bibliography

Adams, E. F. (1932). *Oakland's Early History*. City of Oakland Main Library, Oakland Room.

Allen, A. (1996). Jack London Square. *A Walk Along the Water* Exhibition Labels. Oakland, CA: Oakland Museum of California.

Allen, R. (2000). *The Pan Am Clipper: The History of Pan American's Flying-Boats 1931–1946*. New York: Barnes & Noble Books.

Alsop, J. (1982). *FDR, 1882-1945: A Centenary Remembrance*. NY: Viking.

Ambrose S.E. (2000). *Nothing Like It in the World: The Men Who Built the Transcontinental Railroad, 1863–1869*. New York: Simon & Schuster.

Appleton, D. (1885). *The Annals of San Francisco*. In Jackson, J. H. (Ed.). (1952). *The Western Gate: A San Francisco Reader*. New York: Farrar, Straus and Young. p. 106.

Babyak, J. (1988). *Eyewitness on Alcatraz: Life on the Rock As Told by the Guards, Families and Prisoners*. Berkeley, CA: Ariel Vamp Press.

Babyak, J. (1994). *Birdman: The Many Faces of Robert Stroud*. Berkeley, CA: Ariel Vamp Press.

Babyak, J. (2001). *Breaking the Rock: The Great Escape from Alcatraz*. Berkeley, CA: Ariel Vamp Press.

Bacon, D. (2001). *Walking San Francisco on the Barbary Coast Trail*. Second Edition, San Francisco: Quicksilver Press.

Bagwell, B. (1982). *Oakland: The Story of a City*. Oakland, CA: Heritage Alliance. (Original work published by Presidio Press, Novato, CA).

Baker, J. E., (Ed.). (1914). *Past and Present of Alameda County, California*. 2 Vols. Chicago: S. J. Clarke Company. [Available from California Historical Society Baker Library.]

Beaglehole, J. C. (1974). *The Life of Captain James Cook*. Stanford, CA: Stanford University Press.

Bean, W., and Rawls, J. J. (1988). *California: An Interpretive History*. New York: McGraw-Hill Book Company.

Beatty, R. A. (1996). *The Gardens of Alcatraz*. San Francisco: Golden Gate National Park Association.

Beebe, L., and Clegg, C. (1951). *Cable Car Carnival*. Oakland, CA: Grahame Hardy.

Beebe, L., and Clegg, C. (1995). *The American West: The Pictorial Epic of a Continent*. New York: E. P. Dutton and Co.

Bernhardi, R. (1979). *The Buildings of Oakland*. Oakland, CA: Forest Hill Press.

Bishop, Jim (1974). *FDR's Last Year: April 1944–April 1945*. New York: William Morrow and Co.

Blundell, Nigel (1996). *A Pictorial History of Franklin Delano Roosevelt*. Chelsea, London: Sunburst Books.

Bonnett, W. (1999). *Build Ships! Wartime Shipbuilding Photographs of San Francisco Bay: 1940–1945*. Sausalito, CA: Windgate Press.

Braznel, W. (1982). *California's Finest: The History of Del Monte Corporation and Del Monte Brand*. San Francisco, CA: Del Monte Corp. California Packing Corporation.

Browning, P. (1998). *San Francisco / Yerba Buena: From the Beginning to the Gold Rush*. San Francisco, CA: Great West Books.

Burns, J. M. (1956). *Roosevelt: The Lion and the Fox*. New York: Harcourt, Brace and World.

Burns, J. M. (1970). *Roosevelt: The Soldier of Freedom*. New York: Harcourt, Brace and Jovanovich.

Butruille, S. (1998). *Women's Voices from the Mother Lode*. Boise, Idaho: Tamarack Books.

Cameron, R. (1983). *Alcatraz: A Visual Essay*. San Francisco: Cameron & Co. First printing, 1974.

Canney, D. (1995). *U.S. Coast Guard and Revenue Cutters, 1790–1935*. Annapolis, MD: Naval Institute Press. pp. 98–100.

Clause, F. J. (1981). *Alcatraz: Island of Many Mistakes*. Menlo Park, CA: Briarcliff Press.

Clause, F. J. (1982). *Angel Island: Jewel of San Francisco Bay*. Menlo Park, CA: Briarcliff Press.

Clause, F. J. (1982). *Cable Cars: Past and Present*. Menlo Park, CA: Briarcliff Press.

Collier, P., and Horowitz, D. (1994). *The Roosevelts: An American Saga*. New York: Simon and Schuster.

Cook, B. W. (1993). *Eleanor Roosevelt: Vol. 1, 1884–1933*. New York: Viking.

Cook, B. W. (1999). *Eleanor Roosevelt: The Defining Years, 1933–1938, Vol. 2*. New York: Viking.

Cooper, D. (1996). Birth on the Waterfront. *A Walk Along the Water* Exhibition Labels. Oakland, CA: Oakland Museum of California.

Cooper, D. (1996). Estuary Transformed. *A Walk Along the Water* Exhibition Labels. Oakland, CA: Oakland Museum of California.

Cooper, D. (1996). <u>Hegenberger Road to the Airport</u>. *A Walk Along the Water* Exhibition Labels. Oakland, CA: Oakland Museum of California.

Cooper, D. (1996). <u>Homeless Shelter in Pipe City</u>. *A Walk Along the Water* Exhibition Labels. Oakland, CA: Oakland Museum of California.

Cooper, D. (1996). <u>Key to the Bay.</u> *A Walk Along the Water* Exhibition Labels. Oakland, CA: Oakland Museum of California.

Cooper, D. (1996). <u>Lighthouse on the Move</u>. *A Walk Along the Water* Exhibition Labels. Oakland, CA: Oakland Museum of California.

Cooper, D. (1996). <u>Moore Dry Dock Co. Becomes Schnitzer Steel.</u> *A Walk Along the Water* Exhibition Labels. Oakland, CA: Oakland Museum of California.

Cooper, D. (1996). <u>Oakland Builds an Airport</u>. *A Walk Along the Water* Exhibition Labels. Oakland, CA: Oakland Museum of California.

Cooper, D. (1996). <u>Pioneer Aviators at the Oakland Airport</u>. *A Walk Along the Water* Exhibition Labels. Oakland, CA: Oakland Museum of California.

Cooper, D. (1996). <u>The Government Builds an Island</u>. *A Walk Along the Water* Exhibition Labels. Oakland, CA: Oakland Museum of California.

Cooper, D. (1996). <u>The Transcontinental Railroad Comes to Town</u>. *A Walk Along the Water* Exhibition Labels. Oakland, CA: Oakland Museum of California.

Cooper, D. (1996). <u>Tunnel Becomes Terminal</u>. *A Walk Along the Water* Exhibition Labels. Oakland, CA: Oakland Museum of California.

Cowan, R. E. (1923). *Norton I, Emperor of the United States and Protector of Mexico.* San Francisco, CA: California Historical Society.

Cummings, G. A. and Pladwell, E. S. (1942). *Oakland, A History* [Special issue.] Oakland, CA: The Grant D. Miller Mortuaries.

Daly, R. (1980). *Juan Trippe and His Pan Am Empire.* New York: Random House.

Daniel, C. (Ed.). (1986). *Chronicle of the 20th Century.* Mount Kisco, NY: Chronicle Publications.

Daniels, J. (1966). *The Time Between the Wars: Armistice to Pearl Harbor.* New York: Doubleday.

Davis, K. S. (1971). *FDR: The Beckoning of Destiny 1882–1928: A History, Vol. 1.* New York: G.P. Putnam's Sons.

Davis, K. S. (1985). *FDR: The New York Years, 1928–1933: A History, Vol. 2.* New York: Random House.

Davis, K. S. (1986). *FDR: The New Deal Years, 1933–1937: A History, Vol. 3.* New York: Random House.

Davis, K. S. (1993). *FDR: Into The Storm: 1937–1940: A History Vol. 4.* New York: Random House.

Demoro, H. (1971). *The Evergreen Fleet*. San Marino, CA: Golden West Books.

Duggleby, J. (1990). *Impossible Quests*. New York: Crestwood House.

Dupré, J. (1997). *Bridges: A History of the World's Most Famous and Important Spans*. New York: Black Dog and Leventhal Publishers, Inc.

Emanuels, G. (1994). *California Indians: An Illustrated Guide*. Lemoore, CA: Kings River Press.

Emery, M. (1994). [Photographer]. *From Dry Dock to D-Day: The Return Voyage of the SS Jeremiah O'Brien*. San Francisco, CA: Lens Boy Press.

Envisioning California. *California History*. (Winter 1989/1990). [Special issue.]

Faessel, V. (1996). ARTSHIP. *A Walk Along the Water* Exhibition Labels. Oakland, CA: Oakland Museum of California.

Fehrenbacher, D.E. and Tutorow, Norman E. (1968). *California: An Illustrated History*. New York: D. Van Nostrand.

Ferlinghetti, L. and Petters, N. J.(1980). *Literary San Francisco: A Pictorial History From Its Beginning to the Present Day*. San Francisco: City Lights Books and Harper & Row.

Forbes, A. (1838). An Englishman's Proposal. From Original Edition, London, 1839. In Jackson, J. H. (Ed.). (1952). *The Western Gate: A San Francisco Reader*. New York: Farrar, Straus and Young. p. 77.

Ford, R. S. (1977). *Red Trains of the East Bay*. Glendale, CA: Interurbans.

Frank, S. and Melick, A. D. (1984). *The Presidents, Tidbits and Trivia*. New York: Greenwich House.

Freedmen, R. (1990). *Franklin Delano Roosevelt*. New York: Clarion Books.

Fracchi, C. A. (2000). *San Francisco From the Gold Rush to Cyberspace*. San Francisco: Morcoa Publishing.

Freidel, F.B. and Stauffer, T. (1990). *Franklin D. Roosevelt: A Rendezvous with Destiny*. New York: Little, Brown.

Fulbright, Leslie. Tied to the Bay. *Alameda Times-Star*, Sunday, July 4, 1999. p. 8, special section.

Gandt, Robert L. (1991). *China Clipper: The Age of the Great Flying Boats*. Washington, D.C.: United States Naval Institute.

Garraty, J. A. (1981). *A Short History of the American Nation* (Third Editon). New York: Harper & Row.

Goldberg, M. (1992). *Caviar and Cargo: The C3 Passenger Ships*. Kings Point, New York: American Merchant Marine Museum Foundation.

Goldberg, M. (1993). *Going Bananas: 100 Years of American Fruit Ships*. Kings Point, New York: American Merchant Marine Museum Foundation.

Goldberg, M. (1996). *Stately President Liners: American Passenger Liners of the Interwar Years: The "Sol's"*. Kings Point, New York: American Merchant Marine Museum Foundation.

Goldberg, M. (1996). *Stately President Liners: American Passenger Liners of the Interwar Years - Part I: The "520's"*. Kings Point, New York: American Merchant Marine Museum Foundation.

Goodman, D. K. (1999, December 31). Franklin Delano Roosevelt (1892–1945). *Time Magazine.* pp. 96–113.

Goodwin, D. K. (1994). *No Ordinary Time: Franklin and Eleanor Roosevelt: The Home Front in World War II*. New York: Touchstone: published by Simon and Schuster.

Grafton, J. (1999). *Franklin Delano Roosevelt: Great Speeches*. New York: Dover Publications.

Graham, O. L. and Wander, M. (Eds.). (1985). *Franklin D. Roosevelt: His Life and Times*. Boston, MA: C. K. Hall and Co.

Grover, M. (2001, March 19). Floating Lighthouse Looking for a Safe Port. *San Francisco Chronicle.* p. A18.

Guthrie, J. (2001, May 5). Window to the Bay. *San Francisco Chronicle.* p. A13.

Haller, S. (1997). *The Post and Park: A Brief Illustrated History of San Francisco*. San Francisco, CA: Golden Gate National Parks Association.

Halley, W. (1876). *The Centennial Yearbook of Alameda County*. Oakland, CA. [Available from California Historical Society Baker Library.]

Hansen, G. (Ed.). (1973). *San Francisco, The Bay and Its Cities* (New Revised Edition). New York: New York Hastings House.

Hansen, G. (1994). *San Francisco Almanac*. San Francisco, CA: Chronicle Books.

Harlan, G. (1967). *San Francisco Ferryboats*. Berkeley, CA: Howell North Books.

Halprin, L. (1997). *The Franklin Delano Roosevelt Memorial*. San Francisco, CA: Chronicle Books.

Harrison, J. B. and Sullivan, R. E. (1971). *A Short History of Western Civilization* (Third edition). New York: Alfred A. Knopf. (Original work published 1960.)

Holliday, J. S. (1999). *Rush for Riches: Gold Fever and the Making of California*. Berkeley, CA: University of California Press.

Hunter, S. A. (1940). *Temple of Religion and Tower of Peace: At the 1939 Golden Gate International Exposition*. San Francisco, CA: Temple of Religion and Tower of Peace.

Jackson, I. (1991). Taking a "Liberty" in San Francisco Bay. *Sea Breezes* [Liverpool, England]. pp. 34–41.

Jackson, J. H. (Ed.) (1952). *The Western Gate: A San Francisco Reader*. New York: Farrar, Straus and Young.

Jaffee, W. W., Captain. (1994). *The Last Liberty*. Palo Alto, CA: Glencannon Press.

Jaffee, W. W., Captain. (1995). *Appointment in Normandy*. Palo Alto, CA: Glencannon Press.

Jaffee, W. W., Captain. (1996). *The Track of the Golden Bear: The California Maritime Academy Schoolship*. Palo Alto, CA: Glencannon Press.

Jaffee, W. W., Captain. (1998). *The Presidential Yacht Potomac*. Palo Alto, CA: The Glencannon Press.

Jeremy, C. (1986). Savior of Old Ships: The San Francisco Maritime Museum. *Sea Breezes* [Liverpool, England]. pp. 60, 633–640.

Johnson, M. (1993). *The Second Gold Rush: Oakland and the East Bay in World War II*. Berkeley, CA: University of California Press.

Johnson, P. C. (Ed.) (1964). *The California Missions: A Pictorial History*. Menlo Park, CA. Lane Book Company, Sunset Books.

Kelleher B. T. (1997). *Drake's Bay: Unraveling California's Great Maritime Mystery*. San Jose, CA 95121. (Author/publisher, www.drakesbay.com.)

Kemble, E. C. (1846). *The Brooklyn City's First Newspaper*. In Jackson, J. H. (Ed.) (1952). *The Western Gate: A San Francisco Reader*. New York: Farrar, Straus and Young. p. 97.

Kemble, J. H. (1957). *San Francisco Bay: A Pictorial Maritime History*. New York: Bonanza Books.

Kinder, G. (1998). *Ship of Gold in the Deep Blue Sea*. New York: Vintage Books.

Kingman, R. (1979). *A Pictorial Life of Jack London*. New York: Crown Publishers.

Krupnick, Jon E. (1997). *Pan American's Pacific Pioneers: The Rest of the Story*. Missoula, MT: Pictorial Histories Publishing Co.

Lageson, E. B. (1999). *Battle at Alcatraz: A Desperate Attempt to Escape the Rock*. Omaha, NE: Addicus Books.

Lange, D. and Wollenberg, C. (1995). *Photographing the Second Gold Rush: Dorothea Lange and the Bay Area at War 1941–1945*. Berkeley, CA: Heyday Books.

Lash, J. P. (1971). *Eleanor and Franklin: The Story of Their Relationship, Based on Eleanor Roosevelt's Private Papers*. New York: W.W. Norton.

Lash, J.P. (1972). *Eleanor: The Years Alone*. New York: W.W. Norton.

Lash, J. P. (1976). *Roosevelt and Churchill 1939–1941: The Partnership That Saved the West*. New York: W.W. Norton.

Lavoie, S. (1996). <u>Loading Lumber.</u> *A Walk Along the Water* Exhibition Labels. Oakland, CA: Oakland Museum of California.

Lavoie, S. (1996). <u>Oakland Naval Supply Depot</u>. *A Walk Along the Water* Exhibition Labels. Oakland, CA: Oakland Museum of California.

Lavoie, S. (1996). <u>The Land of Cotton</u>. *A Walk Along the Water* Exhibition Labels. Oakland, CA: Oakland Museum of California.

Lavoie, S. (1996). <u>The Oakland Army Base.</u> *A Walk Along the Water* Exhibition Labels. Oakland, CA: Oakland Museum of California.

Livingston, S. E. (1984). *Historic Ships of San Francisco: A Collective History and Guide to the Restored Historic Vessels of the National Maritime Museum.* San Francisco, CA: Chronicle Books.

Margolin, M. (1978). *The Ohlone Way: Indian Life in the San Francisco-Monterey Bay Area.* Berkeley, CA: Heyday Books.

Minor, W. (1993). *Historic Commercial Buildings of Alameda.* Alameda, CA: Historical Advisory Board, City of Alameda.

Minor, W. (1996). <u>Alameda's Bethlehem Shipyard</u>. *A Walk Along the Water* Exhibition Labels. Oakland, CA: Oakland Museum of California.

Minor, W. (1996). <u>Bridges Become Tunnels</u>. *A Walk Along the Water* Exhibition Labels. Oakland, CA: Oakland Museum of California.

Minor, W. (1996). <u>Cranes Alight at Encinal Terminals</u>. *A Walk Along the Water* Exhibition Labels. Oakland, CA: Oakland Museum of California.

Minor, W. (1996). <u>From Shipyard to Yacht Harbor</u>. *A Walk Along the Water* Exhibition Labels. Oakland, CA: Oakland Museum of California.

Minor, W. (1996). <u>The Alaska Packers</u>. *A Walk Along the Water* Exhibition Labels. Oakland, CA: Oakland Museum of California.

Minor, W. (1996). <u>Victorian Shipyards</u>. *A Walk Along the Water* Exhibition Labels. Oakland, CA: Oakland Museum of California.

Minor, W. (2000). *Pacific Gateway: An Illustrated History of the Port of Oakland.* Oakland, CA: Port of Oakland, Communications Division.

Moore, J. R. (1994). *The Story of the Moore Dry Dock Company* [Private Printing.] Sausalito, CA: Windgate Press.

Navigation Rules, International-Inland. (1983). Washington, D.C.: United States Coast Guard.

Niven, J. (1987). *The American President Lines and Its Forbears 1884–1984: From Paddlewheels to Containerships.* Newark, DE: University of Delaware Press.

Olmsted, N. (1998). *The Ferry Building: Witness to a Century of Change, 1898–1998.* Berkeley, CA: Heyday Books.

Osinski, A. (1987). *Encyclopedia of Presidents: Franklin D. Roosevelt*. Chicago, IL: Children's Press.

Palou, Fray Francisco, O.F.M. (1776). <u>Founding of Presidio</u>. From Bulton, H.E. (Ed.).(1926). *Historical Memoirs of New California*. Berkeley, CA: University of California Press. In Jackson, J. H. (Ed.). (1952). *The Western Gate: A San Francisco Reader*. New York: Farrar, Straus and Young. p. 14.

Parker, D. T. (1994). *Square Riggers in the United States and Canada*. Polo, IL: Transportation Trails.

Perkins, F. (1946). *The Roosevelt I Knew*. New York: Viking.

Phillips, C. C. (1938). *Through the Golden Gate: San Francisco, 1769–1937*. San Francisco, CA: Suttonhouse.

Publication Manual of the American Psychological Association (2001). Fifth edition. Washington, D.C.: American Psychological Association.

Quillen, J. (1992). *Alcatraz from Inside: The Hard Years 1942–1952*. San Francisco, CA: Golden Gate National Park Association.

Reinholt, R. (1973). *Treasure Island*. San Francisco, CA: Scrimshaw Press.

Richter, A. (1996). <u>Birds Find Sanctuary at Lake Merritt</u>. *A Walk Along the Water* Exhibition Labels. Oakland, CA: Oakland Museum of California.

Royce, P. (1993). *Sailing Illustrated: The Best of All Sailing Worlds, Vol. 1*. Newport Beach, CA: Royce Publications.

Royce, P. (1997). *Royce's Sailing Illustrated: The Best of All Sailing Worlds, Modern and Traditional, Vol. 2*. Newport Beach, CA: Royce Publications.

Rogers, J.G. (1995). *Origins of Sea Terms, The American Maritime Library: Volume XI*. Mystic Seaport Museum. Boston, MA: Nimrod Press.

Rowan, R. and Janis, B.(1997). *First Dogs: American Presidents and Their Best Friends*. New York: Algonquin Books of Chapel Hill.

Rubenstein, S. (2000, Oct. 20). <u>Squeaking Under the Span</u>. *San Francisco Chronicle*. San Francisco, CA. p. A1.

Sawyer, L. A. and Mitchell, W. H. (1985). *The Liberty Ships*. London: Lloyd's of London Press, Ltd.

Schlesinger, A. M. Jr. (1957). *The Age of Roosevelt, Vol. 1: The Crisis of the Old Order, 1919–1933*. Boston, MA: Houghton Mifflin.

Schlesinger, A. M. Jr. (1958). *The Age of Roosevelt, Vol. 2: The Coming of the New Deal*. Boston, MA: Houghton Mifflin.

Schlesinger, A. M. Jr. (1960). *The Age of Roosevelt, Vol. 3: The Politics of Upheaval*. Boston, MA: Houghton Mifflin.

Schwendinger, R. (1984). *International Port of Call: An Illustrated Maritime History of the Golden Gate*. Woodland Hills, CA: Windsor Publications, Inc.

Seagraves, A. (1991). *Women Who Charmed the West*. Hayden, ID: Wesanne Publications.

Smith and Elliott (1878). *Illustrations of Contra Costa County, California, with Historical Sketch*. Oakland, CA.

Steinbeck, John and Wollenberg C. (Ed.) (1988). *The Harvest Gypsies: On the Road to the Grapes of Wrath*. Berkeley, CA: Heyday Books.

Style Manual. (2000). Washington, D.C.: United States Government Printing Office.

Tegler, E. (1997, October). USS *Sequoia*. *Naval History: United States Naval Institute*. pp. 38–41.

The Chicago Manual of Style (1993). Fourteenth edition. Chicago, IL: University of Chicago Press.

Thompson, L. (1994). *Rock Hard: The Autobiography of a Former Alcatraz Inmate*. New York: Pocket Books.

Thompson and West (1878). *Official and Historical Atlas Map of Alameda County, California, Compiled, Drawn, and Published from Personal Examinations and Surveys*. Oakland, CA. [Available from California Historical Society Baker Library.]

Ward, G. C. (1985). *Before the Trumpet: Young Franklin Roosevelt, 1882–1905*. New York: Harper & Row.

Ward, G. C. (1989). *A First Class Temperament: The Emergence of Franklin Roosevelt*. New York: Harper & Row.

Westerlin, D. (1996). Containers Transform the Waterfront. *A Walk Along the Water* Exhibition Labels. Oakland, CA: Oakland Museum of California.

Withers, B. (1996). *The President Travels by Train: Politics and Pullman*. Lynchburg, VA: TLC Publishing.

Wollenberg, C. (Ed.) (1970). *Ethnic Conflict in California History*. Los Angeles, CA: Tinnon-Brown.

Wollenberg C. (1978). *All Deliberate Speed: Segregation and Exclusion in California Schools, 1855–1977*. Berkeley, CA: University of California Press.

Wollenberg, C. (1985). *Golden Gate Metropolis: Perspectives on Bay Area History*. Berkeley, CA: University of California, Institute of Governmental Studies.

Wollenberg, C. (1990). *Marinship at War: Shipbuilding and Social Change in Wartime Sausalito*. Berkeley, CA: Western Heritage of California.

Wollenberg, C. (1994). *California's Multiethnic Heritage: A Continuing Tradition*. San Francisco, CA: San Francisco Study Center.

Wood, M. W. (1883). *History of Alameda County, California*. Oakland, CA.

Zauner, P. (1989). *Those Spirited Women of the Early West*. Sonoma, CA: Zanell Publications

List of Photographs and Figures
Photography Credits

The front cover photograph of the *Potomac* was taken in 1995 by John Ravnik, on her post-restoration maiden voyage on the San Francisco Bay, courtesy of Potomac Association.

Photograph of FDR on the inside front cover courtesy of Franklin D. Roosevelt Library, Hyde Park, NY.

Photograph of the author on the back cover was taken by Mia Chambers in 2001.

Photograph of the topsail schooner *Ka'iulani* courtesy of Captain Robert Michaan of the *Ka'iulani*.

Photograph of the *Gas Light* is copyrighted by Mariah Healy of Mariah's Eyes Photography and used with permission.

Photograph of *Lady Washington* by Robert Esposito, Panorama Designs, © 1992, used with permission.

Photographs of the *Alert* tugboat, the car carrier, and a fireboat were taken by Captain Jan Tiura.

Photograph of topsail schooner *Californian* by John Riise of the Nautical Heritage Society used with permission.

Photograph of barque *Eagle* from U.S. Coast Guard Academy brochure obtained from the barque *Eagle* when she visited San Francisco.

Photograph of the *Gold Star* used courtesy of the owner Larry Cullen.

Photograph of *Red Oak Victory* is by Tom Bottomley, Purser, SS *Red Oak Victory*.

Photograph of barque *Star of India* courtesy of Captain John Ruffino, Maritime Museum of San Diego.

Photograph of eight-foot El Toro by Kimball Livingston during the Bull Ship race from Sausalito to St. Francis Yacht Club on April 22, 2001, used with permission.

Historical photographs of the Quinn Lighthouse courtesy of United States Lighthouse Society.

Photograph of the cranes on the arrival ship was taken by David Dibble.

Photographs and text of historical landmarks are from Donald Laird's website www.donaldlaird.com/landmarks. Site contents are copyrighted 1996–1999 by Donald Laird, used with permission.

Photographs and text of the presidential yachts and airplanes are from Helen and Bill King's website http//travel.to/campdavid, used with permission.

Historical photographs from the San Francisco Museum or the National Park Service, used with permission.

The China Clipper photographs from the Pan Am Historical Foundation (PAHF), used with permission.

Chad Malkus took the photograph of the FDR *Potomac* stack/elevator memorial in Cambridge, Maryland.

A number of the photographs of boats are by the manufacturers and used with permission.

Naval vessel photographs are from the U.S. Navy website and are credited.

All other photographs are by David Lee Woods.

For a list of organizations used for research, see Historical Data Sources on page 259.

For a list of websites used for research, see Websites References on page 263.

Table of Figures

Index

Notes

How to Order Book

Cruising Historic San Francisco Bay
with FDR's Presidential Yacht *Potomac*
David Lee Woods
Foreword by Michael Roosevelt

Send your name, address, and phone number
with a check or money order to:

Summerset Books

PO Box 2252
Walnut Creek CA 94595

Email: summersetbooks@aol.com
Phone/Fax: 925-287-8300

Price for each book	$18.95
In California add 8¼% sales tax	$1.55
Add S&H* for first book	$4.95
Add S&H* for each additional book	$0.50

*Shipping and Handling